Day of the Dead
in the USA

LATINIDAD
Transnational Cultures in the United States

This series publishes books that deepen and expand our knowledge and understanding of the various Latina/o populations in the United States in the context of their transnational relationships with cultures of the broader Americas. The focus is on the history and analysis of Latino cultural systems and practices in national and transnational spheres of influence from the nineteenth century to the present. The series is open to scholarship in political science, economics, anthropology, linguistics, history, cinema and television, literary and cultural studies, and popular culture and encourages interdisciplinary approaches, methods, and theories. The Series Advisory Board consists of faculty of the Department of Transborder Chicana/o and Latina/o Studies and Film and Media Studies at Arizona State University where an interdisciplinary emphasis is being placed on transborder and transnational dynamics.

Day of the Dead in the USA

The Migration and Transformation of a Cultural Phenomenon

REGINA M. MARCHI

RUTGERS UNIVERSITY PRESS

New Brunswick, New Jersey, and London

Library of Congress Cataloging-in-Publication Data

Marchi, Regina M., 1965–
    Day of the Dead in the USA : the migration and transformation of a cultural
phenomenon / Regina M. Marchi.
        p.   cm.— (Latinadad : transnational cultures in the United States)
    Includes bibliographical references and index.
    ISBN 978–0–8135–4557–8 (hardcover : alk. paper)—ISBN 978–0–8135–4558–5
(pbk. : alk. paper)
    1. All Souls' Day—United States. 2. United States—Social life and customs.
3. United States—Religious life and customs. I. Title.
    GT4995.A4M36   2009
    394.2660973—dc22   2008040064
      CIP

A British Cataloging-in-Publication record for this book
is available from the British Library.

Visit our Web site: http://rutgerspress.rutgers.edu

Manufactured in the United States of America

For my family and friends, vivos y muertos . . .

Contents

Preface   ix

Acknowledgments   xi

Introduction: A Transborder Communication Phenomenon   1

1. *An Ancient and Modern Festival*   9
   Honoring the Dead   10
   Historical Background on Day of the Dead in Europe and the Americas   11
   Day of the Dead Customs in Various Latin American Countries   15
      Central America   16
      South America   17

2. *Mexico's Special Relationship with Day of the Dead*   21
   Folk and Pop Culture Manifestations   22
      Calavera Imagery   23
      Day of the Dead and Mexican Nationalism   28
   Government Campaigns and Tourism   29

3. *Day of the Dead in the United States*   34
   Mexican American All Saints' Day and All Souls' Day Rituals   34
   A Chicano Tradition Is Born   37
      Early Day of the Dead Exhibits and Events   47
      California and Beyond Adopt the New Celebration   50
      Negotiations over Ownership   52

4. *Ritual Communication and Community Building*   56
   Imagined Community   58
   Communitas   60
   Claims for Public Recognition   64

5. *U.S. Day of the Dead as Political Communication:
   A Moral Economy*   70
   Remembering Migrant Deaths: Protesting Operation Gatekeeper   73
   Remembering Labor Abuses: UFW and the Braceros   78
   Remembering Indigenous Struggles: Genocide and Repression   79
   Remembering the War Dead: A Critique of U.S. Military Interventions   80
   Public Celebrations as Expressions of Unity and Discord   81

6. *Day of the Dead in the U.S. Media:*
    The Celebration Goes Mainstream   83
    Widespread Media Attention   84
    Reasons for Increased News Coverage   90
    News Coverage as a Resource for Financial and Institutional Support   93
    Publicity and Validation for Latino Communities   95

7. *The Expanding Hybridity of an Already Hybrid Tradition*   97
    The American Way of Death   98
    Filling an Emotional Void   101
    New Participants, New Directions, and Debates around Authenticity   106

8. *The Commoditization of a Death Ritual*   115
    Marketplace Offerings   116
        Exotic and Chic Cultural Capital   117
        Day of the Dead as a Tourism/Urban Development Strategy   118
        Longing for the Noncommercial Good Old Days (of the Dead)   120
        Commerce and Culture: A Long History Together   122
    Commercialization versus Authenticity   131

    Conclusion: What We Can Learn from
    U.S. Day of the Dead Celebrations   137

    Methodological Appendix   141
    Notes   149
    Glossary   167
    References   171
    Index   185

Preface

On November 2, 1988, while living in the predominantly Latino Mission District of San Francisco, California, I was invited by a Jewish friend to attend the annual Day of the Dead procession on 24th Street. "You *have* to check this out!" he exclaimed excitedly. As a recent transplant from Boston, I knew nothing about the El Día de los Muertos and listened with interest to my friend's animated descriptions of the annual neighborhood festivities.

As it got dark, we assembled in the symbolic heart of the Mission—the corner of Mission and 24th streets—along with thousands of others, many dressed as skeletons or wearing skeleton face paint. An expanse of flickering candles stretched for blocks, illuminating the faces of paraders as they held photos of deceased loved ones, or giant marionettes, or political signs condemning U.S. military intervention in El Salvador and Nicaragua. One group brandished a large U.S. flag inlaid with a pirate's skull and crossbones to symbolize disapproval of the U.S. government's foreign policy in Latin America. A few individuals wore rubber masks caricaturing President Ronald Reagan. Contingents of schoolchildren dressed as skeletons walked in groups with their teachers and parents. Elderly people spoke in Spanish to each other, politely greeting friends and neighbors in the procession. Giant papier-mâché puppets lurched playfully over the crowd and skeleton-clad stilt walkers tapped out funky beats on tambourines and maracas. *Congueros* drummed in hypnotic synchronicity, while Aztec ceremonial dancers, adorned in shimmering garments and feathers, marked their movements with the swishing sounds of *chachayotl* ankle rattles.[1]

Not sure what to make of this kaleidoscopic scene, I moved with the spirited crowd as it wended its way down 24th. Leaning out of home and store windows on both sides of the parade route, Spanish-speaking children and adults watched and waved, amused by the proceedings below. A playground we passed along the route had been converted into a multimedia electronic installation focusing on the afterlife, and numerous altars for the dead, colorful banners, streetlight decorations, and sidewalk chalk art awaited the crowd at various points along the route. With so many people jammed into a relatively narrow street, procession participants inched forward intimately—shoulders and feet often bumping into fellow marchers, who smiled

understandingly. Some forty-five minutes later, the procession made a collective right turn from 24th Street into the narrow, mural-filled alley of Balmy
Street, passing under multiple arches of flowers and banners. Illuminated with
neon lights that projected hot pink, purple, and green fluorescent designs on
the walls, the alley represented a symbolic passage from this world to the next,
I was told. After traversing the mystical passageway, paraders emerged at
Garfield Park, the ending point of the procession and the beginning point of
other activities.

Curious to learn more about this celebration, I attended my first Day of
the Dead altar exhibit the following day at the Mission Cultural Center for
Latino Arts, and began to gain a better understanding of the meaning of the
tradition. In future years, I would see rural and urban Day of the Dead festivities in Mexico, Guatemala, and El Salvador, while working as a journalist
in the region. I would learn that elements of the holiday were celebrated
throughout Latin America, in ways that were similar to and different from
each other. Even further in the future, as a scholar of communication and culture, I would realize that Day of the Dead—the largest Latino celebration in
the United States—exemplifies some of the paradoxes of life in the postmod-
ern world, where communities are both fracturing and integrating at an
unprecedented rate.[2] The evolution of this ritual observance in the United
States, with links to a network of related celebrations in Mexico and other
parts of Latin America, provides important lessons for those interested in the
study of communication, culture, and politics.

Acknowledgments

The research for this book, much of which was conducted while I was a doctoral student at the University of California, San Diego, was generously supported by funding from UCSD's Center for the Study of Race and Ethnicity (2004), California Cultures in Comparative Perspective Program (2005), and Office of the President (2004–2005). Early research was funded by the Center for Media, Religion, and Culture in the School of Journalism and Mass Communication at the University of Colorado, Boulder (2003–2004). The center provided both financial support and extremely helpful feedback, particularly from Stewart Hoover and Lynn Shofield Clark. Subvention to defray publication costs was provided by the School of Communication, Information, and Library Studies at Rutgers University.

This project benefited greatly from advice given to me by my dissertation committee members, Michael Schudson, Chandra Mukerji, Dan Hallin, David Avalos, and Suzanne Brenner, as well as from thoughtful comments to the manuscript made by Eric Rothenbuhler, Mark Mattern, and my editor, Beth Kressel. Anonymous reviewers also provided helpful criticism.

Of course, the book would not exist without the many people who allowed me to interview them. Although there are too many to list here, I am especially indebted to Tere Romo, René Yáñez, Yolanda Garfias Woo, Maribel Simán DeLucca, Claudio DeLucca, Carmen Lomas Garza, Amalia Mesa-Bains, John Leaños, Tomás Benitez, Barbara Henry, Nancy Chárraga, Patricia Rodríguez, Pita Ruíz, Estela Rubalcava Klink, Louise Torio, Carlos Von Son, Terry Alderete, and Mary Ann Thiem. It is a finer piece of research because of the views and expertise available to me from these individuals; however, any errors or oversights in the text are solely my own responsibility.

Last but not least, I thank my parents, Roberta and Richard Marchi, and my entire family for their encouragement (and their understanding when I couldn't make it to family get-togethers because of working on the book). A special thanks goes to Ignacio Ochoa, with whom I've had years of conversations about Latin American religious and cultural practices, and to Barbara McDonough, Nancy Lee, and Kathleen Collins for their moral support.

Day of the Dead
in the USA

Introduction

HOW DO POPULATIONS WITH LIMITED ACCESS to official channels of power make themselves heard in the public sphere? How do they create the sense of shared knowledge and solidarity necessary to address issues of socioeconomic injustice? These are questions that anyone interested in democratic participation must ask, given the disproportionate influence of affluent and politically powerful stakeholders on the production and circulation of ideas in the public square. This book is about the power of cultural ritual to serve as a medium of political communication, and about the role of cultural hybridity in reconciling feelings of social and cultural displacement, fragmentation, and negation. It is also a story of the key roles played by the mass media and commercial forces in creating, promoting, and maintaining "traditions."

Today, the celebration of Day of the Dead, or El Día de los Muertos, is internationally associated with Mexico. Although assumed to be a timeless ritual that has been seamlessly passed down within Mexican families since precolonial times, it is actually a relatively recent tradition for many Mexicans. Festivities in the United States, the focus of this book, are also recent. They comprise a syncretic mix of both Latin American Indigenous practices and Roman Catholic spiritual traditions that have been reconfigured by Chicanos and other U.S. Latinos to transmit messages of cultural identity and political expression.[1] As we shall see, the survival of this celebration into the twenty-first century has not happened effortlessly, but has been the result of various cultural, political, and commercial initiatives, as well as of abundant media attention. While many contemporary Mexican Americans are familiar with El Día de los Muertos, many others have only recently begun to learn about it and others know nothing about it. In contrast to most Latin American Day of the Dead observances that are primarily family-oriented, religious rituals carried out at private homes and family grave sites, U.S. celebrations are widely advertised, secular "cultural events" held in art galleries, schools, libraries, museums, community centers, and municipal institutions. Outside of the traditional Latin American context, these rituals communicate in radically new ways.

Salient aspects of traditional remembrance rites are reworked into altar exhibitions, street processions, and performances that publicly communicate about Latino histories, cultures, and political struggles. Within a dominant U.S. society that has historically treated Latinos with discrimination, these events are geared more toward asserting a positive Latino presence in the U.S. public sphere than toward fulfilling religious obligations to the deceased. Initiated in the 1970s by Chicano artists who had observed or read about southern Mexico's Día de los Muertos traditions, U.S. celebrations are based on and identified with those of Mexico, although similar rituals occur in other Latin American countries. The process through which the holiday became internationally associated with Mexico will later be discussed in detail, but for now it is sufficient to briefly note a few of the reasons why many people in the United States consider the holiday to be an exclusively Mexican experience.

First, people of Mexican heritage are the largest Latino group in the United States, representing 60 percent of the U.S. Latino population. Mexican Americans were the first to celebrate Day of the Dead in the United States and, until the large influx of Central and South American immigrants in the 1980s and 1990s, were often unaware that the holiday was observed in other parts of Latin America.[2] Second, as the most populous and industrialized of all Spanish-speaking countries in Latin America, Mexico has an extensive tourism industry, highly adept at promoting the country's natural and folkloric assets to national and international markets. Since the 1970s, the Mexican government has sponsored major campaigns aimed at tourists, in which Day of the Dead has been heavily promoted as representing "authentic Mexico." Anthropologist Stanley Brandes notes, "Recognizing that traditional fiestas can further its financial and ideological goals, the Mexican government since the early 1970s has systematically promoted the tourist development of particular religious occasions, including most importantly the well-known Day of the Dead" (1988, 88). Prior to the 1970s, as will be discussed, elaborate activities for Day of the Dead were carried out only in certain areas of southern Mexico, and the celebration was not a national phenomenon. Meanwhile, people in smaller Latin American countries with less developed tourism infrastructure, such as Guatemala, Bolivia, Ecuador, and Peru, have long carried out their Day of the Dead traditions in relative obscurity. Third, Mexico is the largest and closest Latin American neighbor to the United States and therefore has been the most visible and accessible Latin American destination for U.S. tourists, journalists, and researchers. Since the 1920s, U.S. populations have easily been able to travel to Mexico; see Mexico portrayed in plays, movies, books, and music; or visit exhibitions of Mexican art in the United States—an intense level of cultural contact that continues into the twenty-first century.[3]

Although most scholarly and popular publications refer to Day of the Dead as a uniquely Mexican holiday, Latin Americans from other countries, largely unaware of Mexico's celebrations, consider the holiday their own. Bolivians with whom I have spoken refer to the holiday as "*Boliviano*," and friends in Ecuador call the Day "*muy nuestro*" (very much ours). Guatemalan anthropologist Celso Lara, who has spent more than forty years documenting the cultural traditions of Guatemala, calls the holiday "one of the most Guatemalan of all holidays."[4] In reviewing articles and letters to the editor published each fall in newspapers from Ecuador, Bolivia, Nicaragua, Honduras, Argentina, Guatemala, and Panama, it is clear that intellectuals, members of the clergy, and residents-at-large in these countries consider Day of the Dead to be a particularly authentic part of their national culture, which they often contrast with the "invasive" and "foreign" character of Halloween. So, although Mexico became internationally renowned in the twentieth century for Day of the Dead, the celebration is not unique to this country. This is important to keep in mind when discussing festivities in the United States, because some observers hastily conclude that Central and South American immigrants have adopted the "Mexican" holiday. As will be illustrated, these immigrants are instead reencountering and re-creating in the United States practices with which they are already familiar. Nonetheless, it was Chicano artists who first popularized the celebration in the United States and provided the artistic and ritual framework for others to participate in the celebration.

This study is an examination of the political, social, and economic dynamics of Day of the Dead celebrations in the United States, illustrating the complicated intersections of cultural identity, political economy, the mass media, and consumer culture. It focuses on Chicano-style celebrations consisting of art exhibits, community altars, craft workshops, street processions, poetry slams, film screenings, performance art, and other public events, and does not attempt to look at private, family observances. Nor does it rearticulate a detailed history of pre- and post-Columbian Day of the Dead rituals in Mexico, amply discussed elsewhere (Carmichael and Sayer 1991; Childs and Altman 1982; Garciagodoy 1998; Greenleigh and Beimler 1991; Lok 1991; Nutini 1988; Portillo and Muñoz 1988). Instead, it charts the birth and growth of the celebration in the United States, noting continuities and changes over time and place, and elucidating the communicative significance of these developments. Because California has one of the largest Latino populations in the country and was the first place in the United States where Day of the Dead was intentionally planned and advertised as a cultural event (and because I lived there for nearly a decade), my research centers on California celebrations. However, to illustrate certain trends, this book also discusses Day of the Dead events in various regions of the United States and Latin America, using information gathered from newspaper and radio coverage, the Internet, and my personal observations and interviews.

Research for this study involved ethnographic observation of more than 150 U.S. Day of the Dead events as well as formal, tape-recorded interviews with seventy-eight participants. In addition, qualitative and quantitative data analysis was done on information available from a range of historical sources, including newspapers, TV and radio transcripts of U.S. Day of the Dead coverage, popular magazine articles, museum catalogs, Internet Web sites, documentary films, event promotional materials, archival information (at art galleries, museums, and community centers), and more than sixty rolls of film I shot at Day of the Dead events attended from 2000 to 2007 (see appendix for detailed section on methodology). Please see the glossary at the end of this book for definitions of frequently used Spanish terms.

This subject matter bears upon a number of issues relevant to the fields of media studies, communication, cultural studies, anthropology, sociology, ethnic studies, and Latino studies. First, the celebration illustrates that ethnic identity is a malleable social construct, based in practices of community building and shaped by political economic contexts. Although Chicano artists in California adopted and reconfigured Día de los Muertos rituals of southern Mexico as a way to honor Chicano and Mexicano identities, many Day of the Dead celebrations began to expand their focus in the 1980s and 1990s, celebrating a pan-Latino, rather than strictly Mexican, identity, as California became home to vast numbers of immigrants from other parts of Latin America. This dynamic has been repeated in other parts of the United States where diverse Latino populations now live together in the same neighborhoods, with events fostering feelings of solidarity among economically, ethnically, and ideologically diverse groups of Latinos. As we will see, these celebrations sometimes entail tensions and contradictions around issues of group representation, authenticity, and "ownership." The social construction of ethnic identities within concrete political economic contexts, and the historicity and fluidity of these identities, are integral themes that we will return to at various points in the book.

Second, the growing popularity of Day of the Dead rituals among people of non-Latino backgrounds illustrates that expressions of *Latinidad* (Latinness) not only affect individuals of Latin American heritage, but also are reshaping mainstream U.S. culture. The spread of these celebrations to cities across the United States over the past three decades belies prior theories of modernity that assumed an inevitable forsaking of premodern, "nonrational" traditions in favor of Western (Anglo-Saxon) cultural homogenization. The geographical dissemination of the U.S. celebration from two Chicano art galleries in California in 1972 to hundreds of museums, schools, universities, and municipalities across the country some thirty-five years later contradicts prior theories of unidirectional cultural flows from the "center" to the "periphery." This is a case of "third world" practices being reconfigured by a politically marginalized population in the "first world" in ways that have not only influenced mainstream U.S. culture, but have recirculated to Mexico, influencing artistic and political expressions of the holiday there.

A third aim of the book is to illustrate how various forms of mass media, combined with unprecedented levels of transnational communication (through tourism, commerce, and immigration), have transmitted Day of the Dead to a wide public, defying historical dichotomies of local versus global, authentic versus commercial, and traditional versus modern. Rather than obliterating this premodern celebration, the unparalleled flow of information, people, and products that has characterized globalization since the 1970s has revived and sustained Day of the Dead, so that it is more widely known today than ever before.

Finally, as a form of ritual communication, the celebration encourages a rethinking of traditional assumptions regarding the formulation of the public sphere, the definition of "media," and the composition of political communication. For Latino populations that have been traditionally underrepresented and misrepresented in U.S. mainstream media (due to barriers based on race, class, and immigration status), alternative public spheres that do not depend on written language, English fluency, or the attainment of formal citizenship are important arenas for the creation and transmission of alternative and oppositional discourses in the public square.[5]

To understand the significance of Day of the Dead in the United States, it is necessary to have some background on corresponding rituals in Europe and Latin America. Chapter 1 describes these celebrations, providing information on traditions in Argentina, Belize, Bolivia, Colombia, Ecuador, El Salvador, Guatemala, Nicaragua, and Peru, as well as in areas of Europe. Chapter 2 discusses Día de los Muertos celebrations in Mexico, critically examining commonplace tropes about Mexico's "fascination with death" that fuel the modern association of Mexico and Mexicans with Day of the Dead. Exemplifying the social construction of national identity, this chapter sets the stage for the next chapter's discussion of Day of the Dead and Chicano identity.

Chapter 3 discusses the genesis of U.S. Day of the Dead celebrations in California as a key component of the Chicano Movement for political liberation. Noting how Chicanos used both Catholic and Mesoamerican Indigenous symbols to express community identity and encourage feelings of solidarity among diverse groups of Mexican Americans, it also discusses the later participation of Central American, South American, and Caribbean

Latino populations in California festivities. Debates and negotiations in the Latino community around issues of identity and authenticity are also explored, revealing important lessons about the socially constructed nature of ethnic identity and the political significance of tradition.

Chapter 4 examines the ritual communication aspects of Day of the Dead celebrations, in which U.S. Latinos draw upon ancestral forms of social solidarity while at the same time transforming them. Examining changes in meaning that occur when preindustrial, religious rituals are practiced in modern, secular contexts, this chapter shows how the mediums of ritual, myth, and aesthetics are used to create community. Unlike most Latin American Day of the Dead altars that are dedicated to family members, U.S. altar installations frequently honor deceased Latino cultural icons from throughout Latin America and the United States, ranging in diversity from the Venezuelan-born, nineteenth-century, anticolonial champion Simón Bolívar, to the Tejana pop singer Selena. Each Day of the Dead season, a variety of writers, musicians, artists, filmmakers, actors, political activists, and others are commemorated as the collective ancestors of U.S. Latinos. Through public ritual and art, unofficial histories about important cultural and political contributions of Latinos to U.S. society and the world—ignored for decades by schools, museums, mass media, and other mainstream institutions—are publicized and validated.

Chapter 5 illustrates the radicalization of the celebration in the U.S. context, as Chicanos and other U.S. Latinos transformed formerly religious rituals into media for transmitting political messages. A significant number of U.S. Day of the Dead altars, processions, vigils, and other events draw attention to sociopolitical causes of death affecting the Latino community (such as police brutality, unsafe labor conditions, or dangerous border crossings), invoking a "moral economy" form of social protest. Empirical examples describe how the deaths of local individuals honored in U.S. Day of the Dead events serve to personalize abstract political discourses concerning issues of national and global importance, encouraging moral reflection and political action. They illustrate that although contemporary globalization, with its intensified border crossings of peoples and cultures, has created new forms of exploitation, it has also given rise to new cultural practices and solidarities of resistance to racial, gender, and economic discrimination (Sreberny-Mohammadi 1996; Appadurai 1996; Chakravartty and Castañeda-Paredes 2002; Chen 1998; Hall 1998).

Chapter 6 explores and documents the dialectical relationship between Day of the Dead and the media. Unlike in Latin America, where the majority of people are familiar with rituals for remembering the dead on November 1 and 2, in the United States the mass media have played a critical role in educating the public. Radio, TV, films, the Internet, popular magazines, coffee-table books, art posters, T-shirts, museum catalogs, and classroom curriculum guides, among other media, have been crucial in teaching both Latinos and non-Latinos about Day of the Dead, while helping to dispel macabre misunderstandings about the celebration. Since 1972, mainstream news stories about the celebration have grown from nonexistent to common front-page material during the months of October and November. While validating and celebrating the growing presence of Latinos in U.S. society, a significant number of these articles discuss exhibits or events dealing with political topics. Given that Latinos have historically been underrepresented in U.S. news and advertising, and negatively portrayed in television and film, media coverage of Day of the Dead is an important form of mainstream visibility.

Chapter 7 examines the appeal of Day of the Dead for many non-Latinos who annually construct ancestor altars, attend cemetery vigils, view altar exhibits, and walk in Day of the Dead street processions. After tracing historical U.S. attitudes toward death from the belief that death was ever-present (a common mindset before and during the nineteenth century), to a denial of death (widespread during most of the twentieth century), to a search for more dignified, supportive, and collective ways to deal with death (through the hospice and "death with dignity" movements of the late twentieth century and the present), this chapter looks at how Day of the Dead rituals help fill a cultural void in U.S. society by providing a public space in which to tell stories about departed loved ones, collectively mourn, and heal. It also discusses Latino reactions to growing appropriations and modifications of the ritual, exploring concepts of cultural hybridity and authenticity.

Chapter 8 continues examining the issue of authenticity, this time in the context of the commoditization of Day of the Dead rituals, crafts, and products by museums, art galleries, stores, dance clubs, restaurants, tourism industries, and urban redevelopment organizations. Besides being the subject of more than 28 million English-language sites on the World Wide Web, Day of the Dead has been featured in commercial magazines such as *Better Homes and Gardens* and *Ladies' Home Journal,* and in radio and television programs on major networks such as FOX, HBO, NPR, and PBS. This celebration has inspired products and advertising campaigns at major corporations such as Starbucks and Amazon.com.[6] Some see the commodification of Day of the Dead as helpful in promoting Latino culture, but others feel it is exploitative and corrupting. With detailed examples, this chapter traces the historical relationship between the cultural renewal of the folk festivities of Day of the Dead in Mexico and their commodification both there and in the United States.

The most comprehensive scholarly analysis of U.S. Day of the Dead activities to date, this book examines the social, political, and spiritual meanings of the tradition for Latinos of diverse backgrounds, as well as for non-Latinos, who now make up a large proportion of U.S. Day of the Dead participants. In illustrating how the celebration has crossed geographical, racial, ethnic, class, and generational borders in an increasingly globalizing world, it is my hope that this research will stimulate further insights and discussions on the process of identity formation, the dialectical relationship between cultural practices and socioeconomic conditions, and the potential of art and ritual to create alternative public spheres for communication.

CHAPTER 1

An Ancient and Modern Festival

IT IS THE ANNUAL CELEBRATION OF THE DAYS OF THE DEAD. Billowy, white smoke meanders through the air, pungent with the musky-sweet scent of copal incense made of crystallized pine resin, used for centuries by the Indigenous peoples of Mesoamerica to communicate with the spirit world. The area is illuminated with countless candles and marigolds—their dazzling orange color and penetrating aroma said to lure heavenly souls to earth. With a trail of rose petals arranged on the ground as a pathway leading to it, a spectacular altar stands laden with flowers, grains, beans, corn, fruits, and other harvest gifts made to honor family spirits and deities at this special time of year. Along with mementos of the deceased, festive foods such as tamales, *pan de muerto* ("bread for the dead"), and hot chocolate are placed on the altar, together with a glass of water to quench the thirst of ancestral spirits who make the long trip from heaven to earth today. All of these things are offerings, or *ofrendas*, for the deceased. But where? Is this a village in southern Mexico? A community in the highlands of Guatemala? A rural cemetery in El Salvador? No. This event takes place some six thousand miles away in the Oakland Museum of California, with similar events happening at the Metropolitan Museum of Art in New York City, the Smithsonian Institute in Washington, DC, and hundreds of museums, schools, and community centers across the United States.

How did Day of the Dead, virtually unknown in the United States thirty-five years ago, become so popular here? This chapter discusses the fusion of both European and Indigenous remembrance practices seen in Day of the Dead rituals throughout Latin America. By illustrating that these rituals occur in numerous countries in the region, this chapter provides background through which to better understand the discussion of Mexico's Day of the Dead celebrations that will follow in chapter 2 and the emergence of Chicano celebrations discussed in chapter 3.

HONORING THE DEAD

The celebration known in Mexico and the United States as "El Día de los Muertos," or "The Day of the Dead," is a fusion of Indigenous and Roman Catholic rituals for honoring the deceased. In Latin America (and other areas with large Catholic populations such as Spain, Italy, France, Portugal, the Philippines, and Haiti), the "Days of the Dead" (a colloquial term referring to the period of All Saints' Day and All Souls' Day in the Roman Catholic liturgical calendar) are observed, respectively, on November 1 and 2.[1] Although All Saints' Day is officially referred to in Spanish as "El Día de Todos los Santos," and All Souls' Day is called "El Día de las Ánimas," the two days are conceptualized as one holiday throughout Latin America, with both days implied in popular expressions such as "Todos Santos" (All Saints' [Day]) or "El Día de los Difuntos" (Day of the Deceased). In Mexico, the more playful and somewhat less reverent term, "El Día de los Muertos" (Day of the *Dead*), rather than the softer "Day of the *Deceased*" is in popular use.[2] Whether one is speaking in English or Spanish, the term "Day of the Dead" (or El Día de los Muertos) is the only expression used to refer to the artistic and cultural celebrations of the holiday in the United States. In this book, "Day(s) of the Dead" is used to refer to celebrations occurring on November 1 and November 2 in both Latin American countries and the United States.

The observance of Day of the Dead traditions throughout Latin America for more than five hundred years makes this celebration a point of cultural continuity for peoples of diverse Latino ancestries living as racial minorities in the United States. Some 40 percent of U.S. Latinos have ancestry from Latin American countries other than Mexico, and as new Latino immigrant groups participate in Day of the Dead activities, they manifest their regional traditions, transforming these celebrations into pan-Latino events. For example, Honduran and Bolivian immigrants have held Day of the Dead activities featuring their native foods and dances in Cleveland, Ohio; Chilean immigrants erected Day of the Dead altars in Minneapolis, Minnesota, to remember those who were disappeared during the dictatorship of Augusto Pinochet; and the Guatemalan community of San Rafael, California, hosted a Day of the Dead kite flying celebration in a local cemetery.[3] Not only are new Latino populations participating in U.S. Day of the Dead events, but wide-scale Latino migration over the past fifteen years to the Midwest, the Northwest, the Deep South, New England, and other regions of the United States with historically little or no Latino presence has brought the celebration far beyond its U.S. birthplace in the Chicano communities of California.[4] The greater diversity of Latino populations participating in U.S. Day of the Dead celebrations is reflected in newspaper coverage that increasing describes the holiday as "Latino" or "Hispanic" rather than exclusively Mexican:

"The spirits awakened for Día de los Muertos, or Day of the Dead, on Saturday, as Hispanics around Houston gathered at cemeteries to reunite with their loved ones. Derived from ancient Aztec, Mayan and other Indigenous traditions, the celebration is a festive remembrance of the dead."

"The Mexican and Central American tradition of Día de los Muertos dictates that the souls of the dead return every year to visit relatives."

"Día de los Muertos isn't celebrated only in Mexico, but in several other Latin American countries as well, including Guatemala, Peru and Bolivia."[5]

HISTORICAL BACKGROUND ON DAY OF THE DEAD IN EUROPE AND THE AMERICAS

Key practices of the celebration in Latin America include combinations of the following: sprucing up family grave sites by weeding, cleaning, and repainting them; refurbishing old headstones and crosses; placing flowers and candles on graves; constructing home shrines to honor departed relatives; preparing special holiday foods or drinks; and attending Catholic church services. These customs are carried out in diverse ways from country to country and vary from region to region *within* countries. In some areas, the holiday is celebrated with the standard Roman Catholic rituals of All Saints' Day and All Souls' Day, such as attending Mass, participating in novenas, and praying for the dead with rosary beads.[6] In many areas, these official Catholic rituals are mixed with popular practices of folk Catholicism such as shrine making, grave adornment, vigils, and street processions.[7] And in regions with large Indigenous populations, such as in the southern states of Mexico and rural areas of Guatemala, El Salvador, Bolivia, Peru, and Ecuador, the holiday is celebrated through combinations of official Catholic All Saints' Day and All Souls' Day practices, unofficial Catholic folk customs, and pre-Christian Indigenous rituals of honoring the ancestors. The fusion of these diverse religious practices is referred to by social scientists as "syncretism."

Syncretic religious beliefs and practices are found among Indigenous communities throughout the Americas, where people commonly pray to Jesus, Mary, and the saints for protection, while also seeking help from traditional *curanderos/as* (healers) who employ Indigenous practices of communicating with the spirit world. In the worldview of the Aztecs, Maya, Mixtecs, Aymara, Quechua, and other aboriginal peoples of Latin America, maintaining harmony between the worlds of the living and the dead was a crucial belief before the arrival of Europeans to the Americas, and festivals to honor the dead were conducted throughout the calendar year. In contrast to highly individualistic U.S. attitudes of personal space and identity, the worldview in Latin American Indigenous communities is communally oriented, where the maintenance of extensive networks of social relations is considered crucial for physical and psychological survival. It is commonly believed that the spirits of the dead, deities, and saints are always present among the living and must be properly tended to on a daily basis, especially during the Days of the Dead, to ensure the well-being of oneself and one's family.

Practices of honoring the ancestors were so deeply rooted in Indigenous Latin American populations that early Catholic missionaries found it impossible to eradicate "heathen" activities such as altar making, ritual drinking of alcohol, ceremonial dancing, and other oblations for the dead. These practices had similarities with European folk Catholic rituals—vestiges of Europe's pre-Christian religions—with which the Spaniards were already familiar, including customs of shrine making, the offering of food and mementos to the deceased, the adornment of grave sites, nocturnal vigils for the dead, the use of incense and fire to communicate with spirits and deities, and even ritual drinking and partying (at funerals and wakes, for example).[8] Many European folk Catholic rituals, such as costuming, Saints' Day street processions, ceremonial dancing, and mumming, had a playful and joyous feeling that more closely resembled the celebratory spirit of Indigenous Latin American celebrations than the somberness of official church rituals. Across the global Catholic diaspora, the aboriginal practices of native populations have historically been tolerated by Catholic missionaries to facilitate conversion to Christianity. When missionaries in Latin America could not eradicate Indigenous rituals for honoring the dead, they instead relocated them to correspond with the Roman Catholic liturgical dates of November 1 and 2.

The resulting celebrations were fusions of Indigenous customs, official Catholic practices, and folk Catholicism. An example of this amalgamation is the *ofrenda* (altar/offering) tradition of items customarily offered to the dead before the imposition of Christianity. Elements commonly placed on Day of the Dead ofrendas in Mexico, Central America, and South America include pre-Columbian foods such as fruits, legumes, gourds, tuber vegetables, tortillas, tamales, mole, the fermented corn drink *chicha*, the beverage *pulque*, squashes, grains such as quinoa, and various other delicacies, varying by country.[9] In ancient Mesoamerica, marigolds and copal incense were integral elements of altars for the dead, along with valuable commodities such as salt, cacao, shells, and other forms of monetary currency, all of which are still placed on ofrendas today.[10] Pre-Columbian elements are typically combined with images of saints, Jesus, the Virgin Mary, crucifixes, rosary beads, statuettes of angels, devotional candles (in tall glasses embossed with saint images), and other Catholic iconography. Photos of the deceased may be placed on altars.

Before Christianity, in both Europe and the Americas the most elaborate altars to honor the dead occurred at harvest times, when bountiful food offerings were possible. Mesoamericans, like most other peoples of Latin America, lived in agricultural societies where the fertility of the land was crucial for the continuance of family lineages. Believing that the ancestors were deeply involved in a family's ability to reproduce, people constructed ancestor altars at each harvest and performed ritual fertility dances during ceremonies honoring the dead (Lomnitz 2005). Such dances were carried over after Christianity was imposed and have continued to be performed at contemporary Day of the Dead celebrations in areas of South America (Milne 1965; Buechler and Buechler 1971; Coluccio 1991). Like the native peoples of the Americas, prior to Christianity Europeans also believed in a connection between agricultural fertility and human reproduction, as seen in the example of the ancient Celtic harvest celebration of Samhain (celebrated on November 1). At this time of the year, household doors were left unlocked, fires were kept burning in the hearth all night, and gifts of food and drink were arranged for the spirits of the dead believed to visit the living on this date (Santino 1994). Because November 1 was the first day of the Celtic new year and the first day of winter, it was thought to be a transitional time when the gates that separated the worlds of the living and the dead were open.[11] To facilitate converting Europe's "pagans" into Christians, the Catholic Church selected the same date for the liturgical celebration of All Saints' Day, followed by All Souls' Day on November 2.

The importance of the harvest in commemorating the dead illustrates a philosophical worldview in which the living and the dead were intrinsically connected in relationships of reciprocity. Death was not considered the end of life, but rather the continuum of life, necessary for regeneration and rebirth. The symbolic association of life (harvest, fertility, sexuality) and death is visible in past and present rituals for honoring the dead in both Europe and Latin America. In Europe, life-affirming events such as courtship and marriage traditionally occurred around All Souls' Day (Santino 1994, xiii). In Scotland, Ireland, and Wales, from at least the eighteenth century until the early twentieth century, All Souls' Day was the time of the year for making marital matches or engaging in games of divination rituals meant to reveal the name of one's future spouse (Santino 1994, xii; 1998, 117; Rogers 2002, 44–48). In Italy, All Souls' Day is the traditional time of year when marriage proposals are made and engagement rings proffered. Similarly, in Bolivia and Peru, fertility rituals are performed by young people in Indigenous villages during the Days of the Dead (Buechler and Buechler 1971, 84; Coluccio 1991, 115). Particularly in Arequipa and Cuzco, Peru, courtship rituals are performed in which young men bring cake made in the shape of babies to their girlfriends, and in Tomaiquiche, Peru, men go out at dawn on November 2 to serenade their girlfriends (Milne 1965, 163; Coluccio 1991, 117). In Guatemala, teenagers typically meet members of the opposite sex in the cemeteries during the nocturnal festivities of Day of the Dead.[12] In regions of Mexico, Ecuador, Peru, and Bolivia, Day of the Dead bread is made in the shape of babies, symbolizing fertility. The cyclical association of mating (new life) and death is also seen in Mexico, where one of the most common contemporary Day of the Dead motifs is a skeletal bride and groom, donned in white wedding dress and tuxedo.

Over centuries, however, official church doctrine replaced many (but not all) folk religious beliefs in Europe, so that stark distinctions now appear between contemporary European All Souls' Day and Latin American Indigenous celebrations of Day of the Dead. These include differing perceptions of the relationship between the living and the dead. In the official Catholic version of the holiday, dominant in contemporary Europe and among Latin Americans who identify more closely with European than Indigenous ancestry, the souls of children and other sexual innocents are believed to ascend directly to heaven, while those of adults are thought to suffer in purgatory, occupying a lower hierarchical position than the spirits in heaven. The role of the living in this scenario is to pray on November 1 to the saints (souls already in communion with God and thus residing in heaven) for general help with life and, particularly, for intercession on behalf of deceased family members to hasten their journey from purgatory to heaven. November 2 is designated to remembering those souls not yet in heaven and praying for their eventual deliverance. Among Indigenous peoples of Latin America, however, the hierarchical structure between purgatory and heaven is not emphasized. Most people assume that their deceased loved ones are automatically in a positive place, free from the tribulations of life. Both dates are seen as a time of happy family reunion where reciprocal relationships with the ancestors are reaffirmed, social ties between community members are ritually maintained, and the support of the dead in the economic, political, and social lives of the living is ensured.[13] Rather than asking saints to intercede on behalf of their relatives in purgatory, celebrants often ask saints and dead relatives to help them with their worldly affairs.[14]

Another distinction between Latin American and European celebrations revolves around the meanings given to the dates. According to official Catholic doctrine, November 1 is the date when Catholics should pray to the saints, while November 2 is dedicated to praying for the souls not yet in heaven. However, Mesoamerican Indigenous peoples have infused these dates with additional significance, based on the pre-Columbian belief that the souls of children and adults visit the earth on separate dates. The period of October 31 to November 1 is popularly believed to be the time when the souls of children visit the earth, and the evening of November 1 through the dawn of November 2, the time when the souls of adults arrive (Bade 1997, 13;

Carmichael and Sayer 1991, 20; Rogers 2002, 144; Maya and Mixtec celebrants, personal discussion).[15]

There are also major differences between European and Latin American
conceptualizations of death. Christian Europe has historically had finite and
frighteningly apocalyptic formulations of death, including medieval anguish
about the end of the world, the eerie figure of the Grim Reaper clutching a
sickle to sever human life, and notions of hell as a place of excruciating
torment (Reuter 1979, 73–74). In contrast, pre-Columbian cultures viewed
the afterworld as a desirable province offering peace from earthly suffering. It
is this distinct attitude toward death that continues to characterize Indigenous
Day of the Dead celebrations in Latin America. Unlike official Catholic All
Saints' Day and All Souls' Day observances filled with thoughts of suffering
and supplications to free souls from their purgatorial incarceration, Day of the
Dead celebrations in Indigenous regions of Latin America reflect celebrants'
excitement about the homecoming of departed relatives. As one Guatemalan
explained, "Day of the Dead here is similar to Thanksgiving in the United
States, because people travel across the country to be reunited with family
members, living and dead."[16]

Because cultural practices of the Americas, Europe, the Middle East, Asia,
and Africa have influenced each other for centuries, affecting both European
and Latin American Day of the Dead practices, it is sometimes confusing to
determine the origins of traditions. One example is the edible sugar skulls
produced in Mexico each Day of the Dead season. Because of their ubiquity
in Mexico at this time of year, these white skulls, decorated with colored
frosting, have become internationally recognized symbols of Mexico. The
skulls are commonly thought to be Aztec in origin, yet a deeper look reveals
a more complicated story. Although pre-Columbian peoples of Mexico made
flatbreads and sweets with amaranth seeds as offerings for the deceased, the
custom of making sugar-based, skull-shaped sweets for Day of the Dead was
introduced to Mexico by the Spaniards (Brandes 1997, 293). According to
Carmichael and Sayer, the practice dates back to twelfth-century Italy, where
sugar skeletal treats were "affectionate presents for the Day of the Dead, which
were offered to family and friends" (1991, 46). These sweets are still made
today in Italy on November 1 and 2.[17] The fusion of Indigenous and European symbols and rituals is discussed further in the following section, which
provides details on Day of the Dead traditions throughout Latin America.

DAY OF THE DEAD CUSTOMS IN VARIOUS
LATIN AMERICAN COUNTRIES

A description of Day of the Dead practices throughout the Latin
American region is necessary to understand why Latinos of diverse national
heritages are able to identify with the Chicano-initiated Día de los Muertos

celebrations of the United States. Whereas numerous scholarly and photo-graphic books have been produced about Mexico's Día de los Muertos celebrations, relatively little has been published on Day of the Dead rituals in other parts of Latin America. The following descriptions have been compiled from books about the Indigenous traditions of South America, newspaper articles published around the dates of October 31 to November 2 in Central American and South American dailies, my personal observations while living in Central America, and my interviews with people from diverse countries.

Central America

Guatemala provides a good example of how Day of the Dead observances can vary widely within a relatively small country. The towns of Santiago Sacatepequez and Sumpango, for example, are nationally known for their Day of the Dead kite-flying celebrations, in which predominantly Maya Kaqchikel villagers fly giant ornately designed kites (some larger in circumference than most planetariums) in the cemeteries to help traveling spirits find their way back to earth. Notes to the dead are often attached to the kite strings, ascending into heaven as a kind of telecommunication. To the delight of hundreds of participants and onlookers, a festival atmosphere prevails in and around the cemeteries, with vendors selling food, flowers, candles, and the hot corn porridge, *atole de maiz*. Whether elaborate tombs or simple mounds of dirt, graves are lovingly adorned with flowers, candles, and foods for the dead. In the village of Todos Santos, a town literally called "All Saints" (indicating the great importance of the holiday for this town's Maya-Mam inhabitants), November 1 and 2 are special festival days, complete with parades, competi-tive games, and carnival rides. Todos Santos is known for its wild November 1 horse races accompanied by much drinking of chicha.[18] Villagers prepare special foods for the ancestors and place them on family graves as offerings. Later, the food is shared with family and friends (Cameron 1999, 705; Milne 1965, 163; Todos Santos residents, personal interviews).

In the tropical Atlantic Coast region of Izabál, Guatemalans repaint ceme-tery tombs in vivid colors, recarve wooden cross grave markers, lay wreaths of flowers (*coronas*) on graves, and hold family picnics in the cemeteries.[19] In the town of Salcajá, Day of the Dead is celebrated with nocturnal candlelight vigils in the cemetery, where mementos and flowers are brought to the graves and most of the town turns out to await the visiting souls. People carve small gourds, (*chilacayote*) with intricate geometric designs, placing a candle inside to create lanterns for the tombs. Children go door-to-door, ritually begging for candles to illuminate the cemetery, singing, "Candelitas para las ánimas benditas!" (Little candles for the blessed souls!).[20] During the night of November 1, friends and neighbors keep watch by family tombs and reminisce together about the departed. The atmosphere is happy, as children run about, marimba music is played, and the sweetly pungent smells of candles, marigolds, lilies, and copal incense fill the air. A similar nocturnal celebration occurs in the town of Huehuetenango, where people walk from tomb to tomb serenading the dead with their erstwhile favorite tunes.[21] In the capital, Guatemala City, small altars are set up in homes, stores, restaurants, bus terminals, and marketplaces. Trips to the cemetery tend to be more cursory than in rural areas, and greater emphasis is placed on the preparation of a special family dinner in which Guatemala's most famous Day of the Dead food, *fiambre* (a cold dish made of varieties of finely chopped sausages, meats, fish, poultry, and vegetables) is consumed.[22] Guatemalan anthropologist Celso Lara notes that Garifunas (Central Americans of Afro-Caribbean descent living in Guatemala, Honduras, and Belize) observe the holiday by pouring liquor around graves and sending small rafts carrying fire, water, and flowers to sea (1996).[23]

In the country of El Salvador, colorful waxed paper flowers and paper chains adorn tombs, and wreaths made of paper or fresh pine boughs are placed on grave sites for Day of the Dead. *Ojuelas*, sweet, fried tortillas drizzled with honey, are made specifically for this holiday and sold at busy food stands around the cemeteries. Family members leave small mementos by graves and sometimes tape letters to the tombs of loved ones. At a family's request, bands play songs at the tombs of the dead.[24] In Nicaragua, families light candles in the home for each deceased member and prepare *buñuelos* (fried dough pastries) and tamales. In rural homes, candles are arranged as an "altar" on the floor.[25]

South America

The work of Hans Buechler, who has conducted extensive research on the Indigenous customs of the Andes, reveals many similarities between Mesoamerican and Andean Day of the Dead festivities. The following description shows that Bolivian Day of the Dead rituals of the Aymara people have much in common with ofrenda practices of southern Mexico:

> The first of November is a day of food preparation. Any family who "has a warm dead" (i.e., who grieves the recent death of a sibling, parent or child) prepares an "altar" for the soul (or souls) of the deceased relative (or relatives) in the house where he or she lived. First, they shape an arch out of two sugar canes . . . over a table . . . and place two candles on either side; then they heap the table with bananas, oranges, bread, agricultural produce and quinoa or *k'espiña* dough figures and sometimes milk, alcohol and coca. The bread and k'espiña are prepared specially for the occasion. (1980, 80)

Buechler explains that special bread is baked in the shapes of wreaths, ladders, people, babies, and animals. In both its form and use, this bread resembles the pan de muerto made during the Days of the Dead in Mexico.

In the evening, family members, *comadres* and *compadres* (symbolic relatives connected through godparent relationships), friends, and neighbors visit to pray in front of the ofrendas and share in eating the specially prepared foods. "If the deceased liked coca during his lifetime or was inclined to drink beer or white rum," notes Buechler, "the host may offer these items as well" (85).

The praying and eating continue all night, while boys go from house to house singing and collecting bananas and oranges for the deceased (ritual begging) in exchange for their songs. On November 2, Buechler observes, "the entire community gathers in the graveyard. Each family rebuilds the 'altar' with the food not yet distributed the day before on top of the flat-roofed, hut like structures that mark the graves. Renewing their prayers for the souls, relatives move from one grave to another . . . groups of singing boys perform at every grave" (85). Praying, singing, and food distribution in Bolivian cemeteries are sometimes followed by ritual fertility dances in the town plaza (Buechler and Buechler 1971, 84; Coluccio 1991, 115).

Felix Coluccio provides a similar account of Bolivian Day of the Dead ofrenda and cemetery rituals, observing that on the evening of November 1, families leave graveside offerings of breads, fruits, and foods enjoyed by the dead. On November 2, having prayed in the cemetery for most of the preceding night, he notes, the relatives of the dead partake in "abundant food and frequent libations, ending the day with merriment and dancing" (1991, 115). Jean Milne likewise observes, "In the Andean countries it is customary to bring food and people feast, dance and make merry in the cemeteries until dawn of the third [November 3]. In some places, food and drinks are sold at special stands set up on the grounds. Andean Indians often pray to their dead for good crops and set up altars of their favorite foods, of which the dead may partake in spirit" (1965, 162).

Both Milne and Coluccio provide descriptions of Day of the Dead activities they observed in Indigenous communities in Peru, where tombs are adorned with multicolored paper decorations, flower wreaths, and freshly painted crosses. They note that pots are carried to the cemetery, filled with roasted pig, tamales, breads, and other *alma micuy* (meaning "favorite foods" in the Quechua language), presented as offerings for the dead. After a Catholic priest blesses the offerings, the food is later shared with family and friends (Coluccio 1991, 117; Milne 1965, 162–163). On November 2, in the region of Huancavélica, Peru, there are horse races and various types of competitive games, together with more eating, drinking, and partying (Coluccio 1991, 117). Offering a more recent discussion of Day of the Dead practices in Peru, César Abilio Vergara notes that on November 1, in the mountains of southern Peru, ofrendas are made for the dead "for whom dishes and drinks that they most liked in life are prepared, and for whom vigils are held during the night" (57). On November 2, families visit the cemetery offering flowers, candles, and prayers. Headstones are replaced or repaired, and "there is a festive atmosphere on the walkway leading to the cemetery where food and beverage booths are set up, and the population participates enthusiastically and massively" (1997, 57).

Similar festivities have been documented in areas of rural Argentina where, according to Coluccio, from the evening of October 31 through November 2 in the Cochinoca, Rinconada, Santa Catalina, and Yavi regions, kitchen tables are converted into ofrendas of meals, special breads, fruits, jams, cocoa, and chicha (1991, 1995). Vigils and prayers for the souls are held during the night and ceremonies are performed between compadres. Later, the offerings are taken to the cemetery, where part is buried and the rest shared among friends and family. In other areas of Argentina, such as Palermo and Cachi, he notes, a game of chance involving the throwing of "ankle bones" (*taba*) is played while vigils are kept alongside the ofrendas (1991, 113).[26] In the Argentine regions of Tafí and Tafí Viejo, Tecumán, families make ofrendas filled with doll-shaped bread known as *guaguas*, and prepare "the dishes most fancied by the deceased." They carry pots of food to family tombs and arrange portions for the souls of the dead: "It is the belief that the souls partake only of the essence of the food, leaving the meal for their kinsmen, who have spent the night praying, chatting and drinking fig brandy, ingesting coca, and drinking chicha" (114). In Caldimonte, Argentina, he reports, special foods for the dead are left in a room with a closed door "so that the souls can enter without being bothered" (14). The author also observes that in the country of Colombia, cloth is draped over tombs during November 1 and 2, converting them into ofrendas of candles, flowers, and foods "most appreciated by the deceased." A priest is invited to bless the offerings and after much praying, the foods are consumed by participants (18).

In Ecuador, a bloodlike, blackberry drink called *colada morada* is prepared specifically during the Days of the Dead, along with guaguas, found throughout the Andes.[27] The widespread consumption of anthropomorphic breads in the Andean region during the Days of the Dead (also seen in Oaxaca, Mexico) is noted by Brandes (1997, 285) and Rogers (2002, 144). Indigenous Quechuas of Ecuador visit cemeteries to clean and restore grave markers. They place ofrendas of flowers, guaguas, and fresh fruits (particularly bananas, oranges, and apples) on top of family graves, and pray and picnic in the cemetery.[28] In Quito and other urban areas of Ecuador, it is common for both Indigenous people and Mestizos (people of mixed Indigenous and Spanish heritage) to visit cemeteries on November 1 and November 2, to clean, refurbish, and decorate family graves with flowers,

candles, guaguas, and mementos. As one Ecuadorian told me, "The cemeteries are packed on these dates!"

THROUGHOUT LATIN AMERICA, there are ethnic, race, and class differences that
influence one's level of participation in the celebration, and the Day of the
Dead practices considered to be most authentic are those carried out by rural
and Indigenous populations. By comparison, the upper classes (having more
European than Indigenous ancestry) and the upwardly aspiring middle classes
adhere more closely to official Catholic observance. My intention here has
been to illustrate both the presence of this celebration throughout various
areas of Latin America, and the similarities of certain practices across ethnic
and geographical locations. The following chapter reviews the modern history
of Day in the Dead in Mexico, as a way to set the stage for our discussion of
U.S. Chicanos' engagement with the celebration.

CHAPTER 2

Mexico's Special Relationship with Day of the Dead

As MENTIONED EARLIER, Mexico is known internationally for El Día de los Muertos. But, why do people immediately associate Mexico with Day of the Dead? In an internationally lauded essay published in *The Labyrinth of Solitude* (and republished in numerous editions and languages since its first appearance in 1961), Mexican poet and Nobel Laureate Octavio Paz offers an answer. He proclaims that Mexicans, more than any other people, have a "special relationship with death." According to Paz, Mexicans "caress" death, "sleep" with it, "celebrate" it, and consider it their "most steadfast love." He states that "Death enters into everything we [Mexicans] undertake" and "Our relations with death are intimate—more intimate, perhaps, than those of any other people" (1981, 47–64).

Paz contends that contemporary Day of the Dead celebrations are the result of a "death obsessed" national character, allegedly inherited from the Aztecs. In conjuring up this essentialist national image, he ignores the many distinct ethnicities, races, and social classes that make up Mexican society. Yet, his wide renown as a writer has carried these words to Mexican and international audiences for nearly half a century. His essay is habitually cited in articles and films about Day of the Dead, and educators and artists in Mexico and the United States commonly point to Mexico's "special relationship with death" to explain the popularity of Day of the Dead in Mexico.[1] In reality, do Mexicans have a quintessentially death-obsessed national character? Is the contemporary popularity of Day of the Dead a palimpsest of Aztec beliefs and iconography? Such views are contested by scholars who draw attention to the social and political utility of these narratives in achieving nationalist objectives that serve the needs of government, commerce, and the mass media (Brandes 1998a; 2003; García Canclini 1987; Garciagodoy 1998; Lomnitz 2005; Monsiваís 1987; Navarette 1982).

Themes of death—particularly the public commemoration of dead patriots—and the national appropriation of Indigenous customs have historically been central components of nation building (Anderson 1991; Hobsbawm and Ranger 1992; Taussig 1997). Dismissing the notion of death-fixated Mexicans who laugh at *la muerte*, Mexican writer Carlos Monsiváis argues that this theme is a modern construct that arose in the popular imagination during the Mexican Revolution, when the stoicism of revolutionary solders facing government firing squads was widely publicized in newspapers, oral stories, and folk songs. The soldiers' refusal to show fear, he asserts, had nothing to do with Aztec philosophies of the afterlife, but was a typical reaction of captured soldiers anywhere who, out of pride, will deny enemies the pleasure of witnessing their discomposure. Monsiváis contends that the mythic relationship between Mexicans and death is the nostalgic creation of post-Revolution Mexican nationalists who, in forging a new national identity, found it politically useful to compare the triumphant revolutionaries to Aztec warriors. After the revolution, this "mythology . . . was so powerful that it continued, now used by the mass media (the movies, the magazines), and became a game of prefabricated enthusiasm for everyday Mexican experience" (1987, 16).

Anthropologist Néstor García Canclini similarly argues that throughout the twentieth century, Mexico's ruling oligarchies have romanticized Indigenous peoples and traditions as embodying an "authentic" national character to foster feelings of national unity. He notes that such discourses have facilitated the governance of a racially heterogeneous and economically unequal society, allowing the country's elites to advance their own interests while continuing to ignore the needs of Indigenous communities (1987, 1993). Critiquing essentialist assertions from another perspective, Mexican researcher Juanita Garciagodoy suggests that the stereotype of Mexicans laughing at death reinforces a jocular fatalism that ideologically undermines grassroots struggles to improve living conditions and defend human rights (1998). The following section describes Day of the Dead traditions in Mexico and illustrates how these traditions have been disdained, extolled, discouraged, and ultimately hailed again by government officials, artists, and educators. We will see that intervention by Mexican governmental and nongovernmental agencies, commercial interests, and the mass media has been crucial in the metamorphosis of Day of the Dead from a regional to a national holiday. An understanding of how this celebration became synonymous with Mexican national identity will help to contextualize the importance it has had for Chicanos in the United States.

FOLK AND POP CULTURE MANIFESTATIONS

As in most of Latin America, many Mexicans visit cemeteries between October 30 and November 2, to clean, refurbish, and decorate grave sites. *Papel picado* (intricate crepe paper cutouts made for festive occasions in Mexico and Central America to adorn homes, churches, and town squares) are ubiquitous during these days in Mexico, garnishing everything from tombs and altars to shoe stores, fast food chains, schools, discotheques, and hotels. In some areas of the country, nocturnal cemetery vigils are held to await the souls traditionally believed to descend to earth at this time of the year, and home altars are constructed to honor the dead. The southern regions of Oaxaca, Michoacán, Puebla, Chiapas, Vera Cruz, and Yucatán, home to Mexico's highest concentration of Indigenous peoples, are famous for their painstakingly elaborate ofrendas for the dead. These often include tables laden with pan de muerto, salt, grains, coffee, soda pop, alcoholic beverages, favorite foods of the deceased (such as tamales and mole), photos of the departed, mementos, candles, and Catholic iconography. Various sized tables, shelves, or crates may be used to create multileveled altars, which may be crowned with large arches or square frameworks overlaid with marigolds and/or hanging fruits (said to be gateways to welcome the spirits home). These spectacular works of art, carried on by certain Indigenous peoples of Mexico for generations, have gained worldwide attention, attracting millions of tourists each year, including photographers, filmmakers, journalists, and university researchers.

In most of Latin America, including many areas of Mexico, Day of the Dead activities would be classified as folk rituals (observed as a taken-for-granted part of the religious worldview of participants). However, unlike the rest of Latin America, Mexico has both folk and humorous pop culture manifestations of the holiday. In contrast to rural communities that hold muted Day of the Dead processions in which participants walk together from the church to the cemetery holding foods and decorations to place on grave sites, many urban areas of Mexico hold boisterous street parades in which participants carry giant skeleton puppets, dress as skeletons, or wear other motley costumes. Garciagodoy refers to this dichotomy as the difference between "earnest" and "carnivalesque" celebrations, noting that the latter does not necessarily preclude a level of earnestness or gravity. Where folk culture dominates, she notes, El Día de los Muertos consists almost entirely of "earnest" aspects such as visits with the dead and the sharing of ofrendas. Where popular culture dominates, some people observe these aspects of the commemoration, and others do not. In the latter group, "a number ignore the fiesta altogether, especially if their parents or grandparents did not celebrate it" (1998, 79–81).

Calavera Imagery

The most prominent symbol of Mexico's Day of the Dead is the *calavera*, or skull—often made of papier-mâché, clay, wood, plastic, metal, or cutout tissue paper. In particular, edible white sugar skulls decorated with colored icing have become internationally recognized emblems of Mexico. Piled on trays by the dozens in shops and open-air markets, these fanciful treats adorn ofrendas and are often exchanged between family and friends (who may write the donor or recipient's name across the skull's forehead) as tokens of affection. Mexico's Day of the Dead skull art also takes the form of marionettes, gigantic puppets, chocolates, toys, masks, paintings, statues, posters, mobiles, candleholders, and more. With humorous expressions that mimic the living and mock everyday behaviors, these images are said to be reminders of the brevity of life and inevitability of death, urging people to appreciate life today, because death may be just around the corner.

In addition, Mexico has a style of humorous poetry that is also known as "calaveras." Emerging in urban Mexico in the mid-nineteenth century as a carryover from nineteenth-century Spanish lampoons or *pasquines* (Carmichael and Sayer 1991, 58; Tinker 1961, 20), these satirical stanzas are written and published, often anonymously, during the Days of the Dead. The poems may touch on any theme and often take the form of joking "obituaries" for corrupt political leaders and other public figures. The custom of writing satirical verses during the Days of the Dead, also practiced in Guatemala and El Salvador, is part of government-mandated school curricula in Mexico, where local and national competitions are held for the pithiest epigrams.[2] This literary form of social satire originated as a practice of the well educated in Mexico City and to this day is most common in urban areas where literacy rates are highest. (Similarly, in Guatemala and El Salvador the custom is carried out mainly by university students.)

A latter twentieth-century rendition of calaveras to emerge in Mexico is seen in the miniature skeleton figurines known as *calaveritas*. About two inches in height, these mini-skeletons humorously reenact scenes from daily life, including weddings, funerals, sporting events, workplace scenarios, and drunken brawls. Sometimes accompanied by written captions, a significant number of calaveritas express commentary on sociopolitical issues. In tourist shops in Mexico City, Mérida, Cuernavaca, Acapulco, and Tijuana, one may find figurines dressed as police officers, extorting bribes from skeletal motorists, or skeletal waitresses fending off skeletal sexual harassers. Masuoka (1990) and Garciagodoy (1998) document how these miniature figures, crafted by working-class artisans, frequently spoof the wealthy and portray cynicism toward the government, expressing commentaries on political hypocrisy and class exploitation. Collectibles popular with Mexican students, urbanites, and international tourists, calaveritas are three-dimensional, highly accessible manifestations of the tradition of verbal satire expressed in calavera poetry.[3]

As noted earlier, Mexico's humorous Day of the Dead skeletons, found nowhere else in Latin America, are regarded by many as representing a singularly Mexican perspective on death, commonly said to be an inheritance from the Aztecs. This is a point of national pride for those Mexicans and Mexican

Americans who, as a decolonialization strategy, prefer to identify with the country's Indigenous rather than European history. Yet, historical and anthropological sources indicate that associating these skeleton crafts with Aztec imagery is a relatively modern interpretation. According to Mexican historian, Claudio Lomnitz, sugar skulls began to be compared with Aztec *tzompantli* (skull racks) only in the 1920s—"an association that is absent from eighteenth- and nineteenth-century sources" (2005, 48). Anthropologist Hugo Nutini writes that sugar skulls "are a good illustration of the difficulties in determining the functional, structural, and symbolic provenance of elements in a syncretic situation. At first glance, sugar skulls appear to be a survival from pre-Hispanic times. . . . But human skulls as a symbol of death has a long history in Christendom, and it could equally well be that the sugar skulls in the ofrenda are of Catholic origin" (1988, 222).

According to anthropologist Stanley Brandes, there is a lack of evidence to substantiate claims of lineage between ancient and modern Mexican skull iconography (1998b, 185–187). He offers several arguments to support his theory that contemporary Mexico's proliferation of skull art is more a colonial and postcolonial phenomenon than an inheritance from ancient Mesoamerican civilizations. First, he notes that the presence of skull imagery in ancient Mexico was not unique, since other pre-Columbian cultures employed similar iconography. Thus, the mere *existence* of skull iconography in Mexico's ancient past does not explain why Mexico alone came to produce humorous skeletal imagery. Second, he points out that the pre-Columbian Mesoamerican area known today as Mexico was not a single, undifferentiated entity, but a region of distinct cultures that had many different representations of death. Some of these cultures utilized skull iconography to represent death, and others did not. For example, in addition to images of human skulls, Maya cultures also represented death through the distinctive iconography of long black hair tied into the shapes of bows, images of decomposing corpses, and images of dead people shown with open mouths and closed eyes—none of which are present in the popular Mexican art associated with Day of the Dead (190). For the people of the central Mexico area of Teotihuacán, skulls and skeletons were relatively rare motifs (Berrin 1988; Winning 1987). Instead, Teotihuacán artists represented death through images of perforated disks or rings above the eyes or the forehead (Winning 1987, 58). The ancient cultures existing in the present states of Colima, Jalisco, and Nayarít rarely used skeletal representations, and although the Toltec culture at Tula exhibited prominent skull imagery, the artistic design and function were vastly different from contemporary Day of the Dead imagery (Fuente 1974). Aztec iconography included representations of skulls, but did not depict full-length skeletons. Moreover, ancient skull imagery had a stylized rigidity and seriousness vastly different from modern-day calaveras. Brandes concludes, "These archaeological remains display nothing of the playfulness and humor so essential to contemporary Mexican skull and skeletal representations. . . . Contextually, the use of skulls among the Aztecs could not be further removed from that among Mexicans in today's Day of the Dead celebrations" (1998b, 193–194).

In contrast, historical evidence points to a strong connection between Mexico's contemporary calavera imagery and the political caricatures of nineteenth-century Europe. Popular in Spain, France, Germany, Holland, and England, these caricatures, in turn, harked back to traditions of medieval European art rife with skeletal imagery (Brandes 1998b; Carmichael and Sayer 1991; Childs and Altman 1982; Garciagodoy 1998). Given that for hundreds of years Mexico was the political and cultural capital of New Spain and therefore more closely connected to European culture than the rest of Latin America, it makes sense that Mexico alone would develop the humorous calavera tradition. During colonial times, skulls and skeletons were important features of European iconography, as illustrated in the Dance of Death motifs popular across Europe from the fifteenth through the nineteenth centuries. Dance of Death images were highly animated skeletal figures exemplifying a range of human emotions such as gaiety, antagonism, lust, impudence, and sneakiness. Like many of today's Mexican calavera drawings, poetry, and figurines, these macabre depictions were a humorous form of social critique, with skeletons depicted doing human activities. They conveyed a message to the public about death's inevitability and equality before all—the very messages invoked today as being uniquely Mexican.

Boase (1972), Ariés (1981), and Kastenbaum (1989) have documented the popularity of the Dance of Death motif across Europe from the early 1400s through the late 1700s, where they appeared in manuscripts, paintings, and gravestones. Jas Reuter suggests that it was probably in the eighteenth century that images of Death as a comic skeleton were first made in Mexico. At this time, "Puppets and masks, figures made of clay, paper, and cardboard, toys and candies (from little sugar skulls to the bread for the dead) began to fill Mexico's popular markets with the image of the skull and the shape of the skeleton" (1979, 75). Garciagodoy also notes a probable connection between Mexican calaveras and European traditions: "It seems very likely that the spirit of social criticism and the comedy that infused European depictions and dramatizations of the dance of death were taken up and fitted to their new milieu in Mexico" (1998, 134).

The earliest documented example of skeletal imagery in Mexico's literary culture is thought to be the etchings accompanying the tragicomic protonovel, *La portentosa vida de la muerte*, published in 1792 by Fray Joaquín Bolaños and illustrated by Francisco Aguera (Bailey 1979; Garciagodoy 1998). Both the narrative structure and skeleton imagery of this play mirrored the types of writing produced in Spain and other areas of Europe at that time. But the major vehicle for popularizing social and political satire in Mexico was the penny press of the mid nineteenth century (Beezley 1987; Brandes 1998a). One of the earliest examples of skeletal depictions in Mexico's penny press was the short-lived literary magazine *El Calavera*, published in 1847. Providing burlesque and critical commentary on political events, the magazine included drawings of fully clothed, life-like people wearing white skeletal masks. Earlier European publications, such as the French *Voyage pour l' éternité*, published in 1830, also portrayed satirical skeletal figures representing death, and it is known that French and other European magazine caricatures were popular in Mexico at this time.

Although several examples of skeletal imagery in Mexican publications preceded them, the engravers Manuel Manilla (1830–1895) and José Guadalupe Posada (1852–1913), hired in the late nineteenth century by Mexican publisher Antonio Vanegas Arroyo to create graphic images for popular texts, took calavera imagery in new directions. Posada, whose creative style was influenced by Manilla, is credited with originating several key innovations: the representation of death as a skeleton without the usual scythe, the creation of skeletal animals (LaFaye 1979, 139), and the depiction of cavorting skeletons adorned with human apparel (as opposed to prior etchings done in Europe and Mexico depicting fully clothed, in-the-flesh humans merely wearing skull masks). Posada created what has since become the most universally depicted of all calaveras—La Catrina—a female skeleton foppishly attired in the plumed, wide-brimmed hat fashionable with upper class Mexican women during the regimes of President Porfirio Diaz (1876–1880 and 1884–1911). La Catrina satirized the pretensions of the Mexican upper classes and their imitators who, like Porfirio Diaz, preferred the culture of Europe over the Indigenous foods, dress, and customs of Mexico.[4] Art historian Jacques LaFaye notes that the renowned Spanish painter, Francisco de Goya, had earlier made satirical *catrines* (dandies or fops) in eighteenth-century Spain. Whether Posada was familiar with Goya's catrines is unclear, although reproductions of Goya's and other European artists' work were imported in great numbers into Mexico from the eighteenth century onward (LaFaye 1979, 131).[5]

Posada's caricatures addressed issues of a Mexican society in conflict, critically commenting on the changes wrought by modernity, the corruption of government officials, the hypocrisy of the rich, and the suffering of the poor. Childs and Altman observe, "Anyone and everything was likely to be the subject of his illustrations, including political and revolutionary leaders, businessmen, members of the aristocracy, barmaids and others" (1982, 56). In the context of an international artistic movement, Posada and other Mexican artists were part of a repertoire of nineteenth-century urban popular art—prints, peep shows, plays, and fairground attractions—that addressed the historical circumstances of their times (Wollen 1989, 19; Brandes 1998b, 204).

The proliferation of calavera sketches produced by Posada "breathed new life into Death" (Reuter 1979, 75), and repopularized the traditional allegories of medieval Spain with a new twist (LaFaye 1979, 138).

This is not to say that Posada was not influenced at all by Aztec skulls but rather that the tradition of humorous skulls that he made so popular in Mexico had distinct roots in Europe. Posada employed diverse skeletal images, including Christian allegorical skeletons, the conventional pirate's skull and crossbones, and skull images reminiscent of the *tzompantli*, or walls of human skulls displayed in ancient Mesoamerican temples. According to LaFaye, he was one of the first modern artists to incorporate Aztec imagery into his work: "Posada's calaveras, if they are the reflection of the Hispano-Christian tradition, mark also the emergence of the Aztec past into modern Mexican art" (1979, 138).

Day of the Dead and Mexican Nationalism

Forgotten by the Mexican public toward the end of his life, Posada (who died unknown and penniless) was rediscovered after his death when Mexican intellectuals and artists in the post-Revolution 1920s sought to create a new "cultural nationalism" distinct from the historically dominant influences of Spain, France, or the United States (Brandes 1998b, 202–205; Hamill 1999, 81–84; Rochfort 1993, 33–34; White 2001, 17–19). This was the period known as the Mexican Renaissance, when a burgeoning interest in Mexico's popular arts emerged among the country's elite. Seeing both artistic merit and populist charm in the work of Posada—a working-class Mestizo whose art had widely appealed to the urban lower classes—the most important modernist painters in Mexico, including Diego Rivera, José Clemente Orozco, David Alfro Siqueiros, Jean Charlot, and Dr. Atl, hailed his work as the embodiment of Mexico's Mestizo culture and claimed his influence on their own work. Art and film theorist Peter Wollen writes, "Th[e] particular role assigned to Posada was important both in relation to Mexicanism and in relation to Modernism. It gave credibility to claims to be part of an authentically Mexican artistic tradition . . . and, at the same time guaranteed the modernity of the tradition by aligning it with the revival of popular imagery among the European avant-garde. It was a way of solving the classic dilemma of evolutionary nationalism—how to be popular, authentic, traditional *and* modernizing all at the same time" (1989, 16).

With the newfound vogue for Mexico's popular arts in the 1920s came new veneration for the country's Indigenous cultures. This was the point in history when Aztec sculptures first acquired their status as classical art (Delpar 1992; Errington 1998; Lomnitz 2005, 48), and Rivera, Orozco, Siqueiros, and other artists were invited by the Mexican education minister José Vasconcellos (the initiator of Mexico's muralist movement) to tour the newly discovered ruins of Yucatán for artistic inspiration (Hamill 1999, 84). Vasconcellos had served alongside Pancho Villa in the revolution and believed that for Mexico to be a truly independent nation, it needed a revolution in culture that would fully embrace Indigenous music, dance, art, and architecture. Public murals, he realized, were a medium that would not only showcase a new Mexico to the world, but also would affect the way Mexicans thought about themselves (82).

Prior to this period, Diego Rivera had spent most of his professional life living and painting in France and Italy, emulating European artistic styles and subjects. During his 1921 visit to Yucatán, however, he filled his notebook with Aztec sketches and, having closely studied Posada's calavera drawings, later painted three highly visible and celebrated murals depicting Day of the Dead scenes at the National Ministry of Education in Mexico City (1923–1924). These scenes have since been written about and reproduced in countless postcards, books, magazines, posters, album covers, T-shirts, and other media depicting Mexico. National and international anthropologists and other scholars, inspired by the Mexican Renaissance in art and culture, subsequently produced scholarly accounts of Day of the Dead that reinforced claims that the celebration was a one-of-a-kind Mexican phenomenon derived from ancient Aztec culture.

Powerful ideological work is accomplished by asserting claims of lineage from pre-Columbian iconography and rituals to contemporary Day of the Dead practices. This has both positive and negative consequences. On one hand, identifying with Mexico's ancient cultures has helped create a sense of unity, distinction, and cultural pride among Mexicans and, as we shall see in chapter 3, among Chicanos. On the other hand, claims that Mexicans are still linked to an ancient past reinforce essentialized, exotic stereotypes of Latinos, who are typically portrayed in the media as "steeped in tradition," "closer to nature," and "more spiritual" than Anglos. Such associations can hinder Latinos from being seen as capable and cutting edge contemporary actors in the modern world (Dávila 2001). Furthermore, the privileging of Indigenous over European elements of Day of the Dead, common among Mexican nationalists in both Mexico and the United States, decontextualizes the tradition from the effects of five centuries of colonization, forced loss, and the resulting alienation from Indigenous languages and practices.

GOVERNMENT CAMPAIGNS AND TOURISM

Despite the admiration that Day of the Dead received from Mexican artists and intellectuals after the revolution, folk observances of the holiday waned in the early and middle twentieth century, as Mexico continued to modernize (Brandes 1988; Garciagodoy 1998; Nutini 1988). Indigenous-themed murals on public buildings and the government's promotion of Indigenous dances, music, and crafts did not eliminate the pervasive racism of mainstream Mexicans toward Indigenous peoples and practices (Dawson 2004; Friedlander 2006). Because of the contempt with which Indigenous people were treated by Mexico's lighter skinned middle and upper classes (a legacy of colonialism), many rural and Indigenous people who aspired toward middle-class lifestyles distanced themselves from their traditions. In the 1950s and 1960s, those who still constructed Day of the Dead ofrendas were mocked by "educated" Mexicans for their "superstitions."

A nursery school teacher from Puebla, who was interviewed by Carmichael and Sayer in 1989, explains,

> In the 1950s, when I was a child in school, we were ridiculed for believ-
> ing in *ofrendas*. If we admitted having one at home, we were laughed at
> for our incredulity. Those who honoured Day of the Dead, so it was said,
> were the victims of superstition and hallucination. . . . By 1972 . . . the
> authorities revised their views. . . . Now the Government wants to shore
> up our sense of pride and national identity. Mexico's future lies with its
> children: when official policy was reversed, La Secretaría de Educación
> Pública asked schools and nursery schools to promote Mexican culture;
> teachers, who had mocked our traditions, were told to endorse them.
> (1991, 118)

This passage depicts both the lack of public appreciation for Day of the Dead in Mexico in the mid-twentieth century, and the increased national interest in the holiday twenty years later, when the Mexican government began to officially promote it. The government's embrace of Indigenous culture was aimed at increasing economic development and, like the proponents of the earlier Mexican Renaissance, in fostering a united identity among an ethnically, racially, and economically heterogeneous nation (Dawson 2004; Errington 1998; García Canclini 1995).

In the 1970s, the Mexican Ministry of Tourism began to advertise the celebration as part of a concerted push to promote tourism and economic development in the impoverished southern states. Based on his fieldwork in the village of Tzintzuntzan, Michoacán, now a tourist destination for Day of the Dead seekers, Brandes notes that prior to 1971, the town "celebrated the Day of the Dead exactly as did countless other rural communities throughout Michoacán and Mexico as a whole, that is, in a relatively muted fashion" (1998a, 367). He states that before the 1970s, this fiesta was minor in Tzintzuntzan's annual fiesta cycle: "Villagers would decorate home altars in simple motifs. Some bereaved community members would spend several hours at gravesites, especially on the first anniversary of the death of a relative. Otherwise, people paid little attention to the occasion; it certainly attracted few if any outside visitors" (367). In 1971, however, governmental agencies intervened to stimulate tourism. Incentives were offered so that more local people would participate, and activities associated with the fiesta expanded enormously. Brandes concludes, "Tourism has virtually created Tzintzuntzan's Day of the Dead, or at least, embellished the traditional observance beyond recognition" (1988, 89).

By 1980, thousands of tourists attended the Tzintzuntzan Day of the Dead fiesta, in which local townspeople participated but government outsiders ran the show. Heavy traffic became endemic, television cameras flooded the cemetery with glaring lights, and the town became a stage for a "gala performance" of national identity. Brandes notes similar upsurges in Day of the Dead celebrations in other rural areas of Mexico, while folklorists Kay Turner and Pat Jasper also observe that in the 1970s, "the Mexican celebration of Day of the Dead achieved a new status as a tourist attraction, especially in south and central Mexico" (1994, 133).

Today in Mexico City and throughout the country, Day of the Dead is an exuberant commercial festival, complete with televised parades, concerts, theater productions, dance performances, ofrenda competitions, "discos for the dead," and a variety of other secular activities. Businesses, schools, and universities are urged by the government to construct ofrendas, and Day of the Dead is a mandatory part of Mexican educational curricula for school children. Since the 1970s, Day of the Dead tours have been marketed to tourists from North America, Europe, Asia, and Australia, and many celebrations in rural Mexican towns now have more foreigners and television cameras present than native residents. Local traditions have been drastically altered by the intervention of government tourism officials, who disregard the wishes of residents. In a telling example of governmental priorities, the Tzintzuntzan villagers' desire for electricity in the cemetery (instead of fire torches) was overridden by government officials who wanted to satisfy the romantic expectations of tourists (Brandes 1988).

Illustrating the dialectical relationship between culture and political economy, the previous section reveals how policies employed by government and business leaders encouraged people throughout Mexico to embrace as their national heritage provincial Day of the Dead traditions that were previously denigrated by educated persons. This dynamic is vividly apparent in the Mexican-U.S. border region—an area historically more connected to U.S. culture and less connected to Indigenous traditions than anywhere else in Mexico. Until the 1990s, the Day of the Dead traditions of Mexico's Indigenous peoples were not publicly seen along Mexico's northern border, either because settlers to this region had come from non-Indigenous areas of Mexico or because they had abandoned their Indigenous cultural patterns after migrating north.[6] From at least the 1950s onward, Halloween, rather than Day of the Dead, was enthusiastically celebrated in the border regions, and is still popular there today.

For a combination of reasons related to Mexican nationalism, Mexican American cultural pride, and tourist businesses on both sides of the border, southern Mexico–style Day of the Dead celebrations have grown common since the late 1990s in both Mexican and U.S. border towns. Interviews with long-term residents on both sides of the border reveal that public Day of the Dead events organized by schools, community centers, art galleries, city governments, stores, and hotels are recent developments. Middle-aged natives of Tijuana, Mexicali, Ciudad Juarez, Nogales, and Chihuahua, Mexico, for example, have told me that they grew up celebrating Halloween exclusively. The business community's desire for increased tourism and economic growth partly explains the surge of Day of the Dead in northern Mexico, as a fifty-two-year-old Tijuana college professor observes, "Lots of hotels, restaurants and stores noticed that Americans who came here expecting to find Day of the Dead were disappointed when they realized there wasn't anything. So they started organizing activities, making ofrendas, and selling sugar skulls. You never saw these things in Tijuana when I was growing up. Day of the Dead was not something we did at home or learned about in school."[7] This recent phenomenon is the topic of a *San Diego Union-Tribune* article, which notes that vendors in the Mexican border towns of Rosarito, Ensenada, and Tijuana, who twenty years ago did not sell Day of the Dead crafts, now do a brisk year-round business with U.S. tourists. A Tijuana shop employee is quoted in the article, saying, "almost everyone who buys Day of the Dead art is American."[8]

Aside from the commercial motivations of business and government (discussed further in chapter 8), some residents of northern Mexico have embraced Day of the Dead as a way to reject U.S. cultural and political hegemony. The rising popularity of the celebration in northern Mexico coincides with growing feelings of nationalism among Mexicans who resent the expanding U.S. dominance over Mexico's economic scene since the 1994 implementation of the North American Free Trade Agreement (NAFTA). The following *Los Angeles Times* excerpt connects the rise of Day of the Dead in northern Mexico to concerns of cultural imperialism, describing an "aggressive" Day of the Dead campaign promoted by Tijuana's Instituto de la Cultura and city municipal leaders:

> Tijuana has embraced Halloween for decades, something that might seem inevitable in a region where Mexican children grow up closer to U.S. shopping malls than the wellsprings of Mexican culture. But now, schools and culture officials are fighting back with an aggressive campaign to popularize Mexico's venerated Day of the Dead. . . . The campaign is encouraging parents to take the family for a traditional Mexican cemetery picnic in which food is set out to invite deceased spirits to join the living. School children are learning to write the traditional calavera

poems. . . . Before long, sugar skulls and special Day of the Dead breads began appearing in Tijuana markets, officials say. People—and strolling troubadours—began to flock to beautiful candlelit graveyards. A funeral home kicked off the first altar contest . . . now there's a boom. The Day of the Dead movement is part of the emerging identity of a generation of border adults who grew up alongside the United States. . . . To help remember everything, Tijuana officials have an itemized altar checklist.[9]

IN CHAPTER I, we learned that elaborate rituals for remembering the deceased on November 1 and 2 are not unique to Mexico, although it is the only country that is internationally known for its Day of the Dead traditions. To understand the reasons for the international popularity of Day of the Dead in Mexico, chapter 2 has taken a closer look at some of the political and economic motivations of elite actors in the promotion of Indigenous cultural practices during the 1920s and again from the 1970s onward. As a postcolonial, nationalist strategy, Day of the Dead has been strongly associated with the Aztecs, and European aspects of the celebration have been downplayed. Although elaborate Day of the Dead rituals have been observed by some Indigenous communities in Mexico for generations, many Mexicans—particularly in northern and central Mexico—have only recently begun to embrace the celebration. This has come in response to government education campaigns and media coverage portraying the celebration as a proud marker of Mexican national identity. We have seen how Mexican campaigns to promote Day of the Dead as representative of "Mexicanness," were popularized over time through school curricula, public murals, art exhibits, literature, and other forms of media. As we learn about the adoption of the celebration by Chicanos in the next chapter, we'll see how nonprofit organizations, commercial interests, the media, government initiatives, and foundation funding were also key factors in popularizing the tradition to a U.S. population (both Latino and non-Latino) that was largely unfamiliar with it.

CHAPTER 3

Day of the Dead in the United States

MEXICAN AMERICAN ALL SAINTS' DAY AND ALL SOULS' DAY RITUALS

SINCE AT LEAST THE 1890s, Mexican American families in south Texas and the Southwest have visited local cemeteries on November 1 and 2 to clean and decorate grave sites (Gosnell and Gott 1989; Turner and Jasper 1994; West 1989).[1] These customs resembled the grave decorating customs of other Catholic ethnic groups and did not include Indigenous practices of southern Mexico, such as making harvest-laden ofrendas or burning copal incense.[2] Nor were pan de muerto or sugar skulls part of Mexican American traditions. Before the 1970s, most Mexican Americans did not identify with (or know much about) Mexico's Indigenous cultures, and engaged in folk Catholic rather than Indigenous All Saints' Day and All Souls' Day customs.[3] Southwestern customs were carried out because of the religious beliefs of participants and were not performed for a public audience. Sometimes there were parish processions from the local Catholic church to the cemetery, but these resembled the solemn All Souls' Day processions typical of small Latin American towns and lacked the carnivalesque revelry of Mexico's urban Day of the Dead processions.

Attending Mass, having a special family meal, lighting candles for the departed, and making small home shrines for All Souls' Day were practices familiar to most Mexican American Catholics. Although families often brought picnic lunches to the cemeteries when they spent the day cleaning and decorating graves, Turner and Jasper note that food was not a central symbol of Southwestern observances and did not have the same meaning that food had in Indigenous Day of the Dead celebrations (1994, 145). Instead, they argue, picnicking in U.S. cemeteries was related to transportation difficulties, rather than to rituals of offering food to the dead. In an era when private automobiles were rare, a trip to the cemetery was an all-day family outing. It often required walking for miles or taking lengthy bus rides, making it necessary to pack food for the day.[4] As cars became more common after the 1960s, the authors observe, the level of picnicking at grave sites decreased noticeably. Gosnell and Gott similarly observe that until the post–World War II period, it was common for families to "take food and a little chair and stay [in the cemetery] the whole day," yet by the late 1980s their elderly respondents from San Antonio, Texas, lamented the fact that people no longer did such things (1989, 220).

Grave decorating customs were not practiced by all Mexican Americans but mainly by geographically segregated, working-class communities, particularly in south Texas, where many families had lived and died in the same communities for generations (given the long historical presence of Mexicans in this region). San Antonio's San Fernando cemetery (where Gosnell and Gott and Turner and Jasper conducted research in the late 1980s and early 1990s) was located in the lower-income Westside district, "sliced away from the city's heart" by a freeway. This physical separation from the city's Anglo neighborhoods contributed to a distinctly Mexican cultural milieu, whereas "groups in more flexible economic positions—the professional, technical, and managerial Mexican workers—tended to form enclaves away from the poorest sections or move to other parts of the city. The cultural as well as physical separation of the Westside discouraged or slowed acculturation for those who could not afford to leave the barrios" (Gosnell and Gott 1989, 218–219). Over time, younger Mexican Americans, like children of other immigrant groups, moved out of the barrio as a result of their improved educational and economic status, discontinuing the grave-decorating traditions of their parents and grandparents.

Texan John Gonzalez, whose father was the superintendent of cemeteries for the Catholic archdiocese of San Antonio from the 1940s through the 1970s, observed these changes over time from a unique vantage point:

> Our home was on the grounds of perhaps the best known Catholic cemetery here, San Fernando Archdiocesan Cemetery No. 2, in the West Side barrio. Day of the Dead was an annual observance in my back yard. I grew up in the 1950s and 1960s and lived in the cemetery until the early 1970s. We never called it Day of the Dead. It was always All Saints' Day and All Souls' Day. What I observed was nothing like nowadays. Today, throughout Texas, not just in cemeteries, there are more Day of the Dead arts and crafts and other influences from Southern and "interior" Mexico. The stylized skulls and skeletons are relatively new icons. At our San Antonio cemeteries, in the timeframe mentioned above, there were no such artifacts or influences. The observances were simple. They involved bringing flowers (marigolds and mums) to the grave, tidying up around the grave and maybe having a picnic where people sat around for

hours as other relatives came by. . . . The high point was an All Souls'
Day Mass on the cemetery grounds, usually led by the Archbishop. . . .
Many Texan families incorporated Halloween traditions in the 50s, 60s,
and 70s. They continued with grave visits, but the picnics and other long
vigils faded, in my opinion, because that was viewed as a Mexican peasant practice.[5]

Carmen Lomas Garza, a Chicana artist who has created Day of the Dead
altar installations in galleries and museums throughout the United States,
remembers making grave-site decorations of paper wreaths and paper flowers
(dipped in melted wax to protect them) while growing up in Kingsville, south
Texas, in the 1950s and 1960s. She recalls, "On November 2, we would all go
as a family and take our picnic lunch and work clothes and gardening tools
and go to the cemetery and clean off the graves, clean off all the weeds, and
decorate the graves. And while we were doing this, our parents and grandparents and the elders would tell us stories about each of the dead people
whose graves we were cleaning." Like Gonzalez, Garza notes that calavera
imagery was not part of these festivities: "I didn't see any skeletons or skulls
or anything like that at the cemetery. It was mostly flowers and candles. I don't
remember people using copal incense, either."[6]

Researchers at the Southwest Folklore Center at the University of
Arizona, working in the early 1980s in Nogales, Arizona, and Nogales,
Mexico, note that November 1 and 2 customs among Mexican Americans
living in the Arizona-Mexico border region, like those in Texas, did not
include skull imagery, ofrendas, or pan de muerto. They observe that these
elements had recently been introduced to Nogales by immigrants from farther
south and by members of Nogales's intellectual community. The authors
recount a story of a baker who moved to Nogales, Mexico, from Mexico City
and began baking pan de muerto: "The first year he displayed his pan de
muerto, everyone who came into his bakery wanted to know what it was. This
custom was unknown in Nogales. Now, due perhaps to a combination of his
efforts and to continuing immigration from further south, he makes and sells
pan de muerto in a considerable quantity" (Griffith 1985, 12–17).

In contrast to the border communities in Texas and the Southwest, most
Mexican Americans in large urban areas of the United States did not visit
cemeteries on November 1 and 2. Reasons include the greater pressure faced
by ethnic minorities in large cities to assimilate Anglo cultural norms, and the
fact that most city dwellers were migrants who did not have relatives buried
nearby. Therefore, most urban Mexican Americans had little firsthand experience with the cemetery rituals of November 1 and 2, although many attended
Mass and shared a family dinner to commemorate All Saints' Day and Souls'
Day. In an essay about Chicano Day of the Dead celebrations, Latin American

Studies Professor Sybil Venegas notes that Day of the Dead was "virtually unknown" to urban Mexican Americans in the mid-twentieth century (2000), a sentiment confirmed in the interviews conducted for this book. Nonetheless, the cultural importance of remembering the dead, whether through cemetery visits, home shrines, a family dinner, or prayer, was familiar to all Mexican Americans, making it possible for Chicanos to quickly connect with the Día de los Muertos celebrations of Mexico's southern Indigenous communities.

A CHICANO TRADITION IS BORN

The 1960s and 1970s marked a decisive period in U.S. history, when U.S. Latinos and other people of color were deeply engaged in struggles for civil rights, public recognition, and respect from the larger Anglo society. As part of a multipronged political and cultural movement that included literature, music, murals, and other public art forms, Chicano activists in California began to organize Indigenous-inspired Day of the Dead processions and ofrenda exhibits as a way to honor Mexican American heritage. An urban, artistic, and political phenomenon that would evolve into a requisite tradition of the Mexican American community, these celebrations had vastly different purposes than either the All Souls' Day observances of the American Southwest or the Indigenous Day of the Dead rituals of southern Mexico.[7]

Rejecting assimilationist theories that claimed ethnic minorities could become real Americans only through accommodating themselves to Anglo norms, Chicanos adopted Day of the Dead as a way to challenge conventional ideas of what it meant to be an American. Given that Mexican Americans had long been marginalized by mainstream U.S. society, Day of the Dead celebrations were "a momentous statement of cultural affirmation," says Tere Romo, a Chicana curator who has been deeply involved in Day of the Dead exhibits in California, Chicago, and other parts of the United States for more than thirty years (2000, 20). The Chicano Movement of the 1970s "grew out of the combined efforts to establish farm labor unions by Mexican farm workers in California and Texas; to recognize the plight of dispossessed land grant owners in New Mexico; to acknowledge problems facing the urban working class in Mexican American barrios across the Southwest and Midwest; and to integrate the concerns of the growing youth and student movement" (43). At the forefront of the movement were Chicano artists who were responding to the political, economic, and social oppression of Mexican Americans through the medium of *arte contestatario*—art designed to challenge mainstream racist tropes about Latinos (Gómez-Peña 1986, 86).

Emerging at a time of widespread social justice activism by disenfranchised populations in the United States and throughout the world, the Chicano Movement was influenced by Black civil rights activism, the

American Indian Movement, the Women's Liberation Movement, and the Gay and Lesbian Rights Movement. Romo observes that "The Black Power Movement with its emphasis on political autonomy, economic self-sufficiency, and cultural affirmation influenced the Chicano Movement greatly," while the value Chicanos placed on their Indigenous history in the Southwest provided an important link to the American Indian Movement (2001, 93). At the same time, Chicano activists identified strongly with anticolonial liberation struggles happening around the world (e.g., in Puerto Rico, Cuba, Vietnam, and Africa) and proclaimed solidarity with these movements for self-determination. They supported the struggles of elderly Filipinos in San Francisco trying to avoid eviction from affordable housing, striking coal miners in Kentucky, and the boycott of Nestlé's because of that company's aggressive promotion of infant formula to nursing mothers in Africa (Lipsitz 2001).

Prior to the 1970s, public approbation of Latino cultures was rare in the realm of U.S. arts, culture, education, and mass media. When Latino heritage was acknowledged at all, it was only the Spanish ancestry that was lauded. For centuries, both in Latin America and the United States, Eurocentric racism had categorized Indigenous heritage as a shameful impurity that consigned Latinos to inferior socioeconomic status vis-à-vis Whites. As Chicana artist Yolanda Garfias Woo notes, "I grew up [in California] in a time when Latinos were still changing their last names in order to get better jobs and promotions. If you were light skinned and could pass for something else, you did, because it was easier and you had more opportunity. . . . It still happens in Mexico with the class system, where the middle classes are still afraid to associate too much with the Indigenous groups, which they consider to be below them."[8] Nancy Chárraga, who holds Day of the Dead craft workshops at her fair trade store, Casa Bonampak in San Francisco's Mission district, discusses similar experiences: "Mexicans are a fusion of Indian culture and Spanish culture and, as a product of colonization, we have sort of this unconscious psychology ingrained in us that we should hate the Indian aspect of ourselves, and that the European aspect is better. So we really struggle with that and really undervalue our culture."[9]

As a rejection of this Eurocentric mentality, Day of the Dead celebrations and other actions emerging from the Chicano Movement consciously commemorated the customs and beliefs of working-class Mestizo and Indigenous Mexicans. For many Latinos in California, these events represented the first time in their lives that they saw aspects of Latino culture, previously denigrated as "superstitious" and "ignorant," acclaimed in the public sphere as artistically valuable and philosophically profound. Foremost in the model of *Chicanismo* was the integration of culture, art, and politics, not simply for the sake of making art, but for the goal of building community and creating progressive political change in the areas of labor, education, housing, race relations, and U.S. foreign policy. Chicano activists sought to create a cohesive and culturally distinct community identity that would express a collective history, creativity, and idealism. As they searched for methods and symbols, they looked to Mexico's past for inspiration, as the artists of the post-Revolution Mexican Renaissance did in the 1920s. Romo explains, "Though Chicano art had begun by visually articulating the Chicano Movement's political stance, it also had as a central goal, the formation and unification of a Chicano cultural identity. In visualizing this new identity, artists became part of a cultural reclamation process to reintroduce Mexican art and history, revitalize popular artistic expressions, and support community cultural activities" (2000, 7).

The 1970s was a period in which many racial minority groups in the United States were attempting to reclaim their cultural roots—languages, clothing, art, music, rituals, and other ancestral traditions that had been lost in processes of slavery, colonization, reservation systems, and forced assimilation. Because Mexican culture had not been part of U.S. public school or university curricula when they had grown up, many Chicanos began to do historical research and visit Mexico to gain a better understanding of Mexico's traditions (Morrison 1992, 222; Romo 2000; Chicano artists, personal interviews). Some dedicated themselves to learning Indigenous languages, Maya weaving, Aztec *danza*, or other Indigenous Mexican art forms.

Referred to today as Neo-Indigenism (a movement by Chicano activists to reaffirm and celebrate the contributions and achievements of Mesoamerican civilization), the collective espousal of Mexico's Indigenous past became a dominant aspect of Chicano artistic expression. A major influence on Chicanos was the pageantry of Mesoamerican sacred rituals, religious symbols, and spiritual beliefs. At the same time, Day of the Dead in Mexico was rising in national prominence, both as a tourist attraction and symbol of national identity. Chicanos who witnessed Mexican celebrations were captivated by the striking aesthetics and spirituality. They realized that the creativity and devotion involved in remembering loved ones through ofrendas could also serve as a way to publicly commemorate individual and collective experiences of the Mexican American community. For a marginalized community unaccustomed to seeing positive images of itself in the public sphere, the significance of publicly honoring collective experiences and cultural traditions cannot be overstated.

Day of the Dead imagery became one of the most profound expressions of Chicano iconography, as Chicano artists expanded the definition of art to include all activities that affirmed Mexican cultural heritage (Venegas 2000, 42; Romo 2000, 7). Romo states, "The Día de los Muertos observance, including its indigenous philosophy, ofrendas, popular art, and foods, became a focal point in this reclamation process and helped establish direct ties back to Mexican ancestors, both familial and historical" (2000, 7). Just as Mexican

Day of the Dead traditions were a fusion of Indigenous spiritual practices, official and folk Catholic rituals, and European literary traditions, Chicano Day of the Dead events were a hybridization of all of these aspects, plus elements of Mexican and U.S. popular culture and politics.

Given that most Chicanos did not grow up celebrating El Día de los Muertos, their renditions of the commemoration were based on customs they had read about, witnessed as visitors to Mexico, or seen in Mexican films and artwork. Many Chicano artists were inspired by José Guadalupe Posada's satirical calavera caricatures, and began to create stylistically similar drawings that critically commented on California's politicians, urban youth, and other political topics.[10] Others modeled their work on the ofrendas of southern Mexico, creating altar installations of papel picado, family mementos, synthetic flowers, and foods.[11] Still others made altars that portrayed ironic expressions of Catholic iconography as political commentary. Such eclectic and experimental ofrendas had not been done previously in Mexico or the United States.

In most of Latin America, observances of Day of the Dead would be classified as folk culture, which John Fiske defines as "the product of a *comparatively stable, traditional social order*" (1989, 169). This refers to beliefs and practices arising from the organic life of a community, not intended for promotion to a larger audience. A folk belief related to Day of the Dead, for example, is the widespread conviction, whether in Mexico, Guatemala, Ecuador, Bolivia, or elsewhere, that one's own well-being depends in part on respectfully remembering the dead. Whether people construct elaborate ofrendas or simply lay flowers on family graves, these rituals are rooted in a common feeling of moral obligation to the deceased. Meanwhile, within the more secular context of U.S. society (and the museums, galleries, community centers, and commercial areas hosting Day of the Dead activities), the rituals emerged in nonreligious spheres as a form of popular culture. The term "popular" here refers to cultural practices that are derived from folk culture, commodified for intended consumption by mass audiences, and utilized as signifiers of new meanings. This does not mean that U.S. Day of the Dead rituals are devoid of spiritual significance, but that they routinely occur in secular contexts as art, ethnic culture, or political expression, and are not primarily undertaken as acts of religious devotion. Their principal goal is not the fulfillment of moral obligations to the dead, but the public celebration of Chicano/Mexican/Latino identity.

Despite the secular location of U.S. Day of the Dead events, a residual aura of the sacred remains. As Chicanos reached back to an imagined past for symbols with which to confront an oppressive dominant culture, it was the spirituality of Day of the Dead that made it desirable to them. Indigenous spirituality was considered a vital unifying component of Chicano identity and iconography, offering new perspectives on the metaphysical, apart from what many considered to be the restrictive scriptures of a historically oppressive Catholic Church (Romo 2000). As evident in *El plan espirituál de Aztlán* (The spiritual plan of Aztlán), a Chicano Movement manifesto drafted at the 1969 Chicano National Liberation Youth Conference in Denver, Colorado, and subsequently promoted by Chicano artists throughout the United States, a culturally unifying spirituality that incorporated ancient Indigenous beliefs and practices was considered integral to the struggle for cultural resistance against a homogenizing and often hostile U.S. mainstream (Gonzalez 1972, 405; Romo 2000, 40). Romo refers to this as a "spiritual nationalism," which became a unifying force for Chicano farm workers, artists, and community activists (2000, 32). Chicano spirituality was what political theorist Antonio Gramsci would call "religion taken not in the confessional sense, but in the secular sense of a unity of faith between a conception of the world and a corresponding norm of conduct." This conception of religion emphasizes elements of struggle, process, and politics, with the goal of creating a unity of consciousness to aid social development and political action (Gramsci, quoted in Hoare and Smith 1999, 326–328).

Chicano spirituality was a hybrid assemblage of the diverse religious influences that shaped Chicano identity, woven together for the purpose of creating a feeling of cultural unity that would assist in struggles for political justice. Noting the comfortable coexistence in Mexican American communities of Catholic *quinceañera* Masses with Indigenous curandera healing rituals, Romo explains, "Chicano spirituality evolved from multiple sources by way of Spanish Catholicism, Moorish mysticism, African beliefs and a Mesoamerican Indigenous worldview—all filtered through an American-lived experience" (2000, 30–31).[12] U.S. Day of the Dead installations reflect the hybrid nature of Chicano spirituality, as they routinely include Catholic iconography such as crucifixes, Bibles, saints' candles, rosary beads, and pictures of the saints, Jesus, or the Virgin Mary; these items are mixed with Indigenous elements such as copal incense, marigolds, pre-Columbian foods, and Maya or Aztec symbols. Day of the Dead events are sometimes blessed by Catholic priests, Indigenous elders, Aztec ceremonial dancers, or a combination of these people, depending on the orientation of an event's planning committee.[13] For some, the participation of both Indigenous and Catholic officiates is a way to acknowledge the Mestizo history of the tradition and attract the broadest range of participants possible. For others, the involvement of *either* Catholic clergy *or* Indigenous elders is a way to privilege one history over the other. Meanwhile, many Day of the Dead events have neither Indigenous nor Catholic functionaries present.

Romo, who helped organize the first Day of the Dead celebration in Sacramento in 1975, discusses the decision of the Royal Chicano Air Force, a collective of Chicano artists and activists, to include both Indigenous and Catholic ceremonies as part of the celebration:

We had an Indigenous ceremony with dance offerings, along with a Catholic Mass, because there were a lot of older, traditional people there, and it's a holy day of obligation for Catholics. We invited the Guadalupanas because we wanted to get that generation of people involved, like our parents and grandparents.[14] And how do you get them involved if we were doing Indigenous stuff and they might see it as too artistic or not Catholic enough, or respectful enough? Because we were a Chicano reclamation project, we wanted to incorporate all the things that we knew made up the culture. We wanted people to start recognizing the Indigenous connections and foundations of a lot of what we took for granted as our culture. . . . We chose Día de los Muertos because of its specific connection to Indigenous thought. . . . And we also wanted to recognize that there was a segment of the older population that was very Catholic and needed to be part of this, and we wanted to be respectful, in terms of their belief system, but not let one take over the other. And it worked.[15]

The participation of religious leaders in some U.S. Day of the Dead ceremonies does not mean that participants necessarily consider these events within a religious context, although they may. Religious symbols in U.S. Day of the Dead celebrations, although recognizable to most Latinos, are open to a variety of meanings that may be similar to or vastly different from the same symbols in a Latin American context. As anthropologist Claudio Lomnitz-Adler notes, a symbol such as the Virgin of Guadalupe has different meanings for "an atheistic politician than for a proclerical one, for an Indian than for a worker, for a shantytown dweller than a university professor" (1992, 312). Regardless of their personal feelings about Catholicism or Indigenous spirituality, Chicano artists saw themselves as part of a larger community for whom these symbols had historical meaning. The ways in which they mixed Aztec, Maya, and Catholic iconography with American pop cultural items and political symbols created new meanings, distinct from those the items had in Mexico. In the Chicano context, objects of religious devotion were transformed into gallery art that could be both spiritual and political. Meanwhile, Day of the Dead activities done in public schools did not include religious symbols, exclusively focusing on history, language, or arts activities such as calavera poetry, sugar-skull making, and papel picado. Students were invited to bring in photos and objects to commemorate their dead loved ones, and teachers emphasized the anthropological aspects of the tradition.

Chicanos' knowledge of Day of the Dead expanded through cultural exchanges between Mexico and California. Chicano artists traveled to Mexico and brought back artifacts, crafts, and ideas that they shared with others at workshops in the United States. They also invited Mexican artisans to the

United States to hold workshops. Examples of this include numerous visits to California by members of the Linares family of Mexico. The Linareses taught Chicano artists traditional Mexican techniques for making papier-mâché Day of the Dead crafts. In another example, Arsacio Vanegas Arroyo was invited from Mexico to the Centro Cultural de la Raza in San Diego to show Chicano artists the engraving plates and restrike prints of José Guadalupe Posada. Vanegas Arroyo was the grandson of Posada's employer, publisher Antonio Vanegas Arroyo, and still had the old plates Posada used to make his calavera prints. Chicano artists were allowed to print images using Posada's plates. Artist David Avalos explains, "For Chicanos, it was very exciting to have a direct connection with the engravings of Posada. This was stuff we had only seen in Dover Edition publications, and we had the sheets and plates right in front of us!"[16] An exhibit of these prints traveled to Southwestern College in California, the Mission Cultural Center in San Francisco, La Raza Bookstore in Sacramento, the Contemporary Hispanic Arts Consortium in Milwaukee, and the Goez Gallery in Los Angeles, providing direct links to history and a sense of continuity between Mexican and Chicano culture.

The Day of the Dead ofrendas, street parades, and crafts that Chicanos recreated were selectively adopted from a variety of Day of the Dead traditions existing in Mexico. Distinctively Catholic aspects (such as saying the rosary for the deceased or going to Mass, for example) were generally downplayed or omitted in favor of rituals associated with pre-Columbian times.[17] In contrast to Mexican Indigenous peoples who consider El Día de los Muertos to be a Catholic celebration, Chicano observances were (and are) secular, both because most Chicanos want to distance themselves from a religion closely connected with colonialism, and also because they want to make the cultural activities available to a racially and religiously diverse U.S. population through workshops held in publicly funded schools and in nonprofit organizations.[18] Thus, aspects of the holiday promoted in the United States have been those that are most easily adapted to classroom and gallery environments.[19]

Eric Hobsbawm and Terrance Ranger coined the phrase "invented tradition" to refer to newly created practices of a ritual or symbolic nature, "which seek to inculcate certain values and norms" and which "imply continuity with the past." In "using old models for new purposes," they observe, an implied (but fictitious) continuity with the past is key to establishing group cohesion and identity (1983, 1–5). Although the term "invented tradition" often conveys a pejorative tone, connoting a falsification of history or manipulation from "above," U.S. Day of the Dead celebrations exemplify agency from "below." Here, traditions are reenacted, not to provide a dominant group with "the sanction of precedent, social continuity or natural law" (2), but to offer a historically marginalized population cultural resources with which to counter generations of disparagement from the larger society. In California, the Southwest, and increasingly in the rest of the United States, Day of the Dead celebrations help counteract a history of Latino exclusion from the mass media, museum circuits, and academia. They also counteract the psychological harm done by decades of racially segregated public education, where Latino children—historically relegated to substandard schools with no college-track curricula—were taught misleading histories that portrayed their cultures as abject.

Through public rituals that transmitted narratives of cultural pride, Day of the Dead in the United States became a forum for expressing a community's collective experience and memory of itself. This was a space to promote and validate unofficial histories or "hidden transcripts" (Scott 1990) regarding Latino contributions to U.S. society that were long ignored by the mainstream. Chicana writer Alicia Gaspar de Alba has referred to this as the transformation of Day of the Dead "from folk culture to popular culture," where ancient devotional expressions are converted into "ceremonial art whose main function [is] the ritual celebration and preservation of cultural memory" (1998, 76).

Writing about mod, punk, Rastafarian and other subcultural movements, Dick Hebdige contends that subcultures respond to the oppressive ways in which social life is experienced by minorities within the dominant culture. They "express forbidden contents (consciousness of class, consciousness of difference) in forbidden forms," that transgress codes of acceptable thought and behavior (1979, 91). For Chicano activists, the overt skull imagery of Day of the Dead and the act of publicly communicating about death in a society that shunned the topic were ways to express their "consciousness of difference." Similar to the unconventional fashions and commodities embraced by the subcultures of punk (Hebdige 1979), rap (Rose 1994), and hippies (Frank 1997), the shock value of Day of the Dead iconography made the ritual an attention-catching proclamation of identity for the Chicano community.[20] This initially struck (and still strikes) some onlookers as morbid, shocking, or even ghastly, making skull iconography powerfully distinctive. The comments of an Anglo administrative assistant at an art gallery that exhibits Day of the Dead altars illustrates the jolting effect that calaveras can have on people who are unfamiliar with the tradition: "I can't get used to it. I just *can't*. The blatant skeletal symbols bother me. They really do. They're too garish. Too gory! The bones really turn me off. The sugar skulls are too much! It's too reminiscent of a decomposed body. *That's* not the memory I want."[21] Such visceral reactions are not limited to non-Latinos, as the following comments by a Mexican American sales rep from San Francisco illustrate: "I don't celebrate such holidays. Truthfully, it scares the living daylights out of me! Just the weirdness of it. Can you *imagine* people actually celebrating the *dead*?!"[22]

Unlike in Latin American villages where Day of the Dead customs were passed down from generation to generation, the U.S. public was unfamiliar with this celebration and needed to be taught the meanings behind the images and rituals. For Chicano artists, a primary goal of Day of the Dead events was to teach about the meaning and history of the holiday as a way to foster greater public understanding of (and respect for) Mexican traditions. From late September until early November, educational workshops on how to make paper flowers, papel picado, sugar skulls, papier-mâché masks, and ofrendas became a major part of U.S. festivities. These were offered to the public for free or at very low cost in community centers, schools, and art galleries serving largely working-class constituencies of Latinos and other people of color.[23] Today, such educational programming continues to be the medium through which most people (including Mexican Americans) learn about Day of the Dead. Another important way that the U.S. public learns about the celebration is through commercially available books designed for children, teachers, and lay audiences, such as *Making Magic Windows: Creating Papel Picado/Cut Paper Art* (Garza 1999); *Pablo Remembers* (Anaconda 1993); *Barrilete: A Kite for Day of the Dead* (Amado 1999); *The Skeleton at the Feast* (Carmichael and Sawyer 1991); *Piñatas and Smiling Skeletons* (Harris and Williams 1998); and the *Through the Eyes of the Soul* series (Andrade 1999–2003).

Based on a conceptual framework of Latin American Day of the Dead celebrations, U.S. activities include components such as the creation of ofrendas on which tributes to the dead are arranged, participation in candlelight processions (pedestrian cavalcades in which participants carry candles and/or photos of the deceased), and sometimes cemetery rituals where participants may decorate graves, hold vigils, pray, sing, or dance in honor of the dead.[24] (In a particularly southern California rendition of Day of the Dead, artists in San Diego have organized car caravan "processions" to visit ofrendas in public spaces and private homes.)[25] These traditions are integrated with contemporary elements, such as educational workshops, performance art, multimedia installations, and calavera poetry slams (where participants publicly read poems or tell stories about the departed). "Altar installations" (the term used by Chicano artists to describe the ofrendas they make in public spaces) are composed of mixed media such as sculpture, oil paints, silkscreen, mobiles, collage, computers, televisions, sound systems, video footage, and interactive Web sites.[26] U.S. celebrations also include public lectures that educate people about Day of the Dead traditions, or that utilize the seasonal theme to discuss metaphysical topics related to death and the spirit world. They may feature film screenings ranging from documentaries about Day of the Dead, such as *La Ofrenda: The Days of the Dead* (Portillo and Muñoz 1988) and *La Muerte Viva, The Day of the Dead: A Living Tradition* (Llamas 1989); to classic Mexican movies with Day of the Dead scenes, such as *Macario* (Roberto Gavaldon

1960) and *Ánimas Trujano* (Ismael Rodriguez 1962); to films on Mexican folk art such as *Pedro Linares: Folk Artist* (Bronowski and Grant 1975). In some communities, such as in Sherman Heights (San Diego) and Oceanside, California, and in New Brunswick, New Jersey, resident volunteers grow fields of marigolds months in advance as preparation for their Day of the Dead celebrations. The planting, weeding, watering, and harvesting of the flowers becomes a community-building experience for people of diverse ages and ethnicities.

An innovative component of Chicano celebrations has been the inclusion of Aztec spiritual ceremonies and *danza*, a term used to refer to a pre-Columbian style of "dancing in prayer" to communicate with the spirit world. Today, danza performances are frequently part of U.S. Day of the Dead events, although this form of dance was previously not combined with ofrendas during the Day of the Dead. Expert *danzante* Macuilxochitl Cruz-Chavez, who founded the San Francisco Bay Area group Danza Xitlalli in 1982, learned danza as a teen in her native Mexico. She notes that the ancient form of prayer dance was originally done in private rather than public performance spaces: "It was done in the homes. . . . When I lived in Mexico City, the group that I danced with didn't dance on Day of the Dead. When I moved to San Francisco, people weren't doing it. After a few years, I connected danza with the way I celebrated Día de los Muertos in my home, involving food on the altars, like I did in my home. I started to connect the two customs—danza and Día de los Muertos. We were the first group to do this in San Francisco. Now people here think that all danza groups have *always* danced on Day of the Dead. But that's not the case. Other groups began to combine danza with Day of the Dead, and now many groups do this."[27]

Mario E. Aguilar, who began studying danza in 1974 and is the founder of the San Diego group Danza Mexi'cayotl, explains that while danza is a form of honoring the deceased, it was not traditionally part of Day of the Dead observances in Mexico. "The danza tradition is very much a ghost dance in which you honor your ancestors through dance. You have to remember them, recalling them by specific names. But doing danza on Día de los Muertos is a totally Chicano creation."[28]

By combining Aztec ceremonial dancing with the ofrenda tradition in ways that were not done by the Indigenous populations of southern Mexico, Chicanos exercise creative syncretism. Not all U.S. Day of the Dead festivities include Aztec danza, but many do. Wearing synthetic renditions of Aztec clothing and headdresses decorated with colorful feathers, danza performers frequently inaugurate Day of the Dead processions, altar exhibits, and community celebrations in modern re-creations of ancient ceremonies. Sometimes, these events are convened by blowing on a large conch shell, used by the Aztecs as a form of communication. Typically, the four elements (earth, air, fire, and water) and the four directions (north, south, east, west) are saluted, followed by dancing and prayerful singing.

Because U.S. Day of the Dead festivities were created as secular commemorations rather than religious rituals, gallery spaces and altars became key media for communicating messages of Latino cultural affirmation and political consciousness. Besides honoring family and friends, Chicano artists have utilized the holiday's focus on remembrance to criticize dominant power structures by creating installations intended to raise public awareness of the sociopolitical causes of death. In doing so, they expanded a tradition reserved for family members into one that also remembered groups of people not personally known to the altar makers. Romo explains, "The *remembering* and acknowledging of the dead—even if we never knew them—was and continues to be an important component of U.S. Day of the Dead observances. . . . connected to the [Chicano] Movement's political origins."[29] As we shall see in chapter 5, U.S. Day of the Dead rituals and art continue to be thriving media for communicating political critiques.

Early Day of the Dead Exhibits and Events

According to both Romo (2000) and Morrison (1992), and confirmed by the Chicano artists I interviewed, the first recorded Day of the Dead celebrations in California occurred in 1972, organized separately by artists at Self-Help Graphics in Los Angeles and at La Galería de la Raza in San Francisco. Self-Help Graphics, a community-based visual arts center in East Los Angeles, hosted a lively Day of the Dead procession in which people dressed as skeletons and walked to a nearby cemetery. Sybil Venegas notes that none of the Chicanos who helped organize this first ceremony were personally familiar with Day of the Dead, so they took their cues from the three founders of Self-Help Graphics (Mexican artists Antonio Ibañez and Carlos Bueno and Italian American nun Sr. Karen Boccalero), who were familiar with the celebration. She notes, "While these artists were initially unfamiliar with El Día de los Muertos, they were undoubtedly attracted to its potential to generate cultural awareness, ethnic pride, and collective self-fulfillment for the East Los Angeles community" (Venegas 2000, 47). Through the influence of Ibañez and Bueno, the Self-Help Graphics artists were introduced to the Mexican folk art aspects of the festival, such as calavera imagery, and to Indigenous-style ofrenda making. By 1974, the celebration had attracted the participation of a cross section of the larger Chicano artist community, and a plethora of silkscreen prints, posters, paintings, multimedia compositions, performances, and other Day of the Dead–inspired art soon emanated from Chicano artists throughout the greater Los Angeles area.

Composed of artists, local residents, students, and grassroots activists, the Day of the Dead procession at Self-Help became an annual event. It concluded in Self-Help's gallery, where there would be a Day of the Dead art show and community workshops. During each celebration, the gallery sold Day of the Dead art, mementos, and traditional foods such as atole de maiz and pan de muerto. In subsequent years, performances by the Chicano political theater troupe El Teatro Campesino were presented. Over time, the Los Angeles procession grew to include music, Aztec danza, giant calavera puppets, sculptures, banners, "low rider" cars, decorated floats, and more. Because Self-Help Graphics worked with local elementary schools to educate students and teachers about Day of the Dead, and held craft workshops at the gallery each weekend during October, hundreds of children attended the processions, wearing or carrying their handmade Day of the Dead art projects. Workshops teaching the public how to make papel picado, sugar skulls, plaster skeleton masks, and ofrendas would be an important part of the organization's Day of the Dead festivals for decades to come. Inspired by Self-Help, community centers, schools, libraries, art galleries, museums, folk art stores, city parks and commercial districts throughout Los Angeles would later develop Day of the Dead programming for the months of October and November.

In the same year, the Chicano art gallery La Galería de la Raza, located in the heart of San Francisco's predominantly Latino Mission District, held the city's first Day of the Dead ofrenda exhibit. Organized by artists René Yáñez and Ralph Maradiaga, together with other artists, including Carmen Lomas Garza and Yolanda Garfias Woo, the exhibit and related educational activities evolved into a much-awaited annual tradition. In 1981, La Galería organized a small Day of the Dead nocturnal procession with about twenty-five people who walked around the block holding candles. As one woman born in Ecuador and raised in the Mission describes the earliest processions, "They were very quiet and spiritual. People prayed and held photos of deceased family members."[30]

Since then, the procession has burgeoned into an exuberant annual manifestation of thousands. It includes Aztec blessing rituals and danza groups, colorful banners, streetside ofrendas, sidewalk chalk art, giant calavera puppets, portable sculptures, Cuban Santería practitioners, candlelight ceremonies, and a Jamaican steel-drum band on wheels. Over the years, individuals walking in honor of deceased family members and friends have been joined by contingents walking to draw public attention to various sociopolitical causes of death, such as U.S. military interventions abroad, gun violence, and AIDS. Each year, the procession has an official theme, honoring a particular group or cause. Although no longer sponsored by La Galería de la Raza (for reasons discussed in chapter 7), the procession today attracts an estimated twenty thousand participants, spanning all ages, races, and ethnicities—making it the largest Day of the Dead procession in the United States.

La Galería's Day of the Dead exhibits have ranged from traditional ofrendas to high-tech video displays and Web sites, to cross-cultural installations done by students and artists from diverse ethnic and racial backgrounds. From the beginning, the themes and people honored have reflected a broad spectrum between the traditional and the contemporary, including installations honoring Mexican altar-making traditions, feminist ofrendas, commemorations for the victims of U.S.-sponsored wars, or tributes to Latin American and Latino artists.[31] This small gallery would have a profound influence on the future shape of Day of the Dead celebrations in the United States, both in encouraging hybrid experimentation with and "mainstreaming" the altar format. Romo notes that La Galería's "most significant contribution to Día de los Muertos and Chicano art history" was the new direction in which it took ofrendas. By blending traditional rituals with modern materials and designs, she notes, artist René Yáñez, in particular, transformed the altar format into an "environmental space" and pushed altar making into the realm of contemporary art installation while still remaining respectful of the traditional ofrenda as a source of inspiration (2000, 38). La Galería's exhibitions and activities ultimately generated citywide recognition and inspired other parallel celebrations, with the result that many non-Latino museums now dedicate October programming to Day of the Dead as a way to outreach to Latino communities.

While Chicano artists were inspired by Mexican Day of the Dead rituals, they note that Mexico's Day of the Dead expressions were later influenced by Chicano renderings of the holiday. Chicano artists traveled from the United States to Mexico to educate urban Mexican audiences about Day of the Dead by conducting workshops and book talks about the celebration. The esteem these U.S. artists had for the holiday helped elevate it in the eyes of urban Mexicans, many of whom had still looked down on it in the 1970s and 1980s. Ironically, while Chicanos were embracing Day of the Dead, Halloween was gaining popularity throughout Mexico. Artist and visual arts professor Amalia Mesa-Bains, who created an altar at the 1976 Day of the Dead exhibit at La Galería (and many subsequent altar exhibits around the country since), notes, "There was this strange moment where Mexicans were celebrating Halloween and Chicanos were celebrating Day of the Dead. A number of Chicanos began to go back to Mexico and assist in reclaiming the tradition there. . . . In Mexico City and other large cities where there was much more dominance from the U.S. . . . most contemporary Mexican artists were not interested in those traditions because to them they seemed rather old-fashioned. And so we Chicano artists actually valued something that contemporary Mexican artists did not."[32]

Mexican artists have also noted the influence of Chicano Day of the Dead celebrations on Mexico. Sculptor Guillermo Pulido, who was born in Guadalajara, Mexico, and moved as an adult to California in the late 1980s, observed the "regeneration" and "transformation" taking place with Day of the Dead in the United States, and felt that the San Francisco celebration would impact Mexico's with a "recycling of influences back and forth" (Morrison 1992, 362). A staff member at the Mexican Museum of San Francisco expressed similar feelings. On moving as an adult from Mexico to California in 1997, he was surprised to see how Day of the Dead was celebrated in the United States: "Here, because of the Chicano Movement, it's much more political." He felt that Chicano celebrations had inspired more politicized and artistic experimentation with altars in Mexico: "In Mexico, there are new interpretations of altars, and you now see artists doing more experimental things around Day of the Dead."[33] Chicano Day of the Dead celebrations provided new models and inspiration for future generations of artists and "forever changed the tradition not only in the United States, but in Mexico, as well," asserts Romo (2000, 31).

California and Beyond Adopt the New Celebration

Because of their exotic appeal, early California Day of the Dead events soon attracted media attention from local newspapers and television stations—a phenomenon that continues today. The role of the mass media, together with educational workshops and Day of the Dead tourism, all played important roles in promoting the celebration to wide audiences. But why, specifically, did Day of the Dead grab people's attention? Artist and educator Yolanda Garfias Woo, one of the original participants in La Galería's Day of the Dead exhibits, notes that compared with Anglo holidays, Day of the Dead "was *so far out*. It was a shocking kind of thing to be doing. It literally *shocked* the non-Latino community. And that's exactly the emphasis that Chicanos were looking for. They wanted to make a statement and make it big!"[34]

Throughout the 1970s–1990s, Chicano-style Day of the Dead celebrations extended to Sacramento, San Diego, and other areas of California, and also became popular among Mexican American communities in Texas and the Southwest. A 1995 *New York Times* article observed the new trend in San Antonio, Texas: "Rituals that were once shunned are now embraced, becoming a local alternative to Halloween. On November 2, teachers build classroom altars, ethnic, not religious, they say, and bring in pan de muerto. This year, for the first time, a community center arranged for 60 children wearing skeleton masks and makeup to march from an altar at the center to [a] cemetery, where they danced in circles."[35]

The following comments from middle-aged Mexican Americans in California and the Southwest illustrate that Day of the Dead is a new celebration in these areas. Some have adopted it enthusiastically while others consider it a curiosity. A librarian who lived in Tijuana until she was nine (before moving to San Diego, where she has lived for forty years), told me that her family never celebrated Day of the Dead while living in either Tijuana or San Diego, and that she had never heard of the holiday until she saw altar exhibits at the university campus where she worked. A forty-year-old San Diego hairstylist, who spent her childhood in Coahuila, Mexico, before moving as a teen to San Antonio, Texas, learned about Day of the Dead through her children:

> I'm a dedicated Catholic, very active in the church. Growing up, we never celebrated Day of the Dead. We never even heard about it. I don't even really know what it is. It's kind of funny how we people from Mexico don't know about Day of the Dead, but people say it's a Mexican thing. No one in my family ever celebrated it, not even my grandparents. No one I *knew* celebrated it, and I lived in a very Mexican neighborhood. My kids celebrate it now in school though. They go to the Spreckels School, which is bilingual. They make masks and do other things. At first, when they came home talking about Day of the Dead, I didn't respond too positively. I didn't know why the school was teaching my kids about this cult and I didn't like the idea. I thought it was something weird. But they told me it was our Mexican heritage. Well, *I* never heard of it. I still don't know what it is, exactly.[36]

A forty-two-year-old woman, who grew up in Tijuana and moved to the United States to attend college in San Diego, learned about Day of the Dead in the year 2000, when she purchased a home in the San Diego neighborhood of Sherman Heights. As an enthusiastic new home owner, she became active in the Sherman Heights Community Center, where she first saw Day of the Dead ofrendas. She liked the concept so much that she began to participate annually in the Sherman Heights Neighborhood Association's Day of the Dead celebrations:

> My father's family was from Oaxaca and they celebrate it a lot there. But in my neighborhood in Tijuana, we didn't celebrate it. I used to live in Chula Vista [a city with a large Mexican population in south San Diego County] and they don't do it in Chula Vista. I'm surprised. I lived there for ten years, but it's not done. But when I came here and saw the celebration, I really wanted to be a part of it. . . . I feel so much closer to that part of my culture. And I've been able to teach my family about it. My mother is *really* into it now! And my niece. She's ten years old and she's half Caucasian and half Mexican. She really enjoyed learning about it and making the altar with me. She hadn't seen this before and if we hadn't done this, she would never have learned about it.[37]

Similarly, a Mexican American administrative assistant in her midfifties learned about the celebration from the art gallery where she works: "I'm a third generation Mexican American, but we never celebrated Day of the Dead. I mean, we went to church and had a meal, but it was very solemn.

I learned about it working here, and was inspired by all the artists who participate."[38] And Tomás Benitez, a Chicano playwright who was born and raised
in the predominantly Mexican American neighborhood of East Los Angeles,
recounts, "Day of the Dead was really introduced to me by Self-Help
Graphics. Back in the early 1980s . . . I had read a little about it in Chicano
Studies, but never [was active] in a firsthand way of being involved in a
community event or procession."[39]

Thus, despite its renown as a cornerstone of Mexican identity, Day of the
Dead is not something that all people of Mexican heritage necessarily know
about or embrace. Its history is relatively recent in the United States, just as
it is new to many areas of Mexico. In both countries, the celebration has been
shaped by "outside" influences: new elements (e.g., danza, theater performances, political altars) have been added, and hybridized cultural expressions
have emerged. In both places, public attitudes toward the celebration have
changed drastically over time.

Negotiations over Ownership

Despite the fact that traditions of decorating tombs, picnicking in graveyards, holding cemetery vigils, serenading the dead, or altar making are
practiced in various Latin American countries,[40] Day of the Dead has been
hailed as quintessentially Mexican in public media formats such as the murals
of Diego Rivera or the prose of Octavio Paz. With countless English-
language books, newspaper and scholarly articles, documentary films, and Web
sites produced about Mexico's Day of the Dead, and comparatively little information available on the corresponding observances in other countries, most
people familiar with the celebration assume (and sometimes insist) that Day
of the Dead rituals are exclusively Mexican. As one Chicana artist emphatically replied when asked about similarities between Mexican and other Latin
American Day of the Dead customs: "Día de los Muertos is *Mexican. Period!*"[41]

In a sense, she is right. The creation of internationally famous Día de los
Muertos celebrations *is* uniquely Mexican and reflects a mystique around the
holiday that has been produced and perpetuated in Mexico. And Mexican
Americans were the first to bring the celebration to the United States,
providing a cultural resource with which other U.S. Latinos would later
connect. Because Mexican Americans have more political power than smaller
Latino populations to organize major arts and cultural events in the United
States, cultural practices that take place in many regions of Latin America
(such as Day of the Dead traditions, Christmas *posadas*, or the making of *milagros* and *ex-votos*) are often presented to U.S. audiences from a Mexican vantage
point.[42] This is not done in a calculated way to usurp regional cultural practices, but simply reflects the perspective of the United States' largest Latino
population. As mentioned earlier, most Mexican Americans are unaware of

other Latin American observances of Day of the Dead, an ethnocentrism that also exists in Latin America, where people are unfamiliar with Mexico's Day of the Dead.[43]

Non-Mexican Latinos living in California and the Southwest are surrounded by Mexican culture, seen in the types of groceries stocked at Latino markets, the predominantly Mexican programming available on Spanish-language radio and television, and the widespread celebrations of Mexican festivals (e.g., Cinco de Mayo, September 16, and Guelaguetzas).[44] Mexican culture and language predominate in the design of bilingual (Spanish/English) school curricula and university Latino/Chicano Studies programs.[45] Chicanos/Mexican Americans manage most of the Latino community-based organizations; Mexican American leaders are prevalent in the Latino business community; and most Latino government bureaucrats, politicians, and police are of Mexican heritage. Given that people of Mexican descent have lived in California longer than any other population except Native Americans, this ethnic prominence is understandable and accounts for why cultural traditions practiced in much of Latin America are frequently classified as "Mexican."

However, since the early 1980s, as wars and economic restructuring have intensified unemployment and poverty in Latin America and escalated migratory pressures, Mexican American communities have been joined by large numbers of new Latin American immigrants. In fact, so many immigrants from Central America, South America, the Caribbean, and Mexico have migrated to the United States, that there are now more Latinos than African Americans attending U.S. schools (Suarez-Orozco 2001, 40). The traditional segregated settlement of U.S. Latino populations (Mexican Americans in California and the Southwest, Puerto Ricans in the Northeast, and Cubans in Florida) no longer accurately depicts Latino residential patterns. As new waves of immigrants travel both to and within the United States, following job opportunities that draw them far beyond the geographic locations of earlier Latino communities, new educational and social service agencies arise to serve them. These organizations provide administrative support, financial resources, and public space in which to celebrate Latino culture, including Day of the Dead celebrations. Because they are aimed at more heterogeneous Latino populations than in the past, these celebrations often have a pan-Latino tone.

Amid the growing ethnic diversification of California's Latino population, Latino artists and activists appreciate the Chicano Movement's achievements and, at the same time, strive to expand political, cultural, and artistic work toward a greater recognition of diverse Latino populations. Day of the Dead—now the most widely observed Latino celebration in the United States—is one space in which negotiations over cultural representation have occurred. For example, the November 2002 Day of the Dead exhibit, proposed and curated by Tere Romo at the Oakland Museum of California, featured Guatemalan and Salvadoran altar installations along with Mexican ones. Instead of calling the celebration a "Mexican" tradition, as the museum had done in previous years, the exhibit guides and publicity materials described the holiday as "Mesoamerican." Entitled "Espíritu sin Fronteras: Ofrendas for the Days of the Dead," the exhibition featured ofrendas "that explore the Days of the Dead as a Mesoamerican tradition of shared spirituality among the people of Mexico, Guatemala, El Salvador, and their descendents here in California."[46]

This expanded definition of Day of the Dead occurred as a result of discussions between residents of Central American and Mexican descent living in Oakland's Latino communities. A young Guatemalan-born artist, raised in Los Angeles, who worked with the predominantly Mexican American Day of the Dead planning committee to organize the museum's Day of the Dead exhibit, describes the types of negotiations taking place:

> Living in California, of course, there's the Chicano experience. But not very often is the Central American Maya experience recognized. You always get the Mexica-Aztlán-Chicano experience. For me, it was a real priority to have [the Maya] voice heard within this institution, too. So last year was the first year, with the help of Tere Romo, we expanded that part of our identity and incorporated more of the Maya experience and the interpretations of El Salvador and Guatemala. It's hard though. It's definitely a push to get that voice heard. Even just changing the language, because now, instead of saying it's a "Mexican" tradition, we're saying "Mesoamerican" tradition. . . . Internally within the committee, it was a push to get them to do this. There's always resistance when you try to change anything. . . . I guess if you lived in New York, everyone would assume you're Puerto Rican. Here in California, if you're not Mexican, you're sort of invisible.[47]

California is not the only place where Latinos of various ethnicities participate in Day of the Dead celebrations, as can be seen in media coverage of these events from newspapers around the country (discussed in detail in chapter 6). Nor is this celebration limited to major cities, which used to be the only spaces where diverse ethnic groups lived in close proximity. Today, globalizing towns in the U.S. "heartland" also hold Day of the Dead celebrations. In November of 2007, events were held in Lincoln, Nebraska; Cicero, Illinois; Logan, Utah; Kokomo, Indiana; and Winston-Salem, North Carolina.[48] A Day of the Dead celebration held in New Brunswick, New Jersey, in November 2006 included ofrendas and performances by Mixtecs and other Indigenous peoples from the Mexican state of Oaxaca, together with Puerto Ricans, Cubans, Chileans, Maya immigrants from Guatemala, and others who live in New Brunswick and the surrounding farmlands of New Jersey.[49] Individuals of diverse Latin American ancestries living in the United States choose to participate in Day of the Dead for a variety of personal, social, and political reasons, in the process constructing new relationships with each other.

IN SUMMARY, a ritual that came to the United States via Chicanos as a way to honor Mexican culture has been transformed in many communities into a celebration of Mesoamerican, Latino, or Hispanic culture. The participation of diverse Latino ethnic groups in these celebrations, the negotiations over "ownership" of the tradition, and the resulting hybrid interpretations, illustrate how ethnicity is a flexible construct (Aparicio and Chavez-Silverman 1997; Flores 1993; G. Fox 1996; Martínez Nova 2003; Valdivia 2003). Continually being created and negotiated, it is capable of expanding to include new populations as immigration, labor, housing, and socializing patterns change. In the next chapter, we will take a look at some of the ways that ritual communication encourages feelings of solidarity among these diverse populations.

CHAPTER 4

Ritual Communication and Community Building

DURING ITS ANNUAL CELEBRATION of El Día de los Muertos, the Sherman Heights Community Center in San Diego is bustling with activities that neighborhood residents have planned for months. On the front lawn, dozens of children line up to have fast-setting plaster tape smoothed over their faces for Day of the Dead masks. Sitting at nearby tables, youth and adults decorate sugar skulls with colored icing and cut intricate crepe paper adornments called papel picado. In the kitchen, a standing-room-only crowd learns how to bake pan de muerto as the bread's aroma swirls through the building. Today, the center is filled with delicious smells, including those of smoldering copal incense; hand-dipped beeswax candles from the markets of Tijuana; tamales made by neighborhood women; and thousands of pungent marigolds planted earlier in the year by local children who diligently watered, weeded, and harvested them for this special day. Mexican folkloric music plays in the background, followed by Aztec drumming and a danza performance. Although largely Mexican American, the audience includes neighborhood residents from Columbia, Honduras, Nicaragua, Guatemala, Panama, and Puerto Rico, as well as neighbors of Asian, African American, and European descent.

The highlight of the celebration, which fills the center's main salon and overflows into the hallways, is an exhibition of ofrendas created by neighbors who have worked on them nonstop for the past twenty-four hours. Reminiscent of rural Latin American Day of the Dead rituals where people sit by family graves to await the arriving spirits, the altar makers sit next to their ofrendas, chatting with family and friends and answering questions from the public: "What is an ofrenda?" "Who is the person being honored?" "What country are you from?" And always, some deeply moved visitors ask, "Can I make an ofrenda here next year?"

This contagious enthusiasm is something seen time and again at U.S. Day of the Dead celebrations. Since Sherman Heights began celebrating the ritual in 1994, increasing numbers of people have volunteered to make ofrendas every year.[1] The center's former director, Estela Rubalcava Klink, recalls, "We started with two altars. . . . Then more people asked if they could be a part of it. We got people's names and numbers and it kept growing. In the beginning it was altars from Oaxaca, Guanajuato, Michoacán, but then we started having altars from other parts of Mexico, Central America, and the Philippines."[2] The ofrendas tell stories about families and communities, presenting aspects of Latino culture and history to more than two thousand people, including busloads of schoolchildren and tour groups, who annually visit the center during the five-day altar exhibition. Some ofrendas are created in styles typical of specific regions of Mexico or Central America. Others are constructed to honor icons of Latino popular culture or political struggle, such as Mexican artist Frida Kahlo, Argentine revolutionary Che Guevara, Cuban salsa star Celia Cruz, and Salvadoran human rights defender Archbishop Oscar Romero. Participants use symbols and rituals derived from but not identical to Latin American practices to express messages about their lives in the United States.

Because it involves rituals *and* occurs ritually each year, U.S. Day of the Dead is a form of "ritual communication"—a term that refers both to viewing communication processes as rituals and to seeing rituals as an important form of communication (Carey 1989; Rothenbuhler 1998). Influenced by the work of John Dewey, the concept of ritual communication emphasizes the roots of the word "communication" in terms such as "common," "communion," and "community." It focuses on the projection of community ideals through creative public expressions and examines the role of ceremonial presentation and participation in the structuring of people's lives. Dewey contends that artistic presentations (e.g., poetry, drama, novels) are often more accessible and effective than news media in stimulating the social inquiry and public debate crucial to the goal of turning the Great Society into a Great Community (1927, 183–184).

Following Dewey's lead, James Carey writes that the knowledge and consciousness people need to act politically often develop "only by divesting life of its mundane trappings and exposing our common sense or scientific assumptions to an ironic light" (1989, 25). Carey's concept of ritual communication was influenced by Raymond Williams, who argues that in addition to information transmitted in the mass media, communication includes the sharing of aesthetic experience, religious ideas, personal values, and intellectual concepts through art and performance (1961, 1973). These forms of communication, he says, create "structures of feeling," or expressions that convey knowledge through humanization rather than through theory or argument, to reveal "the deepest feelings in the real experiences of the time" (1961, 68; Simpson 1992, 17). Williams suggests that structures of feeling are achieved during a "process of consciousness between the articulated and the lived," or the contrast between dominant ideology and personal experience (1979, 168).

Critiquing the predominant transmission model of communication that narrowly views society as either a political order (a network of power, administration, and control) or an economic order (a network of property, production, and trade), Carey asserts that social life is much more than the dynamics of power and trade. Through ritual communication, he argues, social identities are symbolically constructed and reinforced while engaging the intellectual, spiritual, and/or physical participation of the public. Noting that a ritual view of communication does not exclude the processes of information transmission or attitude change, Carey provides the following general distinction between the transmission model and the ritual model of communication: "The archetypal case of communication under a transmission view is the extension of messages across geography for the purpose of control, the archetypal case under a ritual view of communication is the sacred ceremony that draws persons together in fellowship and commonality" (1989, 18). Embedded in the transmission model is the assumption that communication must convey new information. In the ritual model, however, the act of communication is often effective without relaying new information. It is more likely to be repetitive than unprecedented, recycling deeply felt ideas, values, and experiences to retell rather than report a story. This form of communication has powerful consequences in terms of consciousness raising and solidarity building.

Imagined Community

Because Day of the Dead is an event with which people of various Latin American backgrounds can identify, its celebration in the United States brings together ethnically and racially diverse populations who, whether recent immigrants or native-born U.S. citizens, may face political, social, or economic marginalization by the larger society. Rituals of making altars, walking together in processions, holding vigils, and performing related activities can stimulate feelings of empathy and solidarity that create a sense of "imagined community" or "horizontal comradeship among people who have never met" (Anderson 1991). They create communicative space for the development of "a distinct Latino sensibility, a social and political discourse, and a Latino aesthetic" emerging from the collective experiences of being Latino in the United States (W. Flores 1997, 264).[3] These celebrations also serve as cultural bridges that help increase understanding and exchange between Latinos and the larger U.S. society. Although most organizers and participants in these events are Latinos, Day of the Dead events attract substantial numbers of non-Latino participants and spectators, creating a diverse public audience.

Public celebrations are one of the primary methods through which Latino imagined community is constructed and sustained in the United States (Rosaldo and W. Flores 1997; Cadavál 1998; Sommers 1991). The cultural identity that is exhibited and reproduced during Day of the Dead celebrations illustrates anthropologist Renato Rosaldo's concept of "cultural citizenship"—a phenomenon whereby people organize their values, practices, and beliefs about their rights based on a sense of cultural belonging, rather than on their formal status as citizens of a nation. Cultural citizenship develops during a range of public activities and performances through which historically oppressed minorities exert their place within the larger civic arena (Rosaldo 1994a, 1994b, 1994c; W. Flores and Benmayor 1997).

As "one of the most meaningful yearly celebrations . . . throughout Latin America" (Carrasco 1990, 142), Day of the Dead is a point of cultural continuity for ethnically, racially, and economically diverse U.S. Latino populations.[4] Not all Latin Americans observe Day of the Dead, of course, but most recognize November 1 and 2 as a time of the year when the dead are remembered through certain rituals. Thus, the holiday provides an opportunity for sharing within a familiar cultural framework. As a Puerto Rican resident of San Diego explained, "In Puerto Rico, we don't celebrate Day of the Dead in the way that the Mexicans do, but we do go to the cemetery and bring flowers. Like a lot of people, my mother and grandmother always had a little altar in the house, year-round, so I can relate to the sense of devotion that is felt for certain saints or people we've lost."[5] A Brazilian American commented, "I grew up in the back country of Brazil, in a very traditional type of atmosphere, folkloric, you might call it. So for us, dealing with this is an extension of our own backgrounds. Even though we celebrate it differently than Mexicans, it is something we know something about, and our cultural and aesthetic tastes are drawn to it."[6] The reaction of a native Salvadoran who lives in California illustrates both the taken-for-granted status of the commemoration in Latin America as well as the very different social, cultural, and political perspectives with which individuals raised in Latin America and Chicanos raised in the United States view the celebration: "I think that the reaction of other Latinos is, 'OK, what's the fuss?' Because they're used to it. They wonder why the Chicanos are making such a big deal of it. Yes, you remember your dead, but it's a typical part of Latin American culture."[7]

The concept of an imagined Latino community is discussed by a variety of scholars with a mixture of wariness and hope (J. Flores 2000; W. Flores and Benmayor 1997; D. Lopez and Espiritu 1990; Molina Guzmán 2006; A. Rodriguez 1999; Oboler 1995). On one hand, the umbrella terms "Hispanic" and "Latino," used by corporations, the mass media, and government for data collection and marketing purposes, ignore the ethnic, racial, linguistic, socioeconomic, and political diversity of the U.S. Latino population. On the other, essentialist assertions of ethnicity can fragment the Latino community and reduce its potential for solidarity. Sociologist and professor of Black and Puerto Rican Studies Juan Flores distinguishes between "Latino" as a demographic unit of analysis created by outside institutions, and a "Latino imaginary" fashioned by Latinos themselves for the purpose of sociopolitical solidarity (2000, 198). Despite cultural and historical variation among people of Latin American heritage, including differences in U.S. settlement patterns, political relationships between countries of origin and the United States, and between recent immigrants and those with longer histories in the United States, common experiences of racism and structural inequality form an important basis for an imagined Latino community (J. Flores 2000; Gómez-Peña 1996; Padilla 1985). Flores explains, "The Latino historical imaginary refers, first of all, to home countries in Latin America, the landscapes, life-ways, and social struggles familiar, if not personally, at least to one's people. . . . The Latino imaginary . . . rests on the recognition of ongoing oppression and discrimination, racism and exploitation, closed doors and patrolled borders" (2000, 198–199). He observes that Latino communities are drawn together across ethnic, generational, and other lines by invented traditions that display elements of an "alternative ethos," with cultural values and practices that are self-referential and affirming (200).

Whereas Flores finds a basis for shared Latino identity in the similar political struggles of people of Latin American heritage, historian of religion Davíd Carrasco sees an important basis of Latino identity in what he calls "the religious imagination"—composed of a shared knowledge of symbols from Indigenous religions and Catholicism. Through music, performance, murals, and other expressive and ritual forms, he notes, Indigenous and Catholic symbols are used as spiritual resources to communicate messages of resistance against Anglo-created stereotypes, oppression, poverty, and unequal opportunity (1990). For more than five hundred years, the historical influence of Catholicism in Latin America has been so extensive that, even today, a majority of Latin Americans and U.S. Latinos are at least nominally Catholic—a commonality that draws diverse groups of people together at both social and political events (Sanchez 1993).[8] The familiarity many Latinos have with Catholic iconography has made it possible for Latino artists to reutilize this imagery in novel and politically meaningful ways (Carrasco 1990; Gutierrez 1995; Romo 2000).[9]

COMMUNITAS

While Latin American celebrants observe Day of the Dead rituals because of a sense of religious or moral obligation (to the dead, to the saints, to God, etc.), most people in the United States, whether Latino or not, participate as an optional activity, or as what anthropologist Victor Turner calls "leisure rituals." Leisure rituals "are potentially capable of releasing creative powers, individual and communal, either to criticize or prop up dominant social structural values" (1977b, 42). This does not mean that the rituals are not serious. Chicanos who initiated U.S. celebrations did so out of a felt moral obligation to counter racism and promote sociopolitical change. Yet, they were free from the institutional and social obligations that have traditionally characterized Day of the Dead observances in Latin America. In Turner's words, they had the "freedom to *play*" with ideas and fantasies, blurring the lines between art and politics. "Play frames allow participants to escape from the 'should' and 'ought' character of ritual . . . and see themselves as free to fabricate a range of alternative possibilities of behaving, thinking, and feeling that is wider than that current or admissible in . . . the [obligatory] ritual frame" (1982, 28). Free from the constraints of the traditional ritual frame, creative play allows U.S. Day of the Dead events to express both spirituality and/or politics, commenting on a range of social issues and identities.

The primary intent of U.S. Day of the Dead events (affirming Latino culture) differs from the primary intent of most Latin American based events (fulfilling moral obligations to the dead). But, both types of ritual activity create important opportunities for the cultivation and maintenance of social relationships. Day of the Dead in Latin America, particularly in Indigenous communities, is not simply a remembrance of the dead, but also a reaffirmation of living communities. Rituals such as refurbishing grave sites, constructing altars, or preparing special foods for the holiday require the collaboration of extended networks of family and friends who come together to pray for the deceased, visit each other's ofrendas to pay respects to the dead, and share festive foods. These actions reinforce a sense of collective identity and solidarity.

In the United States, Latinos of various socioeconomic and cultural backgrounds also develop and reinforce a sense of shared community as they gather to plan Day of the Dead celebrations (a process requiring months of meetings and preparatory activities) and engage in altar making, vigils, processions, craft workshops, or other activities. These rituals can have the temporary effect of leveling social hierarchies, exemplifying Victor Turner's concept of "communitas"—a period during ritual celebrations in which the norms governing institutionalized relationships are transgressed. During such events, argues Turner, the powerful and the weak often reverse roles, as individuals have opportunities to "merge with the masses" and experience a sense of equality in the "liminality" of the nonordinary experience (1977a, 202). This status reversal does not bring drastic change in the status quo, but briefly offers a new perspective from which to observe social structure. "What is left," states Turner, "is a kind of social average, or something like the neutral position in a gear box, from which it is possible to proceed in different directions and at different speeds in a new bout of movement" (1977a, 202).

Although Turner originally discussed communitas in the context of tribal societies, he later argues that people in modern, industrial societies who share important characteristics (such as ethnicity, race, or religion) and feel alienated from the larger social system in which they live may "seek the glow of communitas among those with whom they share some cultural or biological feature they take to be their most signal mark of identity" (1977b, 48). Moore and Myerhoff also note the power of ritual to create social solidarity among strangers in industrialized, heterogeneous societies: "Ceremonies that make visible a collective connection with some common symbol or activity can minimize for a ceremonial moment their disconnections and conflicts in a crowd" (1977, 6).

Folklorist Olivia Cadavál has noted this process at work during Latino festivals in Washington, DC, where solidarity is created among Latinos of different social classes, so that "individuals whose heritage may be Latin American but whose regular behavior and cultural patterns are not identifiably ethnic may become Latinos for the day" (1991, 212). Other scholars have made similar observations about the communitas created during U.S. Day of the Dead celebrations. Describing the event at Self-Help Graphics in Los Angeles, Lara Medina observes, "Despite diverse religious affiliations, the sense of a communal identity pervades the celebration" (Medina and Cadena 2002, 85). Romo notes that the celebration has "brought different aspects of the community together: age, gender, geography, politics, etc. Because if some people didn't agree with the UFW [United Farm Workers' Union] or whatever, they would still come to this event. Chicanos can go there with Mexican Americans and Mexican immigrants, right-wing and left-wing people. It's been a great equalizer."[10]

A cross section of Latinos from different ethnic, racial, class, political, and generational backgrounds is typically present at Day of the Dead celebrations. Estela Rubalcava Klink explains how Day of the Dead builds both ethnic and intergenerational connections:

> People who may not even know each other will say, "You're from Michoacán? I am too! Let's do an altar together next year." And they do it. They become almost like comadres and they build an altar together. This event brings people together and gives them an opportunity to talk and act as if they've known each other for a while, when they haven't. It's a way for different generations to interact. I remember one woman who was from Puebla came last year. She was really moved by the altars. . . . She went home and came back later with her daughter, who was twenty years old. She not only showed her daughter the altar, but explained the whole tradition to her, and now she and her daughter want to do an altar from the Puebla region next year.[11]

The phenomenon of communitas during Day of the Dead is particularly interesting with respect to relations between immigrant and U.S.-born Latinos. As has occurred with other ethnic groups in the United States, certain conflicts exist between long-term and newcomer Latino populations. Depicted in films such as *El Norte* and *Bread and Roses* and in prime-time TV shows such as *American Family* and *The George Lopez Show*, and illustrated by political actions such as the approval of the anti-immigrant Proposition 187 by a significant percentage of California's Latino voters, some Latino U.S. citizens have negative feelings toward newcomers and feel that Latin immigrants represent tax burdens or job competition.[12] The fact that Mexican and Central American immigrants have worked as replacement workers, or "scabs," during labor strikes by the United Farm Workers' Union, for example, has historically created resentment among Mexican American farm workers. Inherent in issues of labor and immigration are issues of class. Some middle- and upper-income Latinos (most of whom are U.S. citizens) look down on Latino immigrants, while some newcomer Latinos feel discriminated against by U.S.-born Latinos (Durand Ponte 2000, 106; Omi and Winant 1993, 106).[13] Among U.S. Latino populations, language is a major marker of class: Hispanic media marketers (themselves educated, middle-class Latinos) classify monolingual Spanish audiences in the United States as lower class, while bilingual and monolingual English-speaking Latinos are considered higher class (A. Rodriguez 1999, 50).

However, shared cultural symbols and rituals bring people together in ways they would not otherwise interact. During Day of the Dead celebrations, the social tensions between newcomer and long-term Latinos in the United States temporarily diminish, as both groups reflect on a perceived common cultural ancestry. The celebration is a time when low-income, monolingual Spanish-speaking immigrants can gain admiration, based on the grounds of tradition, from middle-class Latinos who have lived in the United States for generations and for whom the celebration is more an intriguing novelty than a lived reality. After observing community-based Day of the Dead celebrations in San Francisco, California, in the 1980s and 1990s, Suzanne Morrison notes that Latino class hierarchies were temporarily reversed because newcomers often held firsthand knowledge of traditions that most U.S.-born, urban, and middle-class Latinos lacked (1992, 301).

My observations coincide with Morrison's. For example, in a Day of the Dead workshop I attended at a San Diego art gallery in October 2000, Salvadoran immigrants explained the meaning of the holiday to about twenty bilingual schoolteachers. Most of the workshop participants were U.S.-born Latinas who appeared to have little firsthand knowledge of Day of the Dead, judging from the intensity of their note taking. The Salvadoran immigrants, with their heavily accented English, held positions of higher status during the workshop because of their firsthand experiences with Day of the Dead. Similarly, during Day of the Dead workshops at Sherman Heights, monolingual Spanish-speaking immigrants discussed the significance of the ofrendas and demonstrated how to make pan de muerto, while bilingual and monolingual English-speaking Latinos listened intently, often from behind the viewfinders of their home video cameras.[14]

CLAIMS FOR PUBLIC RECOGNITION

While encouraging feelings of community among diverse Latino populations, the holiday's spectacle nature performs another important type of communication: the assertion of claims for public recognition by the wider society. Access to public space is a crucial element of contemporary cultural politics, and public rituals are as much symbolic statements to outsiders about a group's social and political presence as they are consolidations of internal values and meanings for insiders (Baumann 1992; Orsi 2002). The creation of a public sphere through the art and rituals of Day of the Dead has provided a significant aperture for the recognition of Latino culture by the mainstream. Before the 1970s, prestigious museums and galleries in the United States typically shunned the work of U.S. Latino artists, considered neither "American" nor "Latin American" (Dávila 1999). Whether representing magical realism, neo-Indigenist styles, experimental modern art, or revolutionary expressions, U.S. Latino artists were considered jarring to the "legitimate" standards of Western classical art. This began to change in the 1970s, as Day of the Dead exhibits and other public art expressions created in Latino barrios brought Chicano artists invitations to create installations in eminent museums and universities.

While the celebration has helped draw positive attention to Chicano artists, Day of the Dead has also brought some positive mainstream attention to Latino immigrants, who have traditionally been more marginalized by mainstream society and more negatively portrayed in the media than U.S.-born Latinos. Cadavál describes how a Day of the Dead celebration at the Smithsonian Institute in Washington, DC, allowed local Nicaraguan, Guatemalan, Salvadoran, and Ecuadorian immigrants to "take over" social space in one of the nation's most prestigious institutions—historically the realm of the (mainly White) upper middle classes. Although the holiday was not widely observed in DC at the time, its celebration provided an opportunity for ethnically diverse Latinos to collaborate among themselves and simultaneously receive attention from the mainstream (Cadavál 1985, 186). This dynamic has continued in other regions of the country.

In November 2001, Mixtec immigrants from Oaxaca, Mexico, living and working in Oceanside, California, gained attention through public ritual when they participated in the city's first Day of the Dead festival.[15] Unlike most of

California's Day of the Dead events, the idea for the three-day Oceanside celebration was initiated by non-Latinos from the city's chamber of commerce, as
part of a multipronged attempt to encourage cultural tourism and economic
development in the financially struggling city.[16] After contacting the pastor of
St. Mary's Star of the Sea Church (Oceanside's largest Mixtec congregation)
to seek his support and connections with the Mixtec community, the chamber
of commerce invited members of the Binational Oaxacan Indigenous Front
(Frente Indigena Oaxaqueño Binacional) to build seven large altars in store-
fronts throughout downtown Oceanside.[17] Initially surprised by the request,
the Mixtec community accepted the invitation to participate in a citywide
celebration of their Oaxacan culture.

Becoming the talk of the town among both admirers and detractors, the
ofrendas were constructed inside the windows of prominent downtown businesses, and received recognition from city schools, local government leaders,
businesses, the public library, nearby universities, journalists, and artists. The
relevance of this recognition is underscored by the fact that Mixtecs, who face
intense poverty and racism in Mexico, are also the poorest and most marginalized Latinos in California. Of all agricultural workers in the state, they hold
the least desirable and lowest paying jobs, suffer the greatest labor abuses, and
live in the worst housing conditions (F. Lopez and Runsten 2003).

The Mixtec ofrendas were made in the exact styles of ofrendas found in
Oaxaca, with no attempt to be intentionally artistic or political. Although the
Chicano initiators of Day of the Dead avoided making exact replicas of
Mexican ofrendas because "a transplanted Mexican version [would] be unre-
alistic and too removed" from the Chicano experience (Romo 2000, 40),
Mixtec immigrants felt comfortable creating a transplanted Oaxacan version
of the holiday. Unlike Chicanos, they had grown up making such ofrendas and
saw the celebration as a modified continuation of their customary activities,
rather than as a cultural reclamation project. A Mixtec who has lived in
Oceanside for thirty years and helped organize the first citywide celebration,
explains how he felt about building an ofrenda in his restaurant, one of the
most popular eateries in downtown Oceanside:

> I made it just like we always do in my village. I had a lot of food, mole,
> fruits. We had it up for four days and everybody came to see it. We dec-
> orated it with a lot of things, jicama and flowers and everything just like
> over there. Here we have about 95 percent American people as cus-
> tomers, so they were very interested to see it. They never saw something
> like that before. They were asking me what it represented and I explained
> to them that it's something we do over there in Mexico. They really liked
> it. A lot of them came in and later came back and brought more people.
> They brought their camera and started taking videos and pictures. Some

even added things to the altar. Some of them told me they wanted to do it in their homes. A lot of people came in just to see it. They didn't want to buy anything, they just came in to see it, just to learn about it. I'm glad about that because since I left Oaxaca, I've never seen anything like that until now.[18]

In addition to the ofrendas, the Oceanside festival included two other important aspects of the celebration for Mixtecs: a Catholic Mass and a public procession that started at the church and made its way through the downtown streets.[19] On the evening of November 1, 2001, nearly one thousand people attended a bilingual Day of the Dead Mass held at St. Mary's and participated in a candlelight procession through the streets of this "all-American" city, as Oceanside is called on the city's official Web site. Nearly half of the participants were Anglo residents of Oceanside, for whom this appeared to be their first exposure to Day of the Dead; those who were part of St. Mary's parish attended the Mass, while others waited outside for the procession to begin. The rest of the public consisted of recent Mexican immigrants (mainly from Oaxaca) and other Latinos (Mexican Americans, Chicanos, Central Americans) from Oceanside and surrounding towns, many of whom had read about the event in the weekly *San Diego Reader*, *North County Times*, or *Union Tribune*. Non-Latino attendees of the event described it as "interesting," "beautiful," and "different," although some thought it was "strange" and a small group of evangelical Christians protested across from the church, calling the event "satanical."[20]

The following additional comments by the Mixtec restaurant owner illustrate how Oceanside's public Day of the Dead rituals have provided recognition and validation for Mixtecs and, more broadly, for Mexicans and other Latinos:

> When I first moved to the U.S., some Mixtec people would celebrate a very little bit in their home. Just a little bit, just making dinner for Todos Santos. But a couple of years ago, somewhere out there, it started really getting big. I guess everybody knows what it is now. For Latinos and Mexican people, it was hard for them to celebrate their own fiesta before. We thought probably a lot of people wouldn't understand what we were doing, because they never lived it or experienced it. . . . I think before, there wasn't enough people. We didn't have a voice. You couldn't hear our voice then. It was like being in a jungle and screaming and nobody could hear you. The voices just got lost. But now, there's enough people to make it happen.[21]

While hundreds of people waited outside St. Mary's Church (which was packed to capacity) for the start of the Day of the Dead procession, an upper-class Mexican American from the affluent town of Del Mar expressed her delight and gratitude toward the Mixtec community, as she said excitedly, "This is wonderful. This is *absolutely* wonderful! I'm so glad they are doing this!" As a light-skinned, U.S.-born Latina who spoke English better than Spanish and did not grow up celebrating Day of the Dead, she appreciated the Oaxacan immigrants for bringing her closer to customs of her ancestral land. "They" were agents, in a way that she could not be, for publicly revealing the beauty of her ethnic culture to the larger U.S. society. Although coming from a very different racial, linguistic, and socioeconomic background than the Latina from Del Mar, a Mixtec resident of Oceanside noted that Mixtecs and other Latinos at the event felt similar feelings of pride and excitement:

> I know for sure that a lot of Latino people wanted to be there for the church and the procession because that's probably the most important part. I think they felt like part of them came true. All the way from there, it came true, and they just couldn't pass it up. They had to be a part of it. For people who were not Latino, I guess they were just interested and wanted to know what was going on. Just curious, I guess. It made me feel good, because at least they were interested. Like I said, when I heard about it, I just couldn't pass it by, because that's what I did when I was young. I just had to be involved. When I saw all those people, it made me feel like I was back twenty years in my life, as if I was home. It made me feel very nice. There were a lot of newspapers covering it. I was interviewed by a TV station too. It was interesting that they wanted to cover it. If we keep going like that, the younger people can learn things. Like my daughter, she's ten and she says, "Dad, I really like this." In school they are learning about these things now.[22]

As the candlelight procession proceeded through the center of town led by a traditional Oaxacan band, Mixtecs were the center of attention, from TV cameras to speeches by the mayor and other city leaders. Although many members of the Oaxacan immigrant community had privately constructed Day of the Dead altars in their homes in previous years, this was the first public celebration of what, for Mixtecs, is the most important holiday of the year. After the Mass, hundreds of people from different generations, social classes, ethnicities, races, and resident statuses gathered together on the street in front of the church, each holding a candle and remembering someone who was no longer living. The flickering candlelight seemed to connect everyone as a single entity, walking slowly en masse down the cordoned-off streets of the city's commercial district, while stopped pedestrians and motorists watched in bewilderment.

In contrast to the college-educated, highly articulate Chicano artists who initiated Day of the Dead in major U.S. cities known nationally for their cultural diversity and progressive social climate, most Mixtecs in Oceanside speak limited English (some speak limited Spanish) and lack the privileges afforded to U.S. citizens.[23] Because many do not have legal permission to work in the United States, the community has maintained a low profile for reasons of survival, existing tenuously in a predominantly Anglo, politically conservative military town. The Mixtecs of Oceanside did not feel empowered to publicly celebrate their heritage until encouraged to do so by the chamber of commerce. Yet, this mainstream institution would likely not have approached them had it not been for the impact of the Chicano Movement on California's cultural landscape.

Day of the Dead celebrations have been held in Oceanside each year since 2001, growing exponentially to become one of the city's most popular annual events. Mary Ann Thiem, a volunteer who coordinated Oceanside's Day of the Dead festival during the years 2002–2006, describes the intercultural community building she observed during the event:

> Day of the Dead brings a lot of people together who might not normally work together. The planning takes almost a year. There are lots of meetings. So we have businesspeople, artists, Mixtec people, designers, teachers all working together. I'm originally from Nebraska . . . so there's people like me who are new to the community, working with people who've lived here a long time. There's people who speak Spanish and people who speak English and people who speak Mixtec or Zapotec. As I said, there are a lot of Oaxacan families involved. We had the Boy Scouts and Girl Scouts involved. . . . On the day of the event, everyone is working together. . . . People who know about Day of the Dead and those who didn't know about it before all work together.[24]

The Oceanside event exemplifies how communitas operates not only internally among the Latino community, but also externally between Latinos and non-Latinos. Day of the Dead rituals often engage non-Latino audiences in physical, psychological, or spiritual ways that they may not anticipate, creating feelings of unity among peoples of diverse racial backgrounds. Studying the interactions between predominantly White, middle-class audiences and the immigrant organizers of ethnic celebrations, such as Cambodian New Year and Day of the Dead, held at the Smithsonian's National Museum of American Art, Jack Santino observes that spectators were transformed into participants. Although temporary, this liminal experience encouraged audiences toward greater "appreciation, acceptance and understanding" of diverse communities (1988, 125). Anthropologist John MacAloon notes a similar dynamic in Olympic Game ceremonies, where the power of public rituals can transport entire societies outside of their ordinary boundaries of space and time, providing a communitas experience that transcends barriers of language, nationality, class, and ideology. People who come to enjoy the spectacle or to profit from it, he notes, often find themselves involved in the action at levels of intensity and involvement they could not have foreseen (1984, 268–269).

RITUAL COMMUNICATION brings about intensified public mindfulness and togetherness that can serve as a source of creativity and improvisation, but it can also serve as an antistructural force, engendering new social and political forms (Lukes 1977). While Day of the Dead rituals in the United States have helped create a sense of community among U.S. Latinos and gained them admiration in the wider cultural sphere, the imagined community cultivated during these public rituals also creates the kind of fertile foundation needed for political organizing. As we shall see in the next chapter, artists and organizers often have overtly political intentions in mind when they design public ofrendas, processions, and other activities.

CHAPTER 5

U.S. Day of the Dead
as Political Communication

A MORAL ECONOMY

AT THE MISSION CULTURAL CENTER FOR LATINO ARTS
(MCCLA), the largest Latino cultural center in San Francisco, a foreboding
chain-link fence, symbolizing the wall between Mexico and the United States,
partitions the main gallery entrance. Along the fence are blinking red and blue
police lights and life-sized, cardboard-mounted photos of armed border patrol
agents, positioned in wooden stands as if ready to apprehend visitors entering
the exhibit. Printed on the gallery wall is text about the border patrol
program, Operation Gatekeeper, along with a graph illustrating a sharp rise in
immigrant deaths since the program's onset.[1] The walls are lined with somber
depictions of immigrant lives and deaths: "before" photos of people in their
communities of origin prior to attempting to migrate to the United States,
juxtaposed with "after" photos of their dead bodies in the desert. In the center
of the room stands a multitiered ofrenda dedicated to migrants who have died
while trying to cross the border. Conjuring up a desert environment, the floor
around the altar is covered with sand imprinted with shoeprints and strewn
with rocks, scorched branches, cactuses, plastic snakes, mice, and scorpions.[2]

The altar installation mixes traditional ofrenda elements (marigolds,
candles, fruit, gourds, copal incense, photos of saints, crucifixes, Indigenous
weavings) with contemporary items such as books about Operation Gatekeeper, photocopies of "green cards," and symbols of Mexican and Mexican
American revolutionary struggles (Zapatista dolls, the United Farm Workers'
union logo, photos of labor leader César Chávez).[3] In an updated twist on the
tradition of placing a glass of water on the altar to quench the thirst of the
souls, commercially packaged plastic bottles of water—the element most
desperately needed by people in the desert—were placed in the sand and on
the altar. On either side of the wall behind the ofrenda, written in red paint

resembling dripping blood, are the words, "¿Cuántos Más?" (How Many More?) and "¿El Sueño Americano?" (The American Dream?). Boisterous as they entered the building, a few dozen high school students on a Day of the Dead field trip quiet down as they look at the photos, examine the ofrenda, and read the writing on the wall. After providing a brief overview of the Days of the Dead, a gallery volunteer talks with the group about the meaning of the installation and asks how many have ever heard of Operation Gatekeeper. Most, including the teachers, have not. The gallery's guest book is filled with comments from visitors expressing their surprise and sadness about the extent of the border deaths.

Many of the other Day of the Dead installations at the MCCLA also have political themes. Some retain the look and feel of traditional altars, while others are abstract expressions, such as Eva Vargas's *Papel Picado para Digna Ochoa* (Papel Picado for Digna Ochoa). This installation consists of a simple mechanical typewriter on a stand, a blue curtain background, and a photo of Mexican human rights lawyer Digna Ochoa, who was murdered in October 2001 in what is widely believed to be retribution for her investigations into the corruption of top Mexican government officials.[4] Another abstract expression is Jesus Barraza's *Rueda de la Muerte* (Wheel of Death), a colorful Wheel of Fortune–style mechanism that the public was invited to spin, seeing where the arrow would fall. Each of the possible categories represented a form of death or destruction attributed to U.S. foreign or domestic policies, such as "Bombing in Afghanistan," "War in Colombia," and "Destruction of the Rainforests for Hamburger Consumption."[5] According to Patricia Rodriguez, exhibit curator at the MCCLA, the Day of the Dead exhibit is the gallery's best-attended art show each year. In addition to hundreds of visitors from the general public, thousands of students from elementary, middle, and high schools and universities visit the exhibit annually, making the gallery a potent consciousness-raising space.[6]

Encouraging the examination of both macro- and microprocesses of communication and cultural production, media theorist Jesús Martín-Barbero has suggested that communication scholars redirect their focus from typical industry critiques and textual interpretations toward cultural, social, and political mediations occurring within grassroots communicative practices (1993). U.S. Day of the Dead events can be seen as a strategic retort to the marginalization of people of color in the corporate-controlled, mainstream media, as Latino artists, community activists, and everyday citizens exercise cultural autonomy and transmit their perspectives on contemporary issues affecting their lives. Through the medium of public altars, they not only counter historically negative media images of Latinos as people without a valuable culture, but also draw attention to the ways that contemporary events, legislation, and public policies affect the Latino community.

Initiated as one of the most prominent manifestations of the Chicano Movement, Day of the Dead celebrations in California were conceived from the start as media for contesting and critiquing the dominant system of power. At that time, the mere idea of publicly celebrating *any* non-European cultural form in the United States was a political statement against decades of Eurocentric race and class hierarchies. Chicano artists found additional opportunities for political commentary within the framework of Day of the Dead because of the celebration's historical association in urban Mexico with social critique (e.g., ironic skeletal caricatures and the satirical calavera poetry). The holiday's focus on "the dead" made it a fitting occasion upon which to criticize government policies and social practices that caused death on a local, national, or global level, while the spirituality associated with the ofrenda ritual imbued the art installations' secular themes with a sacred seriousness. In contrast to altars traditionally made in people's homes, which were a refuge from the impersonal worlds of politics and mass-produced culture, Chicano public altar installations engaged with and responded to these worlds.

At the same time, Day of the Dead celebrations were designed to be attractive to families and schoolchildren. Thus, they included a combination of aesthetic stimulation, holiday crafts, and political commentary, depending on the orientation of event organizers. Some activities were purely "cultural" (particularly those geared to children), teaching about the tradition of altars or holding craft workshops. Others were overtly political art installations or performances. The same gallery or community center might present both politicized and traditional ofrendas or a combination of radical spoken word events and noncontroversial craft workshops.

As the concept grew in popularity and exhibits spread from Chicano-run galleries to elite museums such as the De Young Fine Art Museum, the San Francisco Museum of Modern Art (MoMA), the Smithsonian, Harvard's Peabody Museum of Archaeology and Ethnology, and New York's Metropolitan Museum of Art, they tended to be less overtly political, rendering them comfortable to predominantly upper-income, non-Latino museum audiences.[7] However, a significant number of Day of the Dead events at community centers, universities, art galleries, public libraries, parks, and even business districts continued to communicate about political issues. Particularly in California and the Southwest, it soon became rare to attend a Day of the Dead exhibit without encountering at least one ofrenda dedicated to victims of a sociopolitical cause of death. Today, politically themed installations are created by Chicanos, other Latinos, and non-Latinos concerned with issues of social justice, and are viewed by thousands of event attendees, as well as by consumers of print and electronic media. The public communication that occurs during annual Day of the Dead events is an important generator of knowledge both within and beyond the Latino community, given the institutional racism and poverty that make it difficult for Latinos and other historically marginalized populations to tell their stories in the mainstream U.S. media.

In his discussion of the "moral economy," E. P. Thompson argues that the working-class uprisings of eighteenth-century England were not merely compulsive responses to economic stimuli but self-conscious behavior modified by custom, culture, and reason, in which people used moral indignation to defend community rights and challenge official descriptions of reality. The grievances expressed by the common people, he explains, were grounded in traditional views of norms and obligations that operated within a popular consensus as to what were legitimate and illegitimate practices among various populations in society (such as workers, consumers, businesspeople, and government officials). The moral economy was a "group, community or class response to crisis" that expressed resistance to exploitation and challenged the authorities, on moral grounds, to attend to the commonweal (1991, 187–188). Tracing the origins of the highly organized English working class to local cultural traditions that emphasized decency and mutual aid, Thompson argues that the widespread participation of common people in traditional rituals and ceremonies sustained collectivist values that in turn allowed the working class to maintain solidarity as they faced difficult social and political conditions.

Similarly, the collective Day of the Dead traditions of Latinos living in the United States foster a sense of cultural solidarity in tough political times—as people face rising unemployment, dwindling affordable housing, the privatization of public resources, and the defunding of health care, social services, public arts, education, and youth programming. Moral arguments are aided by "exotic" rituals that attract the attention of mainstream media and the general public in ways that ordinary political work does not. These rituals create semi-sacred spaces that are simultaneously sites for cultural affirmation (through the enactment of ancestral customs), and political expressions (in which the dead assist the living in the condemnation of injustice). Spurring reflection on the contradictions between people's lived experiences and U.S. ideologies of rugged individualism and equal opportunity, political Day of the Dead rituals express the human cost of government and corporate policies that create the economic desperation necessary for individuals to undertake life-threatening forms of survival. The rest of this chapter describes some common themes of political Day of the Dead activities in the United States, illustrating how they draw attention to the violence, poverty, and exploitation facing Latinos and other minorities who disproportionately experience an unnecessary loss of life.

REMEMBERING MIGRANT DEATHS:
PROTESTING OPERATION GATEKEEPER

Since the mid-1990s, immigration-related issues have been the subject of many Day of the Dead exhibits and events. In the face of an increasingly militarized border and intensifying legislation in California and other states to deny undocumented workers basic needs such as health care, housing, access to public education, or the right to obtain a driver's license, Day of the Dead events have emphasized the ironic contradictions between the United States' appetite for cheap labor and its unwillingness to provide immigrant workers with basic human rights.[8] In San Diego, California, the Interfaith Coalition for Immigrant and Refugee Rights (ICIR), whose members include people of Anglo American, Chicano, Mexican, Guatemalan, Cuban American, Italian, and Filipino heritage, holds annual vigils on the U.S.-Mexican border to protest Operation Gatekeeper. Each November 1, an interfaith service is held and wooden crosses are placed along the border wall listing the names, ages, and places of origin of some three thousand migrants who have died while attempting to cross "the line" since Gatekeeper's inception.[9] Also erected along the border are traditional Day of the Dead altars heaped with fruits, candles, flowers, and pan de muerto in memory of the dead migrants. Because these actions occur within view of the official Tijuana–San Diego border checkpoint for car and pedestrian traffic, they are seen by thousands of daily commuters, tourists, and border patrol agents. Mixing the religious, the cultural, and the political, these rituals force the public to remember the desperate living conditions of millions of people south of the border, and to reflect on the U.S. government's role in maintaining a "favorable business climate" for U.S. corporations that results in poverty wages for most Latin Americans.

Roughly one-third of all corpses found along the U.S.-Mexican border are unidentified. This situation is due, in large part, to the fact that Central American and other non-Mexican migrants typically travel without identification, hoping to pass for Mexican and avoid deportation to their native countries if captured by the border patrol. At present, the nameless cadavers are mechanically inhumed in vacant tracts of land near the border, and family members at home have no way of knowing the fate of their missing kin. In response to this situation, the California Rural Legal Assistance Foundation, together with St. Joseph's and St. Anthony's parishes in Holtville, California, sponsored a Day of the Dead event in the Terrace Park Cemetery on November 1, 2001.[10] In a barren potter's field behind the main cemetery, the cadavers of more than two hundred unidentified migrants found in the nearby desert are buried beneath stark mounds of earth, marked with small cement blocks labeled "John Doe" or "Jane Doe." In an implicit condemnation of Operation Gatekeeper, this event combined a traditional, village-style Day of the Dead procession (in which people sang, prayed, held flowers, and carried candles as they walked from the main street to the cemetery), with a political call for binational efforts to identify the bodies through DNA testing.[11]

At the cemetery entrance was a large sign reading, "This Day of the Dead, 600 families don't even know whether or not they have a migrant to cry for." Organizers gave event participants buttons reading, "Would you walk across mountains and deserts for a job? 1,700 migrants did and died."[12] These message urged readers to identify with migrants and compare their differing life circumstances. The underlying discourse of the event appealed to unspoken but deeply felt concepts of basic human rights, dignity, and dedication to family. Following Latin American Day of the Dead traditions of grave adornment, nearly one hundred participants proceeded to decorate the anonymous graves with marigolds, candles, papel picado, copal incense, and pan de muerto, converting the lonely burial site into a vibrant commemoration of "those souls who have no one to remember them."[13] By publicly honoring the migrants buried in Holtville, participants made demands on state and federal government regarding an international problem. The drama, music, and color of the procession drew media coverage through which working-class Latinos and social justice activists gained access to the public sphere from which they are so often marginalized. Edward Dunn, then the director of ICIR, explains, "This type of ceremony not only educates the public about what's happening on the border, but it recommits people of conscience and our coalition members, some of whom have traveled from Los Angeles, Santa Cruz, and San Francisco to be here today, to the statewide work we do on behalf of immigrants and refugees."[14] Each year, immigrant rights activists across the United States observe Day of the Dead with processions and altars critical of U.S. border patrol policies.[15] Although the weekly and monthly migrant death toll along the border rarely makes the local evening news—and is generally relegated to the back pages of mainstream newspapers when covered—Day of the Dead events often get front-page coverage in the metro, region, and culture sections of major newspapers.

Migrant death along the U.S.-Mexican border was also the topic of a binational Day of the Dead Border Pilgrimage held from October 26 to November 2, 2003.[16] The event was organized by immigrant rights and labor activists from California, Arizona, New Mexico, and Texas to draw national attention to deaths they attributed to NAFTA, Operation Gatekeeper, and its sister program in Texas, Operation Hold the Line. As written in the Border Pilgrimage's promotional materials, news coverage, and Web site, the purpose of the event was "to raise awareness about the deaths on our southern border and the economic policies that contribute to them." The front page of the Web site and promotional flyer states,

> Since Operation Gatekeeper in California and Operation Hold the Line . . . [began] in 1994, there have been over 2,200 deaths of undocumented migrants along the U.S.-Mexico border. Economic realities and aggressive employment recruitment tactics act as a strong push for

the treacherous journey north for migrants from Mexico, Central America and points south. Since 9/11, an attitude that all immigrants are terrorists seems to have permeated the United States. This increases the peril for undocumented migrants and their families in search of a better life.[17]

Consisting of nearly fifty people from across California, a car caravan set out from San Diego, California, on October 26, headed for El Paso, Texas, with daily stops at points along the border to learn about U.S. economic and immigration policies and to remember the migrants who had fallen victim to them.[18] A send-off event was held for the caravan in Larsen Field, a public park in San Diego near the U.S.-Mexican border, where about a hundred people participated in a ceremony honoring the dead. Each participant held a white cross inscribed with the name of a migrant who had died since Operation Gatekeeper's inception, and amid singing, prayer, and speeches on the legal and moral implications of U.S. immigration policies, an altar was assembled on the grass. It consisted of candles, marigolds, crosses, discarded shoes, clothing, stuffed animals, and other mementos representing migrants who had died in the desert.

The next day, the delegation traveled to the All-American Canal, which runs between Calexico, California, and Mexicali, Mexico. Although the canal looks placid on the surface, enticing migrants to swim to the U.S. side, its deadly undercurrent is responsible for 10 percent of all border deaths annually. After reflecting on this site, the delegation crossed over to the Mexicali side of the border to view sewer tunnels where migrants crawl through human excrement to reach the United States. The following day, the group stopped in Douglas, Arizona, and talked to a cattle rancher and his wife whose property runs along the border. The couple discussed the problems they had with migrants, border patrol agents, and vigilante groups waging war on their property since the commencement of Operation Gatekeeper. The delegation then met with an advocacy group called the Border Action Network to learn more about vigilantism and civil rights issues along the border.[19]

On October 29, after meeting with human rights activists in Tucson, Arizona, the delegation crossed the border into Agua Prieta, Mexico, to hear from Alianza Indigena about the impact of U.S. border policies on Indigenous communities on both sides of the border.[20] This meeting was followed by a visit to the Casa del Migrante in Agua Prieta, a safe house run by the Catholic Scalabrini order. Here, food, water, and temporary shelter are offered to migrants who traverse the Sonora desert, before they attempt the final leg of the journey crossing the border into Tucson. Unexpectedly, while the delegation spoke with the priest and staff at Casa del Migrante, a group of migrants arrived, visibly exhausted from their desert trek. As staff provided them with food, water, bathroom facilities, and lodging, several of the migrants shared their stories with the delegation members—who later said this encounter was the most moving experience of the pilgrimage.

On October 31, the caravan stopped in Mesilla, New Mexico, to participate in a Day of the Dead tribute and vigil in the central plaza, while townspeople prepared outdoor ofrendas for the town's annual celebration. That evening, the delegation arrived in El Paso, Texas, where it was joined for a weekend Day of the Dead convocation by a similar caravan that had driven to El Paso from Brownsville, Texas. Attending the convocation were hundreds of participants from areas of Texas and other parts of the country who had flown in for the weekend: immigrant rights activists, labor activists, religious workers, elderly people active in their churches, university students and professors, artists, local residents, and their children. About half of the participants were Latino (a mix of Mexican Americans and Mexican and Central American immigrants) and half were non-Latino (mainly Anglo Americans and several African Americans). Planned nearly a year in advance, the event had been promoted among secular and faith-based organizations working with immigrants, as well as among labor groups, universities, and the general public (through newspaper and newsletter articles, community meetings, church bulletins, and the Internet).

On November 1, the convocation included a day of workshops: Migration, NAFTA, and Economic Policy; Life on the Border; Mexican Reality; Current Border Enforcement Policies; and Border Theology and Spirituality, facilitated by human rights activists, labor policy advocates, and professors from university Border Studies programs. Throughout the weekend, there were also Day of the Dead cultural activities, including satirical calavera poetry readings decrying the abuse of Mexican workers in U.S.-owned *maquiladoras*, and migrants' search for the American Dream.[21] Between performances by folkloric dancers and political musicians, giant calavera puppets danced and sang songs of life and death on the border.

For the convocation's conclusion on November 2, a binational Day of the Dead interfaith service was held in the desert along the border fence. On both the Mexican and U.S. sides, a few hundred people stood in the dusty heat, facing each other through a barbed-wire fence dividing North from South as they sang and prayed in honor of deceased migrants. Divided down the middle by the fence was a traditional ofrenda covered with colorful tablecloths, fruits, marigolds, candles, and photos of the dead, which had been constructed by people on both sides of the border. Unable to see amid the crowd, children climbed the fence, clinging to its top for a better view of the festivities on the other side. The Day of the Dead Pilgrimage was covered by the U.S. Spanish TV network Univisión, as well as by local newspapers in San Diego, El Centro, Calexico, Tucson, and El Paso.

REMEMBERING LABOR ABUSES:
UFW AND THE BRACEROS

Another theme common to Day of the Dead ofrendas in California and the Southwest is the commemoration of the labor struggles of the region's farm workers, most of whom are Latinos. These laborers work in the stifling heat with little protection against the elements or against the pesticides they touch and breathe regularly. There is notoriously little oversight or enforcement of the most basic labor rights in the fields, so that workers often don't get appropriate access to drinking water, bathrooms, food and rest breaks, or health care. Whether in grassroots community centers, art galleries, or museums, farm worker ofrendas usually display photos of deceased UFW founder César Chávez and other farm workers. In a contemporary twist on the tradition of offering harvest crops to the dead, such altars typically contain wooden produce crates, pesticide cans, farming implements (hoes, shovels, work gloves, etc.), grapes (boycotted for years by consumers in solidarity with the UFW), heads of lettuce, pints of strawberries, boxes of tomatoes, and related agricultural items. Drawing attention to the chronic exploitation of these laborers, the ofrendas often include newspaper clippings (either placed on the altars or mounted on nearby walls) and handouts about farm worker strikes and struggles.

In the twenty-first century, a related theme has emerged in U.S. Day of the Dead exhibits—ofrendas commemorating *los braceros*, the 4.5 million Mexican "arms" or hired hands recruited by the U.S. government from 1942 to 1965 to fill manual labor shortages during and after World War II. Admitted as temporary laborers but denied the possibility of permanent residency in the United States, these workers were underpaid by U.S. agrobusiness and government authorities, who withheld 10 percent of their wages for a social security–type program that was to be administered by the Mexican government. Some sixty years later, the vast majority of braceros have not received the benefits of these $36 million in wage deductions, and the funds have disappeared from the Banco Nacional de México. Since 2001, hundreds of surviving braceros have held public demonstrations and filed class action lawsuits, both in Mexico and the United States, in attempts to receive compensation for the braceros, widows of braceros, and their children, most of whom live in poverty today.[22] A braceros ofrenda I saw on November 1, 2003, at the Day of the Dead celebration of the Mayapán Women's Collective in El Paso, Texas, included posters explaining the history of the Bracero Program and informational pamphlets discussing the wrongful wage deductions as well as information on how braceros and their families could join the current legal struggle to win financial remuneration. This celebration, which included live music, performances, and Mexican food, was attended by more than seven hundred people, including family members, students in school groups, undocumented workers, political activists, journalists, and senior citizens, some of whom were former braceros. Illustrating the communicative potential of the ofrenda format, when a few elderly Mexican men lingered in front of the altar, visibly surprised to see public recognition of their experience, a spontaneous discussion ensued between these former braceros and exhibit visitors standing nearby. The men spoke of their previous working conditions and the difficulties they were having in collecting the retirement money that was supposedly set aside for them.[23] Because most Americans have never heard of the Bracero Program, and the issue receives little media attention, such public altar installations are valuable forms of communication.

Numerous agricultural-related altars are created throughout California and the Southwest each year, constructed in schools (elementary, middle, and high), universities, public libraries, museums, and other "high traffic" public areas of learning.[24] These altars simultaneously promote Latino cultural traditions and teach a "bottom up" version of history that is underemphasized in the mainstream collective consciousness. By keeping alive the historical memory of past political struggles and achievements, labor-themed ofrendas simultaneously honor the memory of the dead while upholding concerns about present-day worker exploitation that require the awareness and support of the larger community.

Remembering Indigenous Struggles: Genocide and Repression

Another theme to emerge in U.S. Day of the Dead celebrations is Indigenous rights. It is not uncommon for Native Americans, Chicanos, and Latin American immigrants of Indigenous heritage to come together in solidarity to remember their similar histories of disenfranchisement and exploitation.[25] North American Indians also had vital traditions of honoring their ancestors before having contact with Europeans, and because they were also forced to convert to Christianity in ways similar to their Indigenous peers in Latin America, there are strong similarities between Native American and Latin American Day of the Dead customs. These include elaborate grave-decoration practices, the preparation of special foods and new clothes in honor of the deceased, late-night candlelit vigils in the cemetery, and ritual begging from house to house.[26] In November 1999, Lakota Sioux Indians from the Pine Ridge Reservation in South Dakota, together with Maya Indians from Guatemala, organized a Day of the Dead event in Washington, DC.[27] Held directly across from the White House in downtown Lafayette Park, the event featured Guatemalan Day of the Dead kites, Maya music, dancers, and a series of speeches.[28] Themes included the genocide of native peoples across the Americas, solidarity with the people of Guatemala, calls to free Leonard Peltier, and demands to shut down the U.S. Army's School of the Americas.[29] Participants placed photos and mementos of deceased Indigenous leaders on a community ofrenda, as a way to draw attention to the U.S. government's failure to make restitution for the past and present abuses of native peoples. In an unrelated event the previous year, two thousand Native Americans gathered in Mesa, Arizona, on Day of the Dead to pray and dance in honor of their ancestors.[30] Similarly, on November 2, 2002, Pomo Indians from Northern California traveled more than five hundred miles to Chicano Park, the symbolic center of San Diego's Chicano community, to drum, sing, build a "roundhouse" (Native American ceremonial sauna hut), and communally create a giant ofrenda honoring Chicano and Native American ancestors.[31]

Remembering the War Dead: A Critique of U.S. Military Interventions

Because a major element of the Chicano Movement is solidarity with oppressed peoples, Day of the Dead altar installations focusing on the death and destruction caused by U.S.-sponsored military interventions (in Vietnam, Cambodia, Chile, El Salvador, Guatemala, Nicaragua, Panama, Colombia, and elsewhere) have been a regular part of Chicano commemorations of the holiday. In recent years, events have focused on the U.S. wars in Afghanistan and Iraq. For example, on October 30, 2004, Mujeres against Militarism and the Raza Unida Coalition sponsored a Day of the Dead Vigil against Militarism in the Latino community of Sylmar, Los Angeles. Beginning at four in the afternoon with a procession through residential and commercial sections of Sylmar, in which participants held candles, photos of the dead, and banners of skulls clad in army helmets, participants chanted, "No blood for oil!" and other antiwar slogans in Spanish and English. Onlookers in nearby homes and stores stopped what they were doing to watch.[32]

The procession culminated in a five-hour Day of the Dead vigil outside of Tia Chucha's Café Cultural, a popular gallery-café, where Latino youth (predominantly high school and college students) spoke publicly about the disproportionately high percentage of Latinos dying in Iraq, relative to their numbers in the overall U.S. population. They condemned the aggressive recruiting tactics of the Junior Reserve Officers Training Corps (JROTC) and other military recruitment programs that concentrate heavily in Latino and African American communities, noting that JROTC is rarely found in upper-income Anglo communities. Held on the sidewalk in front of the café, in a busy mini-mall, the vigil area included a wall lined with marigolds and candles, on which hung photos of thirty-eight Latino youths killed in Iraq. Below each photo were the servicemember's name, birth date, and death date, and a description of the youth's accomplishments, goals, and dreams, such as the following: "Amy Lopez was a straight A student who had planned to attend college. She joined the army as a way to help fund her education and see the world. She loved animals and wanted to become a veterinarian. She was killed in a mortar attack in Fallujah. She was 19 years old." Visibly sobered by the memorial, passersby at the mall stopped to look at the photos posted along the lengthy "altar wall." Since the onset of the warfare in 2002, I have seen Day of the Dead ofrendas and vigils in California, New Mexico, Texas, and New York, commemorating both Iraqi and U.S. casualties of the war. They have appeared in Latino galleries and community centers, as well as in major museums and commercially sponsored festivals.

PUBLIC CELEBRATIONS AS EXPRESSIONS OF UNITY AND DISCORD

In addition to encouraging feelings of unity, public rituals within racially structured societies can also be important spaces for expressing a *lack* of consensus felt by a given population toward the larger society. U.S. Day of the Dead ofrendas both celebrate culture and respond to the political periods in which they are created. Altar exhibits created in the 1970s honored farm workers who faced life-threatening situations of pesticide poisoning and inhumane labor conditions. In the 1980s, ofrendas were dedicated to the victims of AIDS as a way to honor the deceased and draw attention to a lack of sufficient research and prevention work. Later altars in the 1980s and 1990s drew attention to the suffering caused by U.S. military intervention in Latin American countries, critiquing foreign policies that supported repressive regimes abroad. In 2001, Day of the Dead installations across the country honored those killed in the September 11 World Trade Center explosions, and have since honored victims of the subsequent wars in the Middle East. Recent events have indicted U.S. immigration policies and the negative social, environmental, and economic consequences of NAFTA.

Day of the Dead in the United States is a contemporary example of a public ritual serving as a medium for communicating political critique messages, but it is not an anomaly. Other ethnic celebrations in the United States have also been public forums for communicating about identity and politics, and have also attracted attention far beyond the intended community. St. Patrick's Day, which began in Ireland as a family-oriented religious observance, became in the U.S. context a public celebration of Irish identity. Given the severe economic exploitation and social discrimination faced by Irish in the United States from the late nineteenth through the mid-twentieth century, St. Patrick's Day parades were initially a public statement that unified people from various parts of Ireland and challenged the hegemony of the dominant Anglo Saxon society. Much later, the holiday became a high-spirited American pastime, where anyone could be "Irish for the day." In the 1990s, the St. Patrick's Day Parade in Boston, the largest annual parade in the city, served as a riveting site for gays and lesbians of Irish descent to struggle for public recognition and acceptance within the Irish community.

Columbus Day began as a day to commemorate the "discovery" of America, but later became a time to celebrate Italian heritage by Italian Americans who, like the Irish before them, initially faced discrimination and hatred from the larger society. It has also been observed as a day of mourning by some Native Americans and others who do not want the public to forget the destruction that the Italian explorer's arrival portended for the original inhabitants of the Americas. Martin Luther King Jr. Day was initiated to honor the Civil Rights Movement and its most prominent protagonist, but became a day for African Americans to celebrate Black culture and discuss problems facing the Black community. At the same time, antiwar activists, connecting with Dr. King's advocacy of nonviolence and condemnation of war, have protested U.S. military invasions on MLK Day (both during the Vietnam War and the present-day wars in Afghanistan and Iraq). In each case, new expressions and collective meanings of public celebrations are made and remade through ritual communication.[33]

In the struggle against racism and other forms of oppression, Chicana writer Gloria Anzaldúa emphasizes the importance of sharing stories as a way to educate each other: "Before the Chicano and the undocumented worker and the Mexican from the other side can come together, before the Chicano can have unity with Native Americans and other groups, we need to know the history of their struggle and they need to know ours. . . . Each one of us must know basic facts about Nicaragua, Chile and the rest of Latin America." For society to change, she argues, people of diverse races and classes need to understand each other's perspectives. This cannot happen without consciousness raising, something that is most stirringly done through ritual communication: "Nothing happens in the 'real' world unless it first happens in the images in our heads" (1999, 108–109).

ALTHOUGH NOT ALL DAY OF THE DEAD participants understand their involvement in the celebration in terms of political or cultural resistance, these rituals in the United States are an important medium for sharing stories that affect the "images in our heads." They illustrate how ritual communication can render the "private" public and stimulate the kinds of understanding necessary to engender feelings of solidarity, whether cross-class and intraethnic solidarity among Latinos, or cross-cultural understanding between peoples of diverse races. As an important subset of Day of the Dead events, politicized ofrendas and processions raise public consciousness on behalf of those in society who are victimized, discarded, and ignored. As we shall see in the next chapter, the aesthetic creativity of these activities attracts media attention that in turn raises mainstream society's awareness of Latino cultural and political issues.

CHAPTER 6

Day of the Dead in the U.S. Media

THE CELEBRATION GOES MAINSTREAM

"TEN YEARS AGO," says an elderly native of San Diego, "I saw just one article, one tiny little mention in the paper saying, 'Come see Day of the Dead.' Now you see feature articles in the newspapers, which ten, fifteen, or twenty years ago, you never saw. Nothing was ever done to honor the Latino culture anywhere here in San Diego County, which is staggering, if you think about it, because we have lots of Latinos here and we're kissing the border."[1]

If the growth of Day of the Dead celebrations and their coverage in mainstream media is news to natives of California, where there has long been a large Mexican presence, it is even bigger news in areas of the United States that, until recently, have had few, if any, Latino residents. Newspaper articles about Day of the Dead were barely on the media radar in the 1970s, but the holiday today is routinely featured in the front pages of the metro, region, culture, arts, and calendar sections of mainstream newspapers across the country, usually accompanied by colorful photos.[2] As the following examples illustrate, the growing popularity of the celebration is itself a topic of headlines:

Homage to the dead in Día de los Muertos draws thousands to Seattle Center—Maria Gonzalez, *Seattle Times*, November 2, 2003, Local News, B1

For a growing number of Atlantans: Navigating life requires honoring the dead—Yolanda Rodriguez, *Atlanta Journal-Constitution*, November 6, 2002, 1E

Celebration carries a legacy; Day of Dead marks launch of new programs—*Grand Rapids Press*, [Michigan], November 2, 2005, City & Region, B4

Day of the Dead celebration is alive and well in Cleveland—Jesse
Tinsley, *Cleveland Plain Dealer*, October 21, 2006, Metro, 3

Día de los Muertos is bustin' out all over the place—Eduardo Cuan,
San Diego Union Tribune, October 28, 2004, Entertainment, 21

This chapter will discuss how media coverage has not only popularized
the celebration among the general U.S. public, but has helped facilitate an
imagined community of Latinos. In seeing themselves and their communities
depicted positively in the mainstream media, commonly in the front pages of
newspapers and magazines, many Latinos feel a sense of cultural pride.
Although Day of the Dead articles are not the only positive stories written
about Latinos, they represent a sizeable number of stories published each fall.
As we shall see, media coverage of Day of the Dead has helped teach about
this celebration, dispelling misunderstandings and legitimizing it in the eyes
of potential funders, the general public, and Latinos themselves. This has
contributed to the growth of the celebration, to the point where it is fast
becoming a new *American* holiday, embraced by Latinos and non-Latinos alike.
In fact, the mainstreaming of Day of the Dead itself is a topic of news:

"From San Francisco to Austin to New Orleans, 'The Day of the
Dead' is becoming more and more widespread. It's not just
something for Latinos anymore."—Anne-Marie O'Connor, Day
of the Dead crosses borders, *Los Angeles Times*, October 31, 1998,
Metro, 1

"Day of the Dead has become an event whose meaning crosses ethnic and social boundaries. . . . The first day of November marks
a transborder happening whose regional popularity rivals that of
St. Patrick's Day."—John Carlos Villani, There's lots of life in Day
of the Dead, *Arizona Republic*, October 29, 2000, A&E, 1

"The holiday was once a rare sight in New England, but will probably become routine for many here."—Raphael Lewis, Locals fete
ancestors with Day of the Dead, *Boston Globe*, November 5,
2000, Metro, B5

WIDESPREAD MEDIA ATTENTION

Media coverage of Day of the Dead comes in a variety of forms. There
have been Día de los Muertos episodes on prime-time television shows such
as PBS's *American Family* (2002 season) and the popular HBO series, *Six Feet
Under* (2002 season) and *Carnivale* (2003 season). A recent John Sayles movie,
Silver City (2004), included a Day of the Dead scene, and the Tim Burton film
Corpse Bride (2005) was filled with Day of the Dead imagery. Widely read

travel publications such as the American Automobile Association's *Horizons* and *Westways* magazines and the *Elderhostel Annual Program* promote Day of the Dead excursions in New Mexico, Texas, and California, while lifestyle magazines such as *Better Homes and Gardens, Ladies' Home Journal, Parent, Travel and Leisure,* and *Holiday Celebrations* have featured articles on the holiday. As mentioned in the notes to the introduction, the celebration is the subject of more than 28.6 million nonprofit, personal, and commercial Internet Web sites geared toward an English-speaking audience. These Web sites serve "regulars" already familiar with the celebration (who simply want to download schedules or directions for events) as well as neophytes searching for information.[3] National news organizations such as the Associated Press, National Public Radio, *U.S. News and World Report,* the *New York Times,* and the *Washington Post,* as well as local TV stations and documentary filmmakers now provide regular coverage of the holiday.

During the "Muertos" season, which in the United States extends from late September through mid-November, a given newspaper may publish multiple Day of the Dead articles and listings, ranging from coverage of children's school activities, to instructions for holiday recipes and crafts, to discussions of avant-garde altar exhibits, community celebrations, political manifestations, or religious syncretism. Unlike family Day of the Dead rituals in Latin America, where cameras would be intrusive, U.S. activities are meant to be publicly showcased. Journalists and members of the general public are allowed and encouraged to photograph the proceedings, which has been an important way of sharing the celebration with wide audiences. The news coverage these celebrations attract is a ritualized opportunity for Latinos to communicate information about themselves to the larger U.S. public.

This media space is significant, given that Latinos have been underrepresented in U.S. media for most of the twentieth century.[4] Historically, news coverage has reinforced negative stereotypes by depicting Mexicans and other Latinos as lazier, less intelligent, less moral, and more prone to crime than Anglos (Carveth and Alverio 1997; Friedman 1991; C. Rodriguez 1997; Wilson and Gutierrez 1985). Although such stereotypes are not as blatant today as in the past, Latinos in the news are still frequently portrayed as lacking agency—presented as objects rather than authoritative subjects of news (Gerbner 1993; Vargas 2000). Moreover, even newspapers attempting to offer positive images of Latinos publish disproportionately high numbers of stories focused on token athletes or entertainers, rather than on the pursuits of everyday people (Kraeplin and Subervi-Velez 2003, 119–121).

The same pattern of underrepresentation and negative representation exists in magazine and television advertising (Combating the network 'Brownout' 1999; C. Taylor and Bang 1997; Wilson, Gutiérrez and Chao 2003) and Hollywood films (Fregoso 1993; Noriega and López 1996;

Ramírez Berg 2002), where Latinos have long been stereotyped in tropes such as the *bandido*, the gang banger, the oversexualized Latin lover, the dangerous temptress, or the dim-witted buffoon. Studies done from the 1960s through the beginning of the 2000s conclude that mainstream U.S. newspaper coverage has reinforced many of the negative stereotypes found in generations of Hollywood films, portraying Latinos primarily within "problem" and "social disadvantage" frames, as people who live in crime-infested neighborhoods, lack basic educational and job skills, and are probably not legitimate U.S. citizens (Carveth and Alverio 1997; Fishman and Casiano 1969; Quiroga 1997; Wilson and Gutierrez 1985). The National Council of La Raza, the largest national Hispanic civil rights advocacy organization in the United States, argues that such media imagery helps legitimize prejudice and undermines public support for policy interventions aimed at addressing discrimination (C. Rodríguez 1997, 18).

Day of the Dead coverage diverges from such portrayals by presenting Latino culture as a vibrant and positive, rather than deviant, part of U.S. society. Moving beyond sports and entertainment tokenism, the news sources interviewed for Day of the Dead articles represent a range of "everyday" Latino voices, including educators, librarians, students, artists, poets, folk dancers, staff of community-based organizations, political activists, homemakers, immigrants, and shopkeepers. As the most widely covered Latino festivity in the United States, Day of the Dead season brings more media attention than usual to Latino cultural and political messages.

From their onset, Chicano Day of the Dead celebrations were formulated as performances of identity whose creators anticipated public viewing. Both Latinos and non-Latinos attending early Day of the Dead events experienced a mixture of surprise, admiration, and awe at the rituals they observed, but Latinos in particular experienced feelings of cultural validation and pride. Media coverage publicized Day of the Dead to millions among the general public who were not personally connected to the Chicano Movement, Latino community centers, the art world, or multicultural education initiatives. For Latinos, this coverage facilitated the development of an imagined community, or "a community of sentiment"—a group that begins to imagine and feel things together, coming to see themselves as people with historical, religious, and social commonalities (Appadurai 1996).

Media coverage of Day of the Dead portrays Latinos as having valuable contributions to offer mainstream society, both in terms of artistic and ritual practices, and in terms of alternative metaphysical views. In a country where the commercial celebration of Halloween begins to occupy people's minds (or at least space in stores, restaurants, schools, and magazine covers) from late August through October 31, news coverage of Day of the Dead has introduced people to an alternative autumn ritual. In fact, articles often portray Day of the Dead as a more meaningful way to engage with the spirit world, as in the following clips:

> "Halloween gets most of the hype, but of this weekend's two spooky holidays, Día de los Muertos has the most heart and soul."

> "For most people who grow up in the United States, Halloween is little more than an excuse to wear tacky costumes, gorge on the plastic waxiness of candy corn and maybe get a few pleasant thrills at the local haunted house. But for many Mexicans and Mexican-Americans, the days at the end of October and the beginning of November are both more solemn and more festive—involving the entire family rather than only the children."

> "For many Americans, the colors of death squeeze into a narrow spectrum. Funeral attire is black, while the pallor of the dead is described as ashen or ghostly. Red, green, blue, fiery orange, deep lavender, the vibrancy of the rainbow—this is not death's palette. That might change for those who take in a new exhibit at Harvard's Peabody Museum on Días de los Muertos (Days of the Dead), a Latin American festival that celebrates the links between the living and the deceased."

> "In Latin America, death is seen as an inevitable, natural part of life. This healthy attitude toward our potentially disturbing fates finds expression in annual Día de los Muertos (Day of the Dead) celebration."

> "This is about an attitude change and looking at life a little differently. Life is short and death is long. Let's enjoy it while we're here."[5]

Unlike Day of the Dead celebrants in Latin America, where the holiday's ritual activities are part of the quotidian fabric of community life, most people in the United States, whether Latino or non-Latino, rely on some form of mass media to get information about Day of the Dead activities.[6] In the weeks preceding November 1 and 2, newspapers announce Day of the Dead events, explaining the "who, what, when, where, and why" of the celebration. Promotional posters are hung in windows of commercial establishments, social service agencies, and schools, while banners and billboards are placed in malls, parks, and university campuses. Early each fall, community centers, art galleries, and museums mail thousands of postcards to their constituents, announcing the dates of their Day of the Dead exhibits, workshops, and related events. Entertainment magazines and the calendar or arts sections of newspapers include Day of the Dead listings, while galleries, museums, universities, folk art stores, and community centers include schedules of their Day of the Dead activities in their Web pages and newsletters. The following examples, showing the types of events typically listed in newspapers, were taken from the *San Diego Reader* during the weeks of October 24, 2002 (in which there were six Day of the Dead events advertised) and October 31, 2002 (in which there were eight Day of the Dead events advertised).

> "*Art for the Dead*: This celebration is at the Chicano Park Gazebo on Friday November 1. Expect to find altar building, spoken word, music and a marketplace to celebrate Days of the Dead. A special offering will be built to commemorate the second cycle of mourning for the twin towers victims. Free."

> "*Día de los Muertos* is being celebrated all over town this week. Bazaar del Mundo has activities planned from Saturday, October 26, through Sunday, November 2, with traditional decorations, activities and artists' demonstrations. Hours 10:00 am to 9:00 pm. . . . Admission is free."

> "*Bring Mementos, Photographs and Objects* that remind you of deceased loved ones. San Diego State University. The event begins with a slide-illustrated lecture . . . and ends with a community altar-making ceremony. The altar will be on view in Love Library through Friday November 22. Free."

> "*The Day of the Dead Festivities* at Casa Familiar Civic and Recreational Center take place on Friday, November 1. There's altar making all day, with the observance getting underway at 6:00 pm and a *velación* [communal vigil for the dead] . . . from 8:00 pm to midnight. Free."

> "*Noche de Muertos*, head to Voz Alta Cultural Center to celebrate life and death with a poetry reading honoring those who have passed away. . . . The event starts at 8:00 pm on Friday, November 1. Free."

During this same period in San Diego, there were also announcements in the *San Diego Union Tribune*, the *North County Times*, *La Prensa San Diego*, and smaller newspapers in San Diego County. Similar listings appeared the same month in newspapers across the United States, such as the *Boston Globe*, the *New York Times*, and the *Village Voice*.

These listings illustrate how, from a primarily internal or family-oriented religious observance in Latin America, Day of the Dead is transformed in the United States into an external, advertised cultural happening, organized primarily by nonprofit organizations that use the mass media to attract participants. Mary Ann Thiem, chief organizer of the annual Day of the Dead

Festival in Oceanside, California, explains, "We advertise it in the *North County Times*, the *San Diego Reader*, and the *Union Tribune*. We have a newsletter that goes out to all our Mainstreet members. Telemundo promoted it. . . . This year we may be working with Uniradio. We're planning to do more advertising on Spanish-speaking stations. It gets written up in *Oceanside Magazine*. Last year the *North County Times* did a huge spread on it. There were something like thirty-three different articles on Day of the Dead, in a huge spread. Not just writing about ours, but other events happening in the county."[7]

Estela Rubalcava Klink notes that while most participants in San Diego's Sherman Heights Day of the Dead events are local residents, the mass media also attract people from throughout greater San Diego County: "It's really grown and we have press releases in local magazines and newspapers. . . . We get people from San Ysidro, North County, Oceanside . . . Los Angeles. There are bus tours that come, organized by another organization. There are tourists, a mixture of Caucasians, African Americans, and Latinos, and professors and students from universities. Last year we were written about in *Smithsonian Magazine* and we were announced in *Night and Day* and the *San Diego Reader*."[8]

Similarly, the owner of the Folktree Gallery in Pasadena, which holds annual Day of the Dead altar exhibits, sells Day of the Dead merchandise, and organizes Día de los Muertos travel tours to Mexico, also notes that media coverage has helped promote Day of the Dead: "There's usually at least one article in one of the local papers about us. The *Star News* and the *Pasadena Weekly*. Once I was on the cover of the *L.A. Reader*. One year we got a blurb in an opera handbook. . . . Oh, and we were in the *New York Times* once. We were also in *Travel and Leisure* magazine and AAA's *Westways*."[9]

In contrast, early California Day of the Dead events were publicized through hand-typed flyers and word of mouth. According to René Yañez, "We were too busy just trying to organize the exhibits. We weren't thinking about publicity."[10] A review of cultural news coverage in the *San Francisco Chronicle* and the *Los Angeles Times* during the 1970s yielded no full-length articles about Day of the Dead events in either paper.[11] However, word of mouth spread quickly, particularly in arts circles, and growing numbers of people attended the Chicano-organized events each year. Neighborhood exhibits attracted the interest of major museums that in turn attracted media attention from newspapers and television stations. Chicana artist and educator Yolanda Garfias Woo, affectionately known in San Francisco circles as "La Madrina" (the godmother) of Day of the Dead for her pioneering work conducting Day of the Dead workshops in California schools, recalls her surprise when all three major television networks covered the opening of an ofrenda exhibit she was invited to create at San Francisco's prestigious De Young Fine Arts Museum in 1975:

It was the first time a major museum was interested in Día de los Muertos, something so ethnically *outlandish*. . . . Channels 4, 5, and 7 were all there with camera crews, filming and asking all kinds of questions that no one on the museum staff could answer. They were doing community interest stories. But channel 7 had an ABC program called *Perspectives* that was an hour long, and they returned and we filmed one hour about the exhibit and the whole history of Día de los Muertos. It was great because since Galería was doing a Muertos exhibit at the same time, we got invited to a lot of TV programs to do a combined effort about the exhibits and about what this *was*. This was a real turning point for the community, as well as for me, in terms of being public.[12]

Other prominent museums began to hold Day of the Dead exhibits by Chicano artists, and as the celebration gained popularity (and legitimacy) in the mid-1980s, full-length articles and photos appeared in newspapers with increasing frequency. As these events became better organized, planners sent press packets to media outlets, held press conferences, and conducted interviews with journalists to educate them about the tradition.

REASONS FOR INCREASED NEWS COVERAGE

The 1980s and 1990s brought an exponential growth in Day of the Dead activities across California, growing from only five organizations holding celebrations in the 1970s, to double that number in the 1980s, and triple the number in the 1990s. By 1990, the Mission District's Day of the Dead celebration was featured on page A1 of the *San Francisco Examiner*, with a large photo of the procession.[13] By the early 2000s, coverage in each of California's two largest newspapers, the *San Francisco Chronicle* and the *Los Angeles Times*, had grown to an average of seven articles annually, almost always accompanied by large photos and detailed listings. The rise in Day of the Dead events during these years corresponds with a growth in financial support for multicultural programming in schools and community-based agencies funded by public and private sources. During an era of energized civil rights advocacy, the Bilingual Education Act (also known as Title VII) was enacted in 1968 and reauthorized several times from the 1970s through the 1990s, to provide federal funding for bilingual and multicultural curricula. Providing learning opportunities in art, poetry, history, social studies, and the Spanish language, Day of the Dead became one of the most popular educational activities in California and the Southwest, later appearing in multicultural teaching curricula used by teachers across the country.

Rising interest in multiculturalism was cited by journalists as an important reason for increased news coverage of Day of the Dead:[14]

"The middle-class white liberal affection for multiculturalism is one reason, as many newsrooms are run by editors who came of age journalistically and politically between the 60s and 80s. It's genuine . . . however, because their view in many ways reflects the view of their readership, particularly in large urban centers."

"The editors of a lot of newspapers realize the importance of diversity and that celebrating diverse cultures will attract readers to their paper."

"I think it's the growing interest in multiculturalism. This is an interesting cultural event that many readers don't know about but might want to see. We also write about the African American Juneteenth celebration and other ethnic celebrations."[15]

Another factor in the growth of Day of the Dead news coverage is the higher number of Latino reporters working at newspapers since the latter twentieth century. Given increased national attention to racial diversity as a result of civil rights work, affirmative action policies at universities nationwide resulted in higher numbers of Latinos graduating from college and attending journalism schools. Editors at news organizations responded to affirmative action requirements by hiring more people of color—previously rare in the historically White and male profession of journalism. Twelve Latino journalists I surveyed indicated that their ethnic background played a role in their choice to write about Day of the Dead: all except one reported that he/she had initiated stories on the topic, pitching the subject in editorial meetings or (in the cases of editors and columnists), simply deciding to cover the subject. The following are a few of their comments:

"I can't and shouldn't cover every Latino event, but I do take care to make sure that I'm not shortchanging Latino events and prominent individuals."

"I brought the idea up, as I do all my stories, to my editor, who is also Latina, and she said Ok. I cover an area that is predominantly Latino, near the San Diego–Tijuana border, and so many of my stories, at least the feature-type stories, are about Latinos."

"I brought the topic up to my editor at the time. There is a fear among some Latino journalists of ghettoizing themselves if they pitch too many articles on Latino culture and life, preventing them from climbing the newsroom ranks. . . . I resist this idea because A) if we don't do it, who will? And more importantly, B) Latinos in the U.S. happen to be the most interesting national story around, if you ask me."

> "I was working the night shift and had the choice of covering two evening events. I picked Day of the Dead because it was something I was familiar with."[16]

Non-Latino journalists also initiated Day of the Dead stories, such as a reporter at the *San Diego Union Tribune*, who said, "I brought up the subject because I cover everything that happens in the city of Oceanside. Although I am not Latina, I am bilingual, did postgraduate work at the University of Mexico, and have been an officer in the San Diego chapter of the California Chicano News Media Association. My editor, also not Latino, was immediately interested."[17] A veteran Latino reporter for more than thirty-five years, working at the *Houston Chronicle*, affirmed that while he initiated writing Day of the Dead stories at his paper, he observed both Latino and non-Latino journalists bringing up stories: "I've initiated any stories I've done on Day of the Dead, but I see my colleagues (both Latinos and not) in other parts of my newspaper doing so as well, like feature writers and arts writers."[18]

Both Latino and non-Latino journalists felt that the record numbers of Latin American immigrants settling in the United States over the past two decades has made the Latino population more attractive as a market for media and other commercial enterprises. Journalists expressed the following thoughts on the relationship between the growing Latino population and increased news coverage of Day of the Dead:

> "I think the media in general is beginning to wake up to the powerful Latino market. . . . The Latino population is really growing and you will be dead in the water in those growing markets if you don't begin doing more to cover Latino issues."

> "[Increased coverage of Day of the Dead] is probably about trying to appeal to Latino readers and advertisers. . . . More and more cities throughout the country are growing in their Latino population [and this] means that media outlets need to hurry and find ways to appeal to those readers."

> "With the Latino population on the rise, more and more people are taking an interest in Day of the Dead as an alternative to the traditional American Halloween. Newspapers reflect this trend."

> "More Latinos are moving to California, graduating from college, and entering newsrooms. More are running community organizations that alert editors of their community celebrations. It's a natural demographic shift. . . . It's also a copycat phenomenon. As more papers watch other papers give it play, they fall in line."[19]

Oaxacan-style Day of the Dead altar in home of an Indigenous Mixtec family. Mexico, 2002.

Decorating graves, picnicking, and flying kites in cemetery. Day of the Dead celebration, Sacatepequez, Guatemala, 2000.

Decorating graves and leaving food offerings in cemetery. Day of the Dead celebration, Otavalo, Ecuador, 2002.

Community altar. Day of the Dead celebration, Centro Mayapán, El Paso, TX, 2003.

Altar for Cuban salsa superstar Celia Cruz. Day of the Dead celebration, California State University, San Marcos, 2004.

Altar for victims of torture, created by high school students. Day of the Dead festival, Santa Fe, NM, 2003.

Altar in memory of rappers Tupac Shakur, Biggie Smalls, and other victims of violent gun deaths. Reggae singer and peace activist Bob Marley is also honored. Oakland Museum of California, 2003.

Altar with papel picado, pan de muerto, marigolds, fruits, and sugar skulls. Day of the Dead exhibit at the New Brunswick public library, NJ, 2006.

Sugar-skull workshop. Folk art store, San Diego, CA, 2005.

"Chalk cemetery" where the public can draw memorials for deceased loved ones. Above hangs the traveling Iraq War Memorial, listing names of U.S. military members killed. Day of the Dead festival, Oceanside, CA, 2005.

Immigrant rights activists decorating graves of unidentified migrants who died attempting to cross the U.S./Mexican border. Holtville, CA, 2001.

Close-up of Holtville grave decorations for "Jane Doe": sugar skull, pan de muerto, marigolds, papel picado (on ground), salt, and copal incense (in bowls). Cross reads, "No Olvidado" (Not Forgotten). Holtville, CA, 2001.

Binational altar in memory of dead migrants (critiquing Operation Gatekeeper and NAFTA). Fence literally divides U.S. and Mexican sides of the altar, separating the Day of the Dead participants from each country. El Paso, TX, 2003.

Guatemalans in Oakland re-creating graves honoring the hundred thousand Mayas murdered in the Guatemalan government's "scorched earth" campaign of the 1980s. Mainstreets Day of the Dead festival, Fruitvale, CA, 2004.

Anti-Iraq War altar, created by North County Coalition for Peace and Justice, and Project YANO (Youth and Non-Military Opportunities). Mainstreets Day of the Dead festival, Oceanside, CA, 2004.

Memorial wall remembering Latino youth killed in Iraq and Afghanistan. Day of the Dead protest event at Tia Chucha Café, Los Angeles, CA, 2004.

Day of the Dead march to the Mexican consulate to demand action on the hundreds of unsolved rapes and murders of the Women of Juarez-female workers at multinational border factories in Juarez, Mexico. El Paso, TX, 2003.

Women of Juarez altar. Day of the Dead celebration, St. Mark's Cemetery, the Bowery, NY, 2007.

Day of the Dead window mural in response to deep state budget cuts to the California Arts Council. Adjacent window had text explaining the impact of the funding cuts. San Francisco, CA, 2003.

Elementary school students celebrate Day of the Dead with songs, art, and poetry. San Francisco, CA, 2005.

Installation honoring urban Latino youth. SomArts Day of the Dead exhibit, San Francisco, CA, 2004.

Day of the Dead poetry slam. Voz Alta art space, San Diego, CA, 2002.

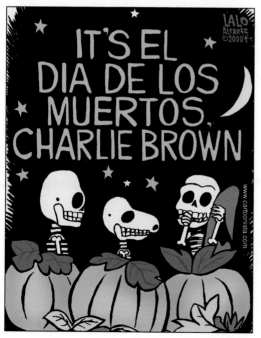

It's El Día de los Muertos, Charlie Brown, reproduced by permission from Lalo Alcaraz, copyright 2004. First published in *LA Weekly* on October 28, 2004, with a subsequent version of the cartoon syndicated in major U.S. newspapers in 2005.

Day of the Dead display of coffee, hot chocolate, cookies, and more. Major multinational coffee chain, San Diego, CA, 2004.

Day of the Dead merchandise for sale in a folk art shop, San Diego, 2002.

News Coverage as a Resource for Financial and Institutional Support

In addition to educating the public about the tradition, media coverage has provided another tangible benefit for U.S. Day of the Dead celebrations: attracting foundation funding and commercial sponsors. This has made it possible to expand activities to new sites and larger audiences. Almost all of the gallery curators and community center staff I interviewed showed me binders, or in some cases compact discs, of collected press coverage of their organization's Day of the Dead events. These displays included newspaper and magazine articles and/or transcripts of radio and TV coverage received over the years. Such media coverage is routinely used as supporting material for grant applications and press packets, indicating the importance of news coverage for the continued public visibility and financial support of Day of the Dead activities. Whereas some event organizers asserted that, regardless of funding, their constituents would continue to engage in Day of the Dead celebrations even if it meant paying expenses out of pocket, others expressed concern that without continued outside funding, the exhibits, workshops, and other activities offered free to the public could not continue. Most spoke of the financial strain that funding cuts to the California Arts Council, the National Foundation for the Arts, and other funding sources had placed on their organization's arts and cultural programming.

Recognizing the power of the media to educate the general public about Latino culture, event organizers have welcomed press coverage of the celebration, both as a way to promote the tradition and to prevent misunderstandings of it. Given the general unfamiliarity of mainstream U.S. audiences in the 1970s with non-Western cultural practices and belief systems, a celebration of "the dead," replete with "offerings," smoldering incense, and other unusual rites, was initially misinterpreted by some as the handiwork of Satan worshippers. For example, in reaction to the 1976 Day of the Dead exhibit at La Galería de la Raza in San Francisco, the word "necrophiliacs" was found scrawled on the front windows of the gallery.[20] People who did not understand the tradition accused the Galería staff of being members of a death cult. René Yañez, who organized the first Day of the Dead exhibit at La Galería, notes, "The Irish captain of the Mission Police Station refused to give me a permit to hold the Day of the Dead procession. He called me a 'devil' . . . [and] said, 'Over my dead body!' People thought we were a death cult. They made references to Charles Manson."[21]

Along with non-Latinos disturbed by what they perceived to be sacrilegious communing with the dead, were Latinos who were unfamiliar or uncomfortable with the Indigenous aspects of the holiday. When she first began teaching schoolchildren about Day of the Dead, Yolanda Garfias Woo was criticized by both Anglo coworkers and a Mexican American school superintendent:

> I taught in an area that was predominantly Black. It was a very difficult area. There were a lot of deaths, a lot of murders, suicides, violence. And because I realized that the students had no outlet, I began doing Muertos in the classroom and found that it was extremely successful in opening things up and being able to talk about death. I was criticized by the staff for teaching "witchcraft," even though the teacher next door to me one year during Halloween was standing in her doorway, wearing a long black gown with a pointed witch's hat, and she said to me, "You know you can't do that in your classroom because it's witchcraft."

Later, when Garfias Woo conducted a teacher's workshop about Day of the Dead, she learned from the teachers that the school superintendent, who was Mexican American, had adamantly resisted the teachers' request for the workshop: "He had told the teachers that it was barbaric and that only the poorest areas of Mexico, only the uneducated people did it, and that it wasn't part of mainstream Mexican culture and had no place in the school curriculum. The teachers fought and fought to get him to approve the workshop."[22]

Whereas some onlookers criticized the festivities as being too "pagan" or too "barbaric," others accused organizers of celebrating a "Catholic" tradition in publicly funded schools. Patricia Rodriguez, gallery curator of the MCCLA in San Francisco, recounts: "I was teaching at the University of New Mexico—doing an altar and talking about the tradition—and the local newspaper wrote me up as being pagan. Others said it was too Catholic, too religious, and that religion didn't belong in the university."[23] Given such misunderstandings and resistance, even among sectors of the Mexican American community, Chicano artists had to work hard to clarify that the celebration bore no relation to zombies, witchcraft, or the devil, and that their renditions of Day of the Dead were cultural, not religious. Communicating the correct meaning of Day of the Dead was important not only in terms of achieving a positive representation of cultural identity, but also in terms of acquiring institutional support. Event organizers regularly clarified the meaning of the celebration when meeting with school groups and other audiences, and published explanations of the tradition in exhibit brochures and museum catalogs. News media helped elucidate the ritual's intention for wide audiences.

Explaining the meaning of the holiday—something that would be unnecessary in Latin America—has been a consistent theme in U.S. media coverage. From the 1980s to the present, articles, television news, and radio segments have observed that the custom is a joyous rather than morbid time, which celebrates life and loved ones, rather than death. Cognizant of the gruesome images that the words "Day of the Dead" might conjure in the minds of people unfamiliar with the tradition, journalists often acknowledge the "strangeness" of the name and preemptively dismiss morbid associations, as in the following front-page examples:

> "Despite its somber-sounding name, el Día de los Muertos, the Day of the Dead, is a day of music, food, and decoration in the Latino community."

> "Although it sounds macabre, celebrating the Day of the Dead is actually about life, affirming the belief that death is the final arc of life's circle, bringing it to its inevitable close. And it is about love, about honoring the people you once knew so intimately that death could not fully take them from you."

> "This is not a grim, morbid affair. With touches of humor and a festive air, it is a form of honoring the dead and acknowledging death as a part of life."

> "Día de los Muertos is not a worship of death, but a recognition that life and death are one in the same, part of the same cycle."[24]

News coverage has helped contextualize U.S. festivities as nondenominational celebrations with roots in the spiritual beliefs of Indigenous Latin American cultures.[25] As more people gain knowledge of the tradition, misunderstandings are less common, although they still exist.

PUBLICITY AND VALIDATION FOR LATINO COMMUNITIES

For politically and economically marginalized populations who do not generally occupy powerful positions as newsmakers, mainstream media coverage provides public validation of their existence to the larger world (Cook and Hartnett 2001; Gitlin 1980; Ryan 1991). For decades, the association of Latinos with crime, drugs, and poverty in the media rendered Latino neighborhoods devoid of the cultural cachet necessary for inclusion in the arts and culture sections of citywide newspapers. However, as Day of the Dead exhibits brought the barrio to the academy, representing the first time, in many cases, that works of Chicano artists were exhibited in prestigious museums, they also brought the academy to the barrio.[26] Exhibits at neighborhood-based Latino art galleries drew art lovers to communities that had long been ignored by the cultural cognoscenti. Coverage of Day of the Dead exhibits in major newspapers encouraged middle-class suburbanites and wealthy city dwellers to venture into Latino neighborhoods for gallery exhibits, Muertos art, or fresh pan de muerto. Today, busloads of schoolchildren and tourists visit

San Francisco's Mission District, East Los Angeles, San Diego's Sherman Heights, and Latino communities elsewhere during Day of the Dead season.

Noting the increased positive visibility that media coverage of the Sherman Heights Day of the Dead exhibit (promoted in the *San Diego Reader*, the *Union Tribune*, *La Prensa San Diego*, and *Fahrenheit Magazine*) brought to this predominantly Latino neighborhood, resident Louise Torio explains, "People from all over the place come to this inner city neighborhood—people who don't know about the neighborhood, or from what they've heard, they think of it as a *bad* neighborhood. Or they haven't been here for thirty years. So with this event, the impression of the neighborhood changes."[27]

Terry Alderete, chief coordinator of the annual Fruitvale Day of the Dead festival in Oakland, California, similarly notes that media coverage of the event (in the *Oakland Tribune*, the *San Francisco Chronicle*, the *Bay Guardian*, television networks, Telemundo and Univisión, AAA's travel magazine, Southwest Airline's in-flight magazine, English-language jazz station KBLX, Spanish radio stations, online news sources, and small local papers) has improved the public's perception of Oakland. Initiated in 1996, Fruitvale's Day of the Dead Festival is the "star" in a lineup of annual cultural events sponsored by the Mainstreets economic development initiative, and now attracts about a hundred thousand visitors annually from throughout the San Francisco Bay Area.[28] It is the largest one-day Día de los Muertos festival in the United States and has not only put Fruitvale on the map of the Bay Area arts scene, but has brought the neighborhood national acclaim, with a listing in the U.S. Library of Congress as a "Local Legacy" for the state of California.[29] Alderete explains, "In the late 1980s, Fruitvale was all boarded up, urban blight, crime. People wouldn't drive here for fear they might get shot at. From the 1970s and into the 1980s, it was like a war zone. . . . [Now] we're getting a lot of publicity and this brings a lot of pride. Our Day of the Dead festival is even listed on the Smithsonian Institution's Web site."[30]

THIS CHAPTER HAS EXAMINED THE ROLE that mainstream news media have played in popularizing what was once a little known tradition, drawing larger audiences and increased public funding. Ritual communication occurs not only when people attend Day of the Dead events in person, but also when they routinely see this tradition positively represented in the major media, strengthening the sense of imagined community felt by Mexican Americans and other Latinos, and giving the general public an opportunity to learn more about Latinos. In so doing, the media have helped turn the ritual into an annual autumn activity for Americans of diverse racial and ethnic backgrounds. But beyond the media attention, what attracts people, particularly non-Latinos, to these celebrations year after year? We will explore this question in the next chapter.

CHAPTER 7

The Expanding Hybridity
of an Already Hybrid Tradition

Day of the Dead is a way of coping with death in a country
where nobody wants to talk about it. . . . For people like me,
who didn't know what to do with death, it's really helpful.
Death hurts and sucks and it's hard. This gave me a place to
put my energy and make something positive and share with
other people.

—An Anglo artist who lost a baby to Sudden Infant
Death Syndrome (SIDS) and now makes an annual
Day of the Dead altar for her deceased child[1]

DAY OF THE DEAD was adopted by Chicano artists as an
expression of pride and politics. Yet, studies of Latinidad should not be
confined to analyses of how Latinos create and fortify cultural ties in response
to the dominant U.S. society. They should also examine how phenomena
considered Latino enter different cultural spaces and change the dominant
culture (Valdivia 2003, 415). The celebration of Day of the Dead in the United
States is not limited to Latinos, but is also enthusiastically engaged in by non-
Latinos, who can make up as many as half (or more) of the participants at
exhibits, processions, and other events. This chapter will discuss the appeal of
this observance for the general population, illustrating how attitudes and practices prevalent in Latin America are influencing non-Latinos who come into
contact with them. It will also present views of some of the Chicano artists
who initiated Day of the Dead events in the United States, regarding the
influx of diverse peoples and practices on the celebration. The views expressed
here reveal valuable lessons about cultural transmission, as well as about the
moral and practical uses of the concept of authenticity.

Over the past eight years, I have seen people of Asian (Chinese, Japanese,
Korean, Vietnamese, Filipino), Native American, African American, Italian,
Jewish, Polish, Irish, Middle Eastern, and other ethnic and racial backgrounds
making Day of the Dead ofrendas at public exhibitions, walking in Day of the

Dead processions, or attending such events as spectators. The mainstreaming of this celebration is an example of the "Latinization" of U.S. culture that has occurred over the past thirty years, as a result of the biggest migration flow in the history of the continent (Suarez-Orozco 2001, 40). As the largest minority population in the United States, Latinos are influencing mainstream America's vocabulary, culinary tastes, music, dance styles, and more. The mass media have played important educational and promotional roles by covering Day of the Dead as a routine autumn activity, but media coverage alone does not explain the appeal of the celebration for so many non-Latinos. A brief historical review of Anglo American attitudes toward death is helpful in understanding some of the reasons.

The American Way of Death

In mainstream U.S. society, death is a topic to be avoided—a kind of obscenity not to be uttered in public. We say someone "passed on" or "slipped away." We put sick pets "to sleep." We outlaw the practice of euthanasia, so that voluntarily choosing to die or assisting someone else in dying become crimes worthy of imprisonment. In contrast to most countries in the world, the relative affluence and technological advancements of the United States have created a sense of invulnerability among the general population, where it is common for individuals to live for twenty or more years without experiencing the death of a family member. This sense of invulnerability fosters a reluctance to confront mortality, so that even when terminal illness strikes, fallacies of likely recovery are often maintained by the sick and their families.

Anthropologists Peter Metcalf and Richard Huntington contend that in societies with harsh living conditions and low social mobility, people hold more accepting attitudes toward death. Seeing it as a peaceful, even joyous release from the hardships of life, they play active roles in preparing bodies for burial, planning funerals, or engaging in mourning and remembrance rituals. However, in the United States, where people are often socially and geographically disconnected from their families, and there is a strong cultural emphasis on individualism, upward mobility, and "winning," people have less accepting attitudes about dying, and tend to play only passive roles in death rituals (1991).

A reluctance to accept death as a natural part of the life cycle seems normal within a consumer culture that emphasizes the new and improved version of *everything*. From ubiquitous antiaging products to constant offers to upgrade technologies rendered obsolete within months, the concepts of physical degeneration and fatality are contrary to dominant U.S. ideologies of competition and productivity. Some critical cultural scholars have argued that the prosperity of modern U.S. consumer society has depended on the continuous promotion of youthful values. In an economic system contingent on ever-expanding production, they note, corporate marketers and media producers enhance selling power by promoting "youth values" such as impulsiveness, immediate gratification, and contempt for authority over "adult values" such as respect for tradition or a willingness to save and sacrifice (Leach 1993; Frank 1997). Contemporary U.S. society is obsessed with looking and acting young, and people are socialized to believe that with the right diet, exercise, and cosmetic surgery, they can be youthful, productive, and *alive* forever. With little social space for thoughts about aging, illness, and the impermanence of life, many U.S. Americans lack positive models for contemplating death or relating to the deceased. Young people in particular often form their earliest notions of death from the ghoulish images of Hollywood slasher films and commercial haunted houses.

With the rise of the funeral industry in the twentieth century, most U.S. Americans became physically separated from their dead. The deceased were no longer cleaned and dressed by family members. Wakes were no longer held at home. Professional morticians transported corpses to funeral parlors for institutionalized viewing and, for the majority of people, active community rituals of leave-taking, mourning, and remembering were lost. Today, most burials are not conducted in front of the public, who are generally led out of the cemetery by funeral professionals before the coffin is lowered into the ground. An underlying reason for this practice is economic expediency, because more funerals can be processed per day when families vacate the cemetery parking lots as quickly as possible. For all of these reasons, Americans today find themselves with fewer opportunities than ever to adequately process the loss of loved ones.

This was not always the case. Until the early twentieth century, death was widely contemplated in the United States and occupied an important place in mass culture, where mourners readily found sources of community support. In the mid-nineteenth century, U.S. religious movements "sought to promote a homely, even domestic view of the world to come" (Metcalf and Huntington 1991, 208). Cemeteries were considered "schools of moral philosophy and catalysts of civic virtue" where the living regularly engaged in meditative promenades to contemplate the shortness of life and learn from the exemplary lives of the interred. Walking, reading, and picnicking in cemeteries were actively promoted by moral leaders as "healthful, agreeable" activities that would inspire individuals to make the most of their lives. So widespread was the desire to stimulate retrospection regarding life and death, that U.S. magazines, newspapers, and advice books of the 1800s encouraged families to take Sunday walks in cemeteries to cultivate "a cheerful association with death" (Meyer 1989, 295).

Visiting the United States in 1847, English writer Harriet Martineau observed that thoughts of death "filled a large space in peoples' minds" (Meyer 1989, 298). As recently as the early twentieth century, the U.S. public still viewed death as an expected part of life. People born in the early 1900s recall that Catholic school students were taught to begin each day by "praying for a happy death."[2] Parents routinely purchased life insurance policies for infants, cognizant of the fact that many children, stricken by commonplace illnesses, would not reach adulthood. As the century progressed, however, life-extending technologies and the move toward scientific rationalization made reflections on death increasingly rare and seemingly morbid.

North America's commercialized version of All Souls' Day—Halloween— is bereft of any serious commemoration of the departed, and Memorial Day, the official U.S. holiday for visiting cemeteries, began as a day to honor Civil War dead and continues to focus primarily on honoring the military dead. As with Flag Day and Independence Day, the U.S. flag is a major symbol of Memorial Day, along with military parades and ceremonies that focus more on patriotism than on celebrating the individual lives of the deceased. The somber tone of contemporary Memorial Day observances stands in stark contrast to the vivid ambiance of Day of the Dead, where altars brim with flowers, fruits, and other colorful symbols of life.

Yet, growing numbers of Americans are feeling dissatisfied with the main-stream culture's method of handling death. Increasingly, individuals are contemplating and preparing for death, as evidenced by the appearance of Death with Dignity legislation in several states, an increase in the popularity of living wills, and a vast rise in the number of hospice care programs.[3] As an indicator of changing public attitudes, only nineteen books were published in the United States on the subject of death during the decade of the 1950s, while more than twenty-six thousand were published on the subject from 1990 to 2000 (McIlwain 2005, 19). Since the 1990s, there has also been a sharp rise in the number of TV programs and Hollywood films revolving around themes of death, the paranormal, and related metaphysical concepts (Clark 2003; McIlwain 2005).

At the same time, there has been growing interest in alternative forms of spirituality. With the Civil Rights Movement, antiwar protests, and cultural revolutions of the 1960s and 1970s, more Americans than ever found them-selves questioning authority, including establishment political and business models and dominant Judeo-Christian belief systems. Those who felt disen-chanted with the accelerated individualism and materialism of the latter twentieth century sought more holistic lifestyles, through practices such as yoga, meditation, mysticism, African and Afro Caribbean religions, Native American spiritualities, and earth-based goddess religions. As one Anglo respondent remarks, "My traditional Catholic upbringing has left me extremely unfulfilled when it comes to dealing with death. In the past few years, I've found myself actively pursuing other culture's rituals and practices around death in an effort to unravel my own feelings."[4] The historical role of traditional Western religions in promoting and profiting from patriarchy, capitalism, and imperialism is troubling to many who have been raised in these faiths. From the 1980s onward, writings by the Dalai Lama, Deepak Chopra, Carlos Casteñeda, Starhawk, and other practitioners of alternative spiritualities have become national bestsellers, inspiring a decentralized nature/spiritual movement known as New Age. These alternative spiritualities have in common the conceptual integration of mind, body, and spirit, along with an emphasis on the interconnectedness between the living and the spirit worlds.

U.S. Day of the Dead celebrations emerged amid this new openness to non-Western spiritualities, and have been embraced by many people who are interested in alternative worldviews. The basic object of the celebration—collectively remembering the dead—is universal enough to appeal to individuals from diverse religious backgrounds as well as to those who identify as atheists. Key concepts of Day of the Dead, such as respect for ancestors, an integrated cycle of life and death, and ongoing communication between the living and the dead, make the holiday readily understood by people raised in non-Western belief systems, where these themes are common. As a Japanese American explains, "My Mom is Buddhist, so I grew up going to Obone. It's pretty much exactly the same celebration—a night where the spirits come to earth to visit, play, eat, and drink. . . . Different cultures, no matter what continent they're on, can relate to the fact that there are different parts of death. The body. The mind. The spirit."[5]

Because of the universality of death, Day of the Dead has a much wider cross-cultural appeal than other ethnic celebrations such as Cinco de Mayo, Kwanzaa, or Chinese New Year, which revolve around historically and culturally specific events. Tere Romo describes the variety of Day of the Dead participants: "It's one of the few exhibits that you can walk into a gallery and see a crowd that is totally diverse . . . African Americans, Asians, Latinos, Whites, all ages, moms with their kids, schoolchildren, old people and every age in between. It has an attraction across generations and ethnic groups."[6] As a new U.S. holiday, Day of the Dead offers Americans an opportunity not only to process the loss of loved ones, but also to respond to the loss of community that has become the hallmark of contemporary U.S. society.

FILLING AN EMOTIONAL VOID

A theme that consistently arose among artists and intellectuals I interviewed is the opportunity that Day of the Dead provides to engage in spirituality outside of organized religion. "There's been a large-scale reaction against organized religion for many in this country," says an Anglo artist who operates a collective art space in the Bay Area. He notes, "Without organized religion, where is the spirit? Day of the Dead gives people something tangible that they can connect to. Everyone has people close to them who pass away.

To have a time to remember them is very healthy and it's a lot easier to access those feelings when a lot of people are visualizing a connection with the spirit world simultaneously."[7]

Today, altar-making activities that thirty years ago were considered superstitious have become widespread, as average U.S. Americans remember the dead by creating public shrines. Examples of mainstream altar-making practices include the unanticipated interaction of visitors with the Vietnam War Memorial in Washington, DC, where individuals regularly place flowers, candles, uniforms, hats, boots, and photos by the wall; the creation of a spontaneous shrine composed of thousands of mementos (stuffed animals, baby shoes, hair ribbons, poems, etc.) tied to the wire fence surrounding the site of the 1995 Oklahoma City bombing; and the hundreds of makeshift public altars (with photos, flowers, letters, candles) that appeared along sidewalks, parks, schools, office buildings, subways, and fire stations throughout New York City in memory of those killed in the September 11, 2001, World Trade Center explosions.[8] Such public acts are efforts not only to honor the dead but to collectively grieve and heal.

The new popularity of public shrine making in the United States (particularly in cases of car accidents, disappeared children, and other tragedies) represents a noticeable shift in U.S. cultural practice from the stoic, private, Protestant-oriented forms of remembrance considered appropriate by mainstream United States during most of the twentieth century. This shift coincides with increased levels of immigration to the United States by Latin Americans and other populations with strong altar-making traditions, such as Filipinos, Cambodians, Vietnamese, East Indians, and Africans. The Latin American custom of erecting roadside shrines to mark the site of a car-related death (previously seen only in the Mexican Southwest of the United States) is now a phenomenon visible in every state in the union and carried out by Latinos and non-Latinos alike (Collins and Rhine 2003, 222). However, it was Chicano artists in particular who consciously transformed familial traditions of altar making into a legitimate public art form, inspiring U.S. Americans of diverse racial backgrounds to express themselves through the altar format.[9]

In a society famed for its rugged individualism, contemporary U.S. Americans find themselves longing for emotionally satisfying community-building experiences to offset feelings of isolation. Day of the Dead celebrations help fulfill this longing by providing a public medium through which to express repressed emotions regarding death. Feelings of gratitude for the opportunity to process feelings about deceased loved ones were frequently expressed by attendees of the annual Day of the Dead procession in San Francisco's Mission District. When asked about the celebration's appeal, a volunteer involved in organizing the procession replied, "During Day of the Dead, there's no negative energy, but an incredible solidarity. A completeness of people coming together to celebrate their loved ones and their own emotions, which rarely happens here. It's a time to acknowledge that we're all human and are dealing with some pretty heavy emotions." She feels that the Day of the Dead procession in the Mission serves as a communal healing process in which the presence of so many people simultaneously remembering deceased loved ones is a healthy form of bereavement: "What makes Day of the Dead unusual is that you're literally walking in the street with hundreds of people, thousands of people who you don't know, but there's a feeling of community. . . . You see strangers hugging each other . . . crying together. It meets a human need for affiliation, on a really elemental level."[10]

In Sacramento, California, non-Latino participation in Day of the Dead events became so prevalent that a roundtable discussion was convened at Sacramento State University to discuss the reasons why. One participant in the discussion explains, "There is no venue in American tradition which lets us honor and celebrate our dead. Once people have died, their memory becomes a private matter for the family. . . . There is no public remembrance past the funeral. It's as if they were swept under the carpet and we move on to the next thing. With Día de los Muertos, the entire community is involved [in a] public acknowledgment of the dead."[11]

The popularity of Day of the Dead among non-Latinos was mentioned by staff from a half-dozen museum shops and folk art stores I visited, where Day of the Dead merchandise is sold. Shopkeepers informed me that Day of the Dead season is their most profitable time of year, and that at least half (or more than half) of the clientele buying Day of the Dead items are non-Latinos. The owner of Back from Tomboctou, a San Diego folk art shop that distributes Day of the Dead merchandise wholesale to retailers across the United States, notes that "Day of the Dead is our busiest time of the year. . . . Probably 65 percent of our clients are non-Latinos."[12] Similarly, the owner of Casa Bonampak, a fair trade craft store in San Francisco, states, "October is our big season. You would be *amazed* at how many sugar skulls we sell here. I sell over a thousand. For a small store, that's *a lot*. I think that everyone I know, at this point, is making altars at home now. It's sort of like decorating the Christmas tree—an annual ritual. Schools have altars. Museums have altars. Companies have altars. I get invited to all kinds of city events. Supervisor Ammiano lost his partner to AIDS a while back, so he does an altar every year in his office in City Hall. I would say my clients are about 50 percent Latino and [50 percent] non-Latino."[13]

The popularity of Day of the Dead among non-Latinos is not limited to California or the Southwest. At celebrations I attended in November 2006 in New York City at the Metropolitan Museum of Art, the National Museum of the American Indian, and El Museo del Barrio, as well as events I attended in the Boston area at Harvard University's Peabody Museum and the Forest Hills

Cemetery, roughly half of the attendees at each venue appeared to be non-Latinos. Non-Latinos are not only attending Day of the Dead celebrations sponsored by the Latino community, but are also organizing such rituals in predominantly Anglo environments. For example, since 1999, the Solana Beach, California, congregation of the Unitarian Universalist Fellowship has held an annual Day of the Dead community-altar ceremony. Each year, worshipers and the general public are invited (through word of mouth, church bulletins, and newspapers listings) to bring photos, stories, and favorite mementos of departed loved ones to share at a communal altar. When I attended this event in November 2001, the fellowship consisted of approximately 150 White, upper middle-class people (predominantly young families and senior citizens). One by one, individuals placed candles, photos, books, jewelry, or alcoholic beverages on the Latin American–style ofrenda (adorned with fruits, tamales, Mexican chocolate, marigolds, pan de muerto, papel picado, Guatemalan tapestries, and El Salvadoran art), then took the microphone to speak about someone they had lost. The atmosphere was both happy and emotional, as people related jokes and stories about loved ones. Numerous participants mentioned that it was the first time they had ever spoken publicly about the deceased since his or her death, which in many cases had occurred years earlier. As a non-Latino celebrating a Latino tradition in a non-Latino space, the organizer of the event states, "I try to stay true to the original intent, giving a history of it. . . . My big fear was that nobody would participate. But every year, I have more people participate than I expect. . . . I've had people tell me they were very moved. They've said things like, 'I wasn't going to get up and say anything, but the level of sharing was just so strong that I decided to do it.'"[14]

All of the non-Latino Day of the Dead participants interviewed for this book discussed what they felt was a dearth of opportunity for honoring the dead in mainstream U.S. society. A Korean American from Los Angeles says, "Americans tend to be morbid and depressed about death, while the Latino culture honors their ancestors and celebrates their life through their death."[15] An Irish American from Boston who had recently lost her father believes that "it's a much healthier version of dealing with death and dying. Making the altar is very healing. It makes a connection with the people who have gone before us and affirms what they did in life."[16] Other respondents, such as a native of Kentucky who participated for four consecutive years in San Francisco's Day of the Dead procession, state that participating in Day of the Dead helped them mourn the loss of family members: "I loved the somber yet celebratory tone of the marchers. I took the time to reflect on the loss of a favorite aunt who died unexpectedly that year. I hadn't been able to go to her funeral. My experience that night gave me some much needed closure on her death. It was wonderful to reminisce about her in such a supportive atmosphere."[17]

The cathartic aspect of Day of the Dead rituals is similarly noted by a U.S.-born respondent of Portuguese-Hawaiian heritage, who participated in a Day of the Dead procession in Chicago:"One thing I thought was neat at a procession at the local cemetery was almost a roll call, where people could call out the name of a dead family member or friend and the entire group would answer 'Presente,' acknowledging their presence among us. It was amazingly soothing for me, as I had just lost my mom and found that many people were just too uncomfortable with death to even talk about it."[18]

All of the respondents described a dichotomy between U.S. American ways of relating to death, which they considered "unfulfilling" or "depressing," and the personalized, communal rituals of remembrance common in Latin America, which they called "celebratory," "supportive," and "healing." An Italian American native of Jersey City explains the dissatisfaction she felt with the U.S. style of privatized mourning:"I've got people who have passed away in my life that mean so much to me, and in thinking about their memory or seeing their picture, it seems so shallow to remember somebody in such a quiet way when they were so important in your life. . . . In the modern world, we have gotten away from our ability to form strong relationships and bonds lasting beyond our physical life. Day of the Dead is a reminder of that. The bonds don't end when our time above ground ends."[19]

The theme of healing was also discussed by Barbara Henry, chief curator of education at the Oakland Museum of California, where Day of the Dead exhibits have been held annually since 1994. Some twenty thousand people attend the six-week exhibit annually, making it the best-attended show in the museum's annual calendar.[20] The event receives enthusiastic feedback in the form of letters, e-mails, and guestbook comments from visitors, and Henry believes that an important part of the exposition's popularity is the opportunity it provides for people to publicly reflect upon and talk about death:

A number of people have said that they don't have anything from their culture that helps them deal with death. One woman sent me a letter about three months after the exhibit closed, telling me how it helped her deal with the death of her mother. We've had a number of grief counselors and people from the health profession who have come here and used this exhibit with their clients to help them process death. There was one group of terminally ill patients. We've gotten written comments from many people telling us about how coming to this exhibit has become an annual tradition for their family.[21]

Another employee at the Oakland Museum also comments that the exhibit is a "healing tool" for visitors: "We've received lots of letters from people thanking us and saying that it's helped them reflect, or telling us how they've adopted the tradition. Not just Latino people. One of the great things we have here is a wall of reflection, where you can write messages to people who have passed on. I've seen families crying, hugging each other. So there's something we can offer people who are in pain, to help them heal."[22]

In Oceanside, California, now some thirty thousand people attend the city's annual Day of the Dead Festival, begun in 2001.[23] David Avalos, a visual arts professor at the California State University at San Marcos, who created an altar for his father at the 2002 festival, describes the variety of participants at the celebration: "It was a mixed crowd. There were Oaxacan Indians mixed with the kind of folks you'd expect to see at the Del Mar Fair."[24] He notes that Day of the Dead provides spiritually nourishing opportunities to learn about and publicly share family histories: "For students who aren't of Mexican ancestry, and even for those who are of Mexican ancestry and don't practice the tradition, it gives them an opportunity to connect with their own personal history, and that's a spiritual resource that we're often denied. When you find out more about dead relatives, you find out more about yourself."[25]

NEW PARTICIPANTS, NEW DIRECTIONS, AND DEBATES AROUND AUTHENTICITY

How do Chicanos and other Latinos feel about the mainstreaming of Day of the Dead, particularly about the participation of so many non-Latinos in the events? Nearly everyone I interviewed expressed pride that the celebration is now observed in many places across the country. However, several Chicana artists expressed mixed feelings about the impact of non-Latinos on the celebration, concerned that they were misinterpreting and altering the rituals in ways that strayed too far from the original tradition. The word "tradition" is regularly used in discussions of Day of the Dead, even though there is not one but many traditions emanating from diverse geographical regions and Latino populations. In the U.S. context, what does "tradition" mean for a celebration that is relatively recent? Does it mean recreating, as closely as possible, the ofrendas made by rural Mexican families? Does it mean consciously designing artistic and radical renditions of ofrendas for the purpose of making critical commentary? Does it mean embodying the frolicking humor of Day of the Dead festivities in urban Mexico? Does it mean keeping the celebration within the Latino community?

The annual Day of the Dead procession in San Francisco's Mission District is the site of major debates around these questions. The first one, organized by René Yañez in 1981, consisted of a few dozen local residents walking around the block holding candles and photos of deceased loved ones; however, "by the third year, it became massive, with thousands of people."[26] The procession now attracts some twenty thousand participants annually, of whom at least half appear to be non-Latinos.[27] In addition to local residents and schoolchildren, it draws stilt walkers, jugglers, steel drummers, and people carrying New Age symbols or political banners. Feeling that the procession had gotten out of hand, staff at La Galería stopped organizing the event after Yañez took a job elsewhere. It was then organized for a few years by the Mission Cultural Center, whose staff also decided it was too large to handle and eventually discontinued sponsorship. Despite the fact that the procession lacked a sponsoring organization, thousands of people spontaneously showed up the following year, illustrating that the event had become a beloved San Francisco ritual, existing independently of the Chicano artists who first organized it.[28]

Expressing the resentment some Latinos feel toward the large non-Latino presence in the procession, a fifty-three-year-old native of Ecuador who grew up in the Mission District told me that she no longer attends because she feels the procession is "too gringo." A forty-two-year-old Salvadoran American who has lived in San Francisco since she was seventeen was also turned off by the procession's metamorphosis: "I stopped going for a number of years. But then we started again because my daughter's school participates. The kids dress up like skeletons and make a giant skeleton puppet and her friends and teachers are there, so we go." About half of the San Francisco Latinos I interviewed share the feelings of the following Chicana artist: "When René started the processions at Galería de la Raza, they were real. It was somber, sad, and beautiful, like the processions that happen in Mexico. . . . But in San Francisco, everyone who wasn't part of the tradition jumped in with their drums, jumped in with their caricatures, cartoons, skates, and puppets that have no meaning to the procession. So it turned into a kind of carnival. It has no meaning. Not in a real sense. . . . It's just cool and popular to be there."[29] Another Chicana artist explains, "People come [to the procession] from all over the Bay Area, which is a good thing, but . . . perhaps unintentionally when people like something, they begin to change the very essence of what it is. Something becomes very popular and very hip, but there is a way we can appreciate the essence without changing it."[30]

Commenting on the participation of non-Latino artists in Day of the Dead altar exhibitions, a Chicana artist in her midsixties states, "The only thing that worries me is when I think that the person doing the installation actually misunderstands what [El Día de los] Muertos is. It concerns me only because I don't want the tradition to get lost. It was so hard to find it, to get it in the first place."[31] The previous comments come from people who remember a time before Day of the Dead was popular in the United States, a time when Latinos were automatically treated as second-class citizens by the dominant society. These words reflect their personal knowledge of how difficult it was to initiate the celebration, given the racism and rejection they encountered from the larger society and, sometimes, from within their own community. As cultural midwives of a U.S. ritual practice that was intended to honor Mexican culture, these artists feel a strong sense of ownership regarding appropriate and inappropriate observations of the tradition.

However, there are divergent views within the Chicano community about "appropriate" and "inappropriate" observances of the holiday. These include debates not only about the effect of non-Latinos on Day of the Dead, but also about the repercussions of artistic expressions by Latinos who have taken the rituals in unconventional directions. Some feel that U.S. celebrations should mirror the aesthetics of rituals in Indigenous Mexican villages, while others feel they should reflect the cultural fusion of peoples and experiences found in the United States. Yañez, for example, has welcomed nontraditional interpretations of Day of the Dead from the celebration's onset, curating unique and provocative exhibitions, such as his famous "Rooms for the Dead" at the Mission Cultural Center and Yerba Buena Cultural Center and "City of Miracles" at the SomArts Cultural Center. With "Rooms for the Dead" (1990–1993), Yañez transformed the concept of altars into themed rooms for the dead, and invited Latinos, Anglos, Blacks, Asians, and others to create room installations. In "City of Miracles" (2001) he pushed the room concept a step further, developing the idea of a dreamlike labyrinth of rooms and passages, complex theatrical lighting grids, and brilliant sheaths of cloth wafting in a gentle breeze. Yañez has consistently recruited nonartists as well as artists to create altar installations, an innovative approach not taken by most curators: "I'll ask housewives, and go to hospitals and recruit nurses and different people to make altars, who wouldn't normally participate."

Receiving both admiration and criticism for his work as an artist and curator, he notes, "Some people think it's too far out. . . . They want to see paper cuts and traditional altars." When he began inviting people from different cultures to participate in Day of the Dead exhibits, Yañez received negative reactions from some of his Chicano peers:

> I got a deluge of objections from people in the community who wanted to keep it Latino. First it was Chicano and Mexican only, and I started opening it up to other Latinos and there was an objection to that. Then the objection went. Then I opened it up to other people and there were more objections and debates. I started feeling pressure from people, mostly academics, who were saying, "You should keep it strictly Latino, Chicano, Mexican American." I wasn't comfortable with that, because part of the process and evolution that happened was that children from all over the city would come see the Day of the Dead in their schools and with their families. And when those kids were growing up and coming to me and saying, "I want to participate," I didn't feel comfortable telling them, "No you can't participate. You're Black."[32]

Like any other community, the Latino community is heterogeneous.

People have diverse views about Day of the Dead and a variety of spiritual, social, educational, and political reasons for participating. And like any other cultural form dislocated from its original context, this celebration takes on vastly different meanings in its new context, reflecting the intersections and interactions of the host community with the mainstream culture. Some Latinos object to the introduction of new elements in Day of the Dead celebrations, believing that authentic traditions can be identified and should be preserved. This group equates cultural change with assimilation and cultural extinction. Others feel that Day of the Dead has survived for centuries precisely because it has adapted to changing cultural environments. They argue that incorporating new elements increases the celebration's contemporary relevance and is, in fact, crucial for its continued survival.

Paradoxically, many Chicano intellectuals and artists who adopted the celebration as adults are more stringent about maintaining "pure" traditions than people who grew up with the custom in Mexico or elsewhere. For example, although Halloween symbols such as plastic jack-o'-lanterns and orange and black paper decorations are periodically seen on ofrendas made by Indigenous families in Mexico, as well as on those made by working-class Mexican immigrants in the United States, most Chicano artists I interviewed expressed alarm at such cultural mixtures.[33] They considered the presence of these elements on ofrendas as cultural imperialism, while Indigenous families I spoke with considered plastic pumpkins and other Halloween toys as pretty additions to their ofrendas. A Chicana artist who visited southern Mexican schools to view Day of the Dead altars expresses the following with dismay: "I got to one classroom and I said to the young man, 'There's something wrong with this altar, do you know what it is?' And he said, 'No, I can't see what you mean.' And I said, 'You've picked up the Halloween colors. Why is your altar done in orange and black?' He said, 'Oh, Maestra, because it's very popular here.' I said, 'Honey, you've got the wrong colors! Those are Halloween colors. You shouldn't be including them in your altar.'"[34]

There are also Chicanos who do not want to be associated with Day of the Dead at *all*, and resent what they feel are rigid and exoticized discourses about racial difference. They wince at the automatic associations of Mexicans with calaveras and ofrendas, and eschew commonplace assertions that Mexicans are intrinsically more connected with the spirit world than other populations. When I contacted one prominent Chicana artist to ask for an interview, she declined, saying, "I don't *do* Day of the Dead."[35] A Mexican-born artist who has had a successful career in the United States for more than fifteen years stated emphatically, "I *hate* Day of the Dead! I only do Halloween. With Halloween, you have much more freedom to do whatever you want."[36] This artist held Halloween art exhibits in his gallery as a way to reject common assumptions (on the part of the art world and the general public) that artists of Mexican heritage must make Day of the Dead altars each fall. Other Latino artists noted that although Day of the Dead season brought them invitations to create installations for galleries and museums, providing them with income and opportunities to have their work seen by large publics, it also pigeonholed them in certain ways.

Affirming that tensions over "tradition" are not limited to Latino versus non-Latino dichotomies, David Avalos notes, "Even young people of Mexican ancestry here in the United States bristle at the constraints they feel are imposed on them by an older generation. They want to make art that reflects and informs their Chicano identity in ways that are different than some recipe handed down from 1970."[37] New generations of Latino artists, who have grown up seeing Day of the Dead celebrated in U.S. schools and communities, approach the event from a different perspective than "old school" Chicano activists. While maintaining respect for the groundbreaking work of earlier generations of Chicanos, many of the younger generation seem less concerned with the gatekeeping of authenticity. In fact, a group of young Latino artists enthusiastically praised the very procession scorned by older Chicanos, expressing excitement rather than concern at its nontraditional aspects. In contrast to the middle-aged Chicana who said, "Everyone who wasn't part of the tradition jumped in with their drums, jumped in with their caricatures, cartoons, skates, and puppets that have no meaning to the procession," a Chicana artist in her early twenties who helps organize the Mission District's Day of the Dead procession exclaims, "Last year, we had people dancing all night! We had fire dancers and people sharing food with one another. A lot of musicians came out, bagpipe players and drummers. It's so cool . . . people of all ages and cultures . . . people really get *into* it. Wearing all kinds of costumes, using all kinds of creative props, music, anything you can think of!"

The same young artist also discusses feeling a "pull" from older Chicanos to adhere to tradition, while feeling an inner desire to embrace the multiple cultures that constitute her world: "People have views of how it *should* be. . . . You have your elders, whom you need to respect, who have their rituals and their understanding of the way it should be. . . . For me, being Latina, it's been a bit of a struggle. I'm of Mexican descent, but I don't speak very good Spanish. So sometimes I'm accepted by the community, sometimes I'm not." She compares the common reliance on Spanish fluency as a marker of Latino authenticity, to calls by older Chicanos for keeping Day of the Dead "traditional," stating that neither stance allows room for the hybrid experiences of U.S. Latinos. "In the United States you have your different types of cultures, often within the same person. You have one side and another side in you and a constant pulling. In doing Día de los Muertos, I want to experience a minimal amount of pulling." Regarding the differing factions and opinions about Day of the Dead, she continues, "There's a lot of political bullshit that's deeply rooted in artists that have been here for like thirty-five or forty years—since we've been alive!—that I can't even begin to understand. But I understand that in order to do a community event, you need to work together with lots of different people."[38]

Ironically, while Chicano traditionalists strive to maintain the Mexican authenticity of U.S. renditions of the celebration, Mexicans who see Chicano altars comment on how "un-Mexican" they are. As a native of Mexico City, who first saw Chicano altar exhibits in San Francisco in the mid-1990s, told me, "Most of these aren't the traditional altars with 'the three levels and the five elements that every altar must have,' [smiling] but that's just different interpretations. What happens in California with Mexican American, Chicano, and Latino artists is really different. It's not Mexican. It's not Latin American. It's a whole different thing."[39] Carlos Von Son, also from Mexico City and a professor of Spanish at the California State University at San Marcos, felt similarly when he first observed Chicano Day of the Dead celebrations. He shares the following reflections on authenticity:

> Sometimes, if I use terms that are Spanglish, my family in Mexico laughs and says, "Look how *pocho* you are," because they think I'm not speaking real Spanish.[40] The same thing happens here with Day of the Dead. Mexicans sometimes laugh when they see the cultural celebrations we do over here . . . because they feel they're not authentic. . . . Being honest, I felt the same way when I first came to the U.S. My instinct was to correct [Mexican American] people for the way they spoke Spanish, or tell them they were making quesadillas the wrong way. When I would see Day of the Dead celebrations here, I would say, "Don't use those elements that are foreign to the way it is in Mexico." But it didn't take me long to realize that these things are not wrong. It's not a degeneration of the original. . . . I started looking more closely at the changes and loving the way that culture gets adapted to new surroundings.[41]

Chicano playwright Tomás Benitez observes that the cultural diversity of Chicanos themselves naturally leads to diverse interpretations of Day of the Dead. Benitez is part Irish (and still keeps in touch with relatives in County Cork, Ireland), while his son is half Jewish. They celebrate Day of the Dead as well as Hanukkah and Passover. "That doesn't take away from my Chicanismo, it adds to it," he states. "Day of the Dead is the same way." Noting that racial and cultural diversity have been integral parts of U.S. Day of the Dead celebrations from their beginning, he adds, "Let's not forget that our experience, which is only about thirty years old, is predated by an experience in Mexico that was several hundred years old. So we're already knocking off. What we're talking about is the authenticity of how Chicanos celebrate it. Which means there's a flexibility to it to begin with. . . . From the get-go [at

Self-Help Graphics] we were a mixed group of Chicanos and Mexicanos with a Franciscan nun who was an Italian girl with a Jewish stepfather, and a couple of other nuns from other places. Right away we had exchanges with Black organizations and Asians and an Australian group. That's hybridization of culture."[42]

Along similar lines, René Yañez feels that opening Day of the Dead to a variety of people and forms of expression keeps it germane to the lived experiences and sociopolitical reality of Latinos and everyone else who participates:

> Death doesn't discriminate. As a Chicano-Latino curator, we started Day of the Dead to create alliances of Chicano culture and work together with other people. I've worked with people from Chinatown. I've worked with Black groups in Oakland. I've worked with mainstream groups. This allowed me to learn about how other cultures think and feel and where we fit in the scheme of things. Because if you're going to be a Chicano curator and not learn from other cultures, then you're very isolated, and not being relevant to your own culture. . . . Irish, Korean, Japanese, African people all bring something to the table. Other Latinos bring something to the table. It's a chain reaction.[43]

In this age of intensified globalization and cultural cross-pollenization, it is not possible to maintain neat categories of ethnicity and corresponding cultural practices. Day of the Dead in the United States illustrates how diverse groups of participants are deepening the hybridity of an already hybrid subject. Quests for authenticity stem from a profound longing for meaning in a demystified, hyperrationalized society. They aim to recover phenomena whose loss is realized only through modernity, and whose recovery can be undertaken only through modern methods and resources. Because they are oriented toward the past, notions of authenticity embody a conservatism that tends to shun new concepts, practices, or participants as illegitimate. In so doing, discourses of authenticity uphold the fallacy that cultural purity, rather than hybridity, is the norm (Bendix 1997, 8–9). Particularly for people who have felt their ethnic culture devalued and threatened, maintaining cultural practices that reflect a perceived faithfulness to the past feels urgent. For others who inhabit different generational, social, or national locations (such as young Latinos who have benefited from the political and artistic legacies of older Chicano artists and have grown up seeing Latino culture validated in their schools and in the media, or for recent Mexican immigrants who do not feel the need to prove their "Mexican-ness"), there is generally less concern about adhering to set traditions.

Conversations and negotiations over Day of the Dead ("growing pains," as one respondent called them) are ongoing and ultimately productive, as they serve to enhance intraethnic and intergenerational understanding. The crucial question, according to folklorist Regina Bendix, is not "what is authenticity?" but rather "who needs authenticity?" and "how has authenticity been used?" (1997, 21). Historically, in Latin America and elsewhere, notions of Indigenous authenticity have been used to advance both progressive and regressive sociopolitical agendas. Thus, it may be most useful to think of authenticity, regarding Day of the Dead and other cultural traditions, as the *quality* of an experience and the feelings it evokes. Most Latinos interviewed agreed that the intentions that people bring to the rituals—a spirit of remembrance and respect for the dead—is ultimately more important than the actual format of the activities or the ethnic/racial backgrounds of participants. Although members of the Latino community do not agree on which, whether, or how much innovation is appropriate, the U.S. celebration is an important space for reflecting on issues of cultural innovation and conservation.

In a sense, anyone who creates a Day of the Dead altar in the United States is an innovator, and the push and pull between the traditionalists and the nontraditionalists is mutually beneficial. The work of the former group in researching the tradition's origins, and observing, documenting, and recreating aspects of premodern Day of the Dead customs has provided the groundwork for educating the public about the celebration. Without this work, there would be no foundation from which the nontraditionalists could transform and redeploy the celebration's rituals. And without the modifications of the nontraditionalists and new participants, there might be less incentive for new generations of traditionalists to research and teach about the origins of the celebration. As sociologists Ron Eyerman and Andrew Jamison note, "traditions are constructed and reconstructed through a continuing dialogue between the upholders of the past and the spokespeople for the future" (1998, 41). The symbiotic tension between these two groups is integral to keeping Day of the Dead alive in the twenty-first century.

EVEN BEFORE THE ENCOUNTER BETWEEN SPAIN AND THE AMERICAS, rituals for honoring the ancestors were in flux, as various Latin American Indigenous populations came into contact with each other. Over the past five hundred years, at least, these rituals have also been influenced by Africans, Europeans, Asians, and others who traded with Indigenous peoples or settled in the region. The celebrations of southern Mexico, which today are widely considered to be the most authentic of Mexico's Day of the Dead traditions, are themselves the hybridized results of diasporas and cultural clashes of Zapotecs, Aztecs, Mayas, Mixtecs, and others, later influenced by Spanish Catholicism and, in the twentieth century, by elements of U.S. popular culture. Summarizing his feelings about tradition and change, Carlos Von Son concludes, "I have learned to see the beauty of cultural changes happening here and now, and it makes me think of how things must have changed one thousand or two thousand years ago, and I'm part of those changes."[44] In the final chapter of this book, we will continue to consider concerns about the authenticity of Day of the Dead traditions, this time in light of their commodification in the marketplace.

CHAPTER 8

The Commoditization
of a Death Ritual

In San Antonio, with its historic and current Hispanic influence, you'll become acquainted with El Día de los Muertos—an extraordinary celebration which honors the past and celebrates the future. Explore the evolution of Indigenous and Hispanic traditions into a friendly family festival. You'll construct a traditional altar . . . take a field trip to San Fernando Cemetery to take part in the day-long celebration, and taste foods prepared only for this special day. . . . Oct. 30–Nov. 3, 2004—$444.00 double, $564.00 single. (Elderhostel 2004, 14)

AS DAY OF THE DEAD HAS GROWN more popular in the United States, its material culture and rituals have become increasingly commoditized—a process in which everyday objects or resources that were traditionally not considered "commodities" are transformed into objects exchangeable in the market for monetary or other advantage. This has provoked consternation among those who feel that commoditization jeopardizes the celebration's authenticity. A look at the marketing of Day of the Dead events and products provides us with an opportunity to consider differing perspectives regarding the commoditization of culture—a phenomenon that is alternately praised or lamented by observers. Although commoditization does not always involve monetary exchange, the related process of commercialization (the act of involving something in commerce) is done expressly for financial gain. As this chapter will reveal, these are distinct processes that occur in a variety of social and economic contexts, resulting in a variety of consequences that do not automatically correlate with cultural degeneration or exploitation. What follows is a closer look at some of the paradoxical ways that consumer culture in the United States and Mexico has intersected with Day of the Dead traditions, both capitalizing upon and revitalizing them.

MARKETPLACE OFFERINGS

In the United States, folk art vendors, museum gift shops, and South-western tourist areas sell Muertos merchandise such as sugar skulls, Day of the Dead coloring books, T-shirts, calendars, mouse pads, tequila glasses, coffee-table books, posters, paintings, sculptures, greeting cards, skeleton figurines, papier-mâché skeletons, skull-themed jewelry, educational videos, and do-it-yourself altar kits in a box.[1] All seven of the Latin American folk art shops I contacted reported that Day of the Dead season was their most lucrative time of the year, outpacing even Christmas sales. Amazon.com and other Internet sites sell many of these goods, as well as more unique collector's items such as Day of the Dead handbags, night-lights, and calavera cuff links.

From late September until early November in cities from Anchorage to Topeka and beyond, Mexican folk crafts that were traditionally learned from family relatives (i.e., how to make paper flowers, bread for the dead, and altars) are taught to U.S. audiences in advertised workshops. Nonprofit art galleries and community centers based in Latino neighborhoods offer such workshops to predominantly working-class, minority constituents, but for-profit galleries and folk art stores charge higher prices for the same workshops, catering to middle-class families and professionals (especially teachers), who are often non-Latino. As a point of comparison, community centers offer workshops for free (or for a nominal cost, such as a dollar per person) on how to make altars, sugar skulls, and pan de muerto. For-profit vendors charge an average of ten to fifteen dollars per person for sugar-skull workshops; as much as twenty dollars per person for "Dead Bread" workshops; and twenty-five to fifty dollars per person to make personal-sized mini-altars (*nichos*).[2] Attending a Day of the Dead exhibit at a community center or Latino art gallery is free, while attending a similar exhibit at a museum typically costs from five to fifteen dollars per person.[3]

While many people who buy Day of the Dead merchandise create home altars and enthusiastically incorporate the holiday into their lives as an annual time to remember loved ones, others purchase these objects simply because they are considered "quirky" and "cool." Day of the Dead motifs have come to signal ethnic chic, and are now found year-round in contexts that have no connection to the celebration. For example, Día de los Muertos embroidery packets (with designs of skulls, bride and groom skeletons, candles, marigolds, and the Virgin of Guadalupe) can be purchased on the self-described "Hip Embroidery" Web site, www.sublimestitching.com. Advertising that "Embroidery Rocks!" and "This Ain't Your Gramma's Embroidery," the site aims to make an oldfangled craft stylish by selling nontraditional patterns. The Día de los Muertos kit is featured at the top of the home page, next to embroidery kits for flaming race cars, electric guitars, goth designs, and yoga symbols.[4]

In similar fashion, Dunlop Musical Instruments advertises Day of the

Dead guitar straps among other "full-throttle, in-your-face images" (such as "Beelzebub" and "Japan Tattoo") aimed at jazzing up an otherwise mundane product.[5] Meanwhile, the popular computer game, Grim Fandango, marketed by George (*Star Wars*) Lucas's company, Lucas Arts, is based on Day of the Dead imagery. The game's designer, Tim Schafer, explains, "I wanted to do a game that would feature those little papier-mâché folk-art skeletons from Mexico. I was looking at their simple shapes and how the bones were just painted on the outside and I thought . . . it'll be cool!"[6] Winner of the 1998 Game of the Year award from the Web site Game Spot, Grim Fandango is described on the Lucas Arts Web site as "a homage to Mexican folklore with a film noir twist."[7]

Exotic and Chic Cultural Capital

The relatively recent fashionability of Day of the Dead products has occurred in the context of two related phenomena. The first was the secular commercialization of Catholic material culture that emerged after the Second Vatican Council (1962–1965), when attempts to modernize the Church deemphasized the presence of Catholic material culture. With fewer Catholics displaying religious statues, votive candles, or pictures of the saints in their homes than in earlier times, the door was opened for humorous "kitsch" reappropriations of these devotional symbols by non-Catholics and non-practicing Catholics (McDannell 1995). The second phenomenon was the commodification of "Southwestern style" (e.g., Native American and Mexican colors and designs) that emerged in the United States in the 1980s and remains popular today. In both cases, vernacular objects were detached from their original social and devotional functions and marketed to the mainstream public as emblems of a "hip" lifestyle. Like glow-in-the-dark rosary beads and holograms of Joan of Arc, Latin American religious icons (such as the Virgin of Guadalupe or Cuban orishas) and Southwestern folk art (such as wooden masks, pottery, and weavings) are purchased by consumers to convey a cosmopolitan knowledge of "exotic" others, while demonstrating a social and intellectual detachment from the traditions being appropriated. Pierre Bourdieu calls this "aesthetic distancing," in which items popular among lower socioeconomic classes are appropriated by the affluent, who distinguish their class position by displacing interest from an object's content to its form (1984, 34). Arjun Appadurai refers to this phenomenon as "commoditization by diversion," where the value of objects is enhanced by diverting them from their native contexts to atypical contexts (1986, 28). As fashion accoutrements, Day of the Dead objects represent cultural capital that communicates the social status of a well-traveled connoisseur of diverse cultures.

Since the late 1990s, bars and restaurants in California and the Southwest have advertised Day of the Dead festivities, usually consisting of live music or discounts on food and drinks. A recent example is On Broadway, described in

America Online's City Guide as the "most exclusive nightclub in San Diego." The club hosted a "Día de los Muertos Party" on October 28, 2004, showcasing Muertos decorations, salsa, merengue, and Spanish rock. Amid its exotic sushi bar, zen lounge, and "retro-futuristic chill-out bar," the Day of the Dead theme enhanced this hot spot's trendy image.[8] In the same year, the coffee colossus Starbucks began placing Day of the Dead displays of Mexican coffee and cocoa, calavera cookies, plastic calavera pails, and information about the holiday (printed on colorful posters and take-away cards) in their California and Southwest cafes.[9]

Illustrating the celebration's arrival in the mainstream, the all-American magazines *Ladies' Home Journal*, *Better Homes and Gardens*, and *Holiday Celebrations* have promoted Day of the Dead decorating ideas, crafts, and recipes as the latest fun fashion. Headlined on the fall 2002 cover of *Holiday Celebrations* (alongside articles about Christmas, New Year's Eve, and Hanukkah), Day of the Dead received an eight-page photo spread depicting altars, Day of the Dead cookies, marigold wreaths, and calavera art. The accompanying article offers recipes for Aztec chocolate custard, mole, flan, salsa, and other Mexican specialties hailed as "festive enough to make anyone feel alive." The magazine's readers (mainly middle-class White women) are encouraged to replace "humdrum Halloween parties" with Day of the Dead "soirees" where guests can "party till the ghosts come home" (Trim 2002, 63–64).

Several respondents active in education and the arts told me about annual Day of the Dead parties they either hosted or attended, and on November 2, 2003, I was invited to such a party at the home of a San Francisco artist. In the entrance of her apartment was an elaborate, candlelit altar, and every room of the flat was decorated with papel picado cutouts and cardboard calaveras hanging from the ceilings. Offering plenty of Latin American food and salsa music, the party attracted about a hundred people, many of whom were prominent artists, writers, and political activists in the Bay Area. In talking with other guests, I learned that this party was considered one of the "places to be" after the yearly Day of the Dead procession in the Mission. The growing popularity of such home parties was noted by several owners of folk art stores that sell Day of the Dead decorations. Maribel Simán DeLucca explains, "There's an amazing number of people who have Day of the Dead parties now. . . . I don't mean Chicanos. I mean Anglo people. There are people who have a party every year, and there are Day of the Dead party groupies [laughs] who attend the party, and people later come and bring us photos of their altars. People spend a whole month planning for what they're going to do with their altar."[10]

Day of the Dead as a Tourism/Urban Development Strategy

Over the past decade, the flamboyance of Day of the Dead has made the celebration a tourist draw for U.S. cities and historical sites seeking to highlight their Mexican heritage. For example, since 1998, stores and restaurants in San Diego's Old Town State Park (which commemorates Mexican and "Old West" heritage) have offered annual Day of the Dead activities from late October until early November. These include altar displays, music and dance performances (from Mexico, Guatemala, Spain, and the Andes), Day of the Dead crafts for sale, and sugar-skull workshops. Each November 2, the park's nineteenth-century Campo Santo cemetery is the site of a well-attended nocturnal Day of the Dead event. This dusty graveyard (a plot of dry, cracked earth punctuated by cacti and Old West tombstones), is brought to life with hundreds of candles, papel picado decorations, myriad marigolds, ofrendas, and live music performed by Los Californios, a group specializing in the Spanish and Mexican music of early California. Predominantly non-Latino visitors are guided from grave to grave by non-Latino volunteer guides from the San Diego Historical Society, who explain the history of Old Town's interred early settlers.[11] Event organizers see the celebration a way to educate the public about California's Native American, Spanish, and Mexican history. Local merchants like the fact that it attracts visitors to Old Town's commercial area. Similar Day of the Dead festivities take place in the historic Mexican plazas of the towns of Mesilla and Santa Fe in New Mexico; San Antonio, Texas; and Olvera Street (El Pueblo de Los Angeles Historical Monument) in Los Angeles, California. Increasingly, one-day and multiday paid tour excursions are organized to these Day of the Dead destinations.

In a new twist on Day of the Dead tourism, the celebration has become an urban redevelopment strategy for blighted communities. The first example of this strategy occurred in 1996 in the predominantly Latino Fruitvale district of Oakland, California, when the Fruitvale Unity Council's Mainstreet Program sponsored a weekend-long Day of the Dead Festival.[12] The event was designed as the highlight of an annual calendar of public cultural events meant to draw visitors to Fruitvale from throughout the San Francisco Bay Area (many of whom would not otherwise sojourn to this predominantly low-income community, known more for crime and abandoned properties than for cultural vitality). The festival chairperson explains, "This is the biggest event we do all year. . . . The business people and community people wanted to plan street festivals and events to draw people to Fruitvale. They figured this was unique and would highlight Fruitvale's Latin culture. It started off with about five thousand people coming, then it grew to ten thousand, then twenty-five thousand. Now we get over eighty-five thousand people coming!"[13]

Sponsored by some forty corporations and local businesses, the event has become the largest Day of the Dead festival in the United States.[14] Each year, ten blocks of the neighborhood's central boulevard are blocked off to traffic and transformed into a festival space offering four performance stages, an international food court, and five entertainment and craft pavilions. Free activities include altar installations, Latino cinema, craft workshops, face painting, dance performances, clown shows, amusement rides, theater, music, puppetry, a participatory drumming circle, and an art exhibit. Because of its success in attracting large crowds, the model was reproduced by Mainstreets organizations in other cities. Exemplifying the chain reaction, when a member of Mainstreets Oceanside (California) observed Fruitvale's success, the idea was adopted in Oceanside, which began hosting Day of the Dead festivals in November 2001. Oceanside Mainstreets members (who received guidance and technical assistance from the Fruitvale Mainstreets group) were later invited by the Sherman Heights Neighborhood Council in San Diego to share their success stories and offer advice, motivating the council to organize Day of the Dead walking tours in collaboration with local businesses, artists, and residents. Other communities are being inspired to organize Day of the Dead festivals as part of neighborhood revitalization.

Longing for the Noncommercial Good Old Days (of the Dead)

Not everyone is enthusiastic about the commoditization of the celebration, as illustrated by the McMuertos altar installation, created by young Chicano artists and displayed in San Francisco museums during the Day of the Dead seasons of 1998, 1999, and 2000.[15] A critique of the commercialization of Day of the Dead, this installation drew parallels between the exploitation of Latino culture and the exploitation of workers in the fast food industry, and was reminiscent of the lampooning calaveras of José Guadalupe Posada. It featured skeletons dressed in McDonald's-like uniforms, working behind a fast food counter decorated in McDonald's-like colors and designs. On the wall behind the counter, a large "McMuertos McMenu" offered entrees such as "McMuertos Meals," "Super-Size Death Combos," "Beaner Babies," and the smiling Ronald MacDonaldesque skeleton clown, "Ronnie Calaca."[16] The following is an excerpt from the exhibit's text:

> Here at McMuertos we care about you and making your preparations for the festive celebration of Día de los Muertos (dee-ah day lohs mwert-toes) as quick and hassle-free as possible. We have perfected the process of providing you with the rapid delivery of a uniform mix of prepared products necessary for your altar in an environment of obvious cleanliness, order, and service with a smile. For starters, we've decorated McMuerto outlets with care to reflect the charming folk traditions of papel picado (pah-pail pee-kah-doh) and luminarias (loo-mee-nah-ree-ahs). The cheerful brown workers have been hand picked and brought all the way from romantic Mexico (may-hee-ko) just to serve you. . . . Our products improve on the cryptic ritual items of primitive Mexico—now you can buy your sugar skulls and candles in pre-packaged variety packs that save you time and money; we assure you they are prepared under

hygienic conditions, are top-quality, and packaged fresh! Be sure to check out the complete line of McMuerto products.[17]

The exhibit parodied the ironic position of Latino immigrants in the United States who are often treated as criminals, denied rights and social services, and exploited in minimum wage jobs, while the commodification of Latin American music, dance, art, food, spirituality and other traditions is a multibillion-dollar business. With phonetic spellings of Spanish words, directed at a non-Spanish speaking audience, and a description of "cheerful brown workers" serving an implied White public, the critique was aimed not only at the commodification of the celebration's rituals and symbols in general, but also at its consumption by non-Latinos in particular.

Looking back, artist John Leaños explains, "By the time we did Mc-Muertos in 1998, we were kind of a group of cynical Chicanos looking at the whole scenario, how the [Mission] procession had turned into a parade and got hippy-ized with all these hippy drummers and big puppets and stuff, and you couldn't tell if it was a Muertos parade or an antiglobalization march. And we were saying, 'What *is* this?!' So we started having conversations about the changes, the commercialization of the celebration north of the border. We reasoned that when you cross a border, the celebration's going to come into a capitalist society so it's going to take on some of those paradigms, it's going to be co-opted in some way."[18]

For its striking creativity, humor, and social commentary, the McMuertos installation was a hit, and ran for three consecutive years at three major art institutions in the Bay Area. It aptly underscored the ways that commercial interests capitalize on ethnic peoples and practices. Yet, the commoditization of culture is a process rife with contradictions. These contradictions, many of which can be seen with Day of the Dead, complicate the frequently taken-for-granted dichotomy between "commercial" and "authentic" culture.

First, it is important to keep in mind that not all forms of commoditization are the same. The sale of Day of the Dead products, the display of altars in museums and galleries, the promotion of the celebration by cities and businesses for economic purposes, and the appropriation of Day of the Dead imagery to sell completely unrelated products are distinct processes with multiple outcomes. As we have seen in the preceding sections, cultural practices may be commoditized (turned into commodities) for financial profit or for community-building and educational purposes. This commoditization can yield financial benefits and nonfinancial benefits—such as increased cultural pride, cross-cultural understanding, and ritual communication. Sometimes, both kinds of benefits may occur at the same time.

Second, "authentic" ethnic traditions are commonly thought to exist apart from consumer culture, until "outsiders" begin to appropriate and

commoditize them. Such a position ignores the ways in which cultural traditions and commerce often sustain each other, and overlooks the constructive
uses that commoditized events and products may have for ethnic minorities.
Although the forces of global capitalism and acquisitive consumerism can disin-
tegrate traditional communities, they can, paradoxically, also offer people a way
to construct ethnic identities in response to the displacement and isolation of
modern life. Ethnic festivals, museum exhibits, and commercially sold ethnic
products produced by both corporate and cottage industries can provide individuals with a sense of ethnic belonging, particularly for second and third
generations who may lack linguistic or geographical connectedness to their
cultural heritage (Halter 2000; Belasco 1987; Stern and Cicala 1991).

Moreover, the commoditization of cultural traditions is not something that
is done exclusively by "outsiders." Criticizing the consumption of Day of the
Dead by non-Latinos, as the McMuertos exhibit jokingly does, not only
assumes fixed racial categories (ignoring the racial and ethnic heterogeneity of
many Latinos), but also implies that Latinos themselves do not engage in
processes of commoditizing and consuming their own cultural practices.[19] In
reality, about half of the consumers of Day of the Dead merchandise in folk
art stores and museum/gallery shops are Latinos seeking to identify with their
Latin American heritage. In a further irony of consumerism, it is often feelings
of disdain for and alienation toward the modern preponderance of commercialized, mass-produced culture that inspires individuals to connect with their
cultural roots through purchasing ethnic merchandise and activities. While
cultural symbols and practices are commercialized by entities with no interest
in or connection to a given cultural community, they are also commercialized
by ethnics themselves, often as a strategy for cultural and economic survival.
This can be seen, for example, in the revival of strong Cajun, Hawaiian, and
Polynesian ethnic identities brought on by the commercialization of aspects of
these cultures by tourism, the music industry, and restaurants (Mattern 1998;
Ivory 1999; Halter 2000). The promotion (and affirmation) of ethnic cultural
events by dominant institutions (museums, universities, businesses, or municipal governments) can have powerful educational and social effects that serve
to strengthen, rather than weaken, ethnic traditions by providing economic
support for endangered practices and helping to counter assimilationist pressures and stigmas attached to being an ethnic minority.

Commerce and Culture: A Long History Together

To dismiss the commoditization of Day of the Dead as mere cultural
exploitation fails to consider the history of how consumerist imperatives have
helped promote and sustain the celebration, both in Mexico and the United
States. Most people interviewed for this book believed that Day of the Dead
in Mexico was free from commercial influences and became commoditized in

the United States. They were unaware that it is Mexico's most commercialized holiday, or that it was being commoditized there even before the celebration became popular in the United States. Romanticized ideas about Mexico's Indigenous peoples, widely disseminated in the mass media, have masked the dialectical relationship between culture and political economy—the ways that commercial forces can sustain, revive, and in some cases invent cultural traditions. In reality, the commoditization of Day of the Dead in Mexico has played a key role in the twentieth-century popularization and "nationalization" of ofrenda rituals that were previously practiced only in certain regions of the country. The following section reveals how Mexico's Day of the Dead traditions have survived and thrived in large part *because* of commercial forces.

Before discussing the commercialization of the holiday in Mexico, we should first have an understanding of the historical importance of the marketplace during the Days of the Dead. Anthropologists have long noted that economic expenditures are important aspects of reaffirming social relationships. Because these celebrations in Latin America are reaffirmations of relationships between extended family and friends—living and dead—they have always involved considerable economic exchange. As described earlier in the book, rural families in Mexico, the Andes, and elsewhere invest enormous amounts of time, energy, and money to purchase the commodities necessary to adorn family graves and altars. Market expenditures have traditionally been (and are still) made not only to purchase special foods and other ofrenda offerings for the deceased, but also to comply with the custom of making all kinds of renewals—symbolically associated with the cycle of death and rebirth—at this time of year. These may include buying new shoes, clothing, cookware, table coverings, furniture, and other home items, as well as repainting the house. Garciagodoy notes the importance of purchasing new products to honor the dead in Mexico: "Many traditional ofrendas include new items of clothing, new work implements, or new miniature clay images of tools laid out on a new petate [straw mat], along with candles, food, and incense on a bed of coal in a new incense burner" (1998, 118). Carmichael and Sayer also describe the spending involved: "Expenditures for *Todos Santos* can be a heavy burden for a family. . . . The *ofrendas* for those who have died within the last year can be especially costly and elaborate" (1991, 56). Anthropologist Claudio Lomnitz notes that the earliest Mexican government documents pertaining to the Days of the Dead relate to the marketplace. For example, in 1735, the mayor of Mexico City described Day of the Dead sales at stalls and shops: "There is nothing equal, or even similar, to it in the entire year" (2005, 292).

Today, many rural families still go into significant debt to meet their ritual obligations to the dead, as they purchase special holiday breads (which are mainly bought in bakeries, not baked at home), alcoholic beverages, soft drinks, enormous loads of flowers, apples, oranges, bananas, pomegranates, and other fruits that are often not grown locally (making them quite expensive by local standards), chocolate, and other specialty items needed for the ofrendas. Although my interviewees made comparisons between "commercial" Halloween and "noncommercial" Day of the Dead, expenditures by U.S. families buying candy or costumes for Halloween pale in comparison with the expenditures of Indigenous families preparing for Day of the Dead (in relation to annual income).[20] Thus, there has long been a situation in which Day of the Dead products (sugar skulls, candles, flowers, bread for the dead, etc.) have been commercialized to the public—a public that evolved over time from rural and Indigenous families to a wider public that also included collectors, tourists, teachers, and others. By the 1970s, the commoditization of Day of the Dead *celebrations*, rather than simply the sale of associated products, was initiated by Mexican government agencies and tourism businesses—playing a crucial role in the revival and survival of traditions that might otherwise be unknown today (Brandes 1988; Nutini 1988; Carmichael and Sayer 1991).

This did not happen overnight. The commoditization of Day of the Dead celebrations was preceded by the systematic commoditization of Indigenous folk art by the Mexican government after the Mexican Revolution. For the revolutionary government and its supporters, Indigenous crafts, previously disdained by the country's elites, symbolized a new, homegrown Mexican national identity, distinct from the Eurocentric identifications of earlier ruling regimes (Delpar 1992). Starting in 1921, the Mexican government organized national and international campaigns to promote an appreciation of Mexican folk art, opening state stores that sold Indigenous crafts, and sponsoring exhibitions to highlight the "art of the people."[21] These efforts were enthusiastically supported by members of the Mexican art world, including Diego Rivera, Frida Kahlo, Alfonso Caso, Miguel and Rosa Covarrubias, and others who "awakened public functionaries, educated persons and the popular classes to the taste for Mexican products" and helped "display the richness of Mexico's folk art before the eyes of the world" (Espejel 1986, 9).

After the construction of the Pan-American Highway in the 1940s, national and foreign artists and intellectuals increasingly traveled as tourists to southern Mexico, where they came into greater contact with Indigenous peoples, and found Mexico's folk art to be intriguing and "campy." Because of a romanticized nostalgia for "the primitive" that continues to accompany the secularization, standardization, and industrialization of modern life, urbane city dwellers purchased as souvenirs the weavings, pottery, masks, and other crafts that were originally produced for daily use by Mexico's Indigenous inhabitants. But, while the "art of the people" was extolled by some government officials, artists, and intellectuals, the practices of Indigenous Mexicans continued to be disdained for most of the twentieth century by the country's middle and upper classes, who considered the "superstitions" of their rural compatriots to be hindrances to the country's ability to modernize. The revulsion that "educated" Mexicans felt toward "Indians" and their Day of the Dead celebrations had existed in Mexico since colonial times (and is not completely gone today). During the late nineteenth to mid-twentieth century in particular, Day of the Dead was considered a mortifying anachronism by those Mexicans who wanted their country to become a more "advanced" and westernized nation.[22]

Tourism, government educational campaigns in the public schools, and museum patronage helped change public attitudes in Mexico, reviving rural traditions that had disappeared or were fading. By the mid- and latter twentieth century, folk crafts that were previously made in small quantities for personal consumption, such as wooden toys or ceremonial masks, were produced in mass quantities and in new colors and styles that appealed to tourists (Barbash and Ragan 1993; Brody Esser 1988; Chibnik 2003a; Graburn 1976). Not infrequently, entirely new crafts were invented to please tourist desires for "Indian" artifacts, and marketed as "timeless" Mexican customs. For example, Mexican woodcarvers modified traditional designs and motifs to please nonlocal buyers, mass reproducing objects, including Day of the Dead skeleton carvings, that sold best with tourists (Barbash and Ragan 1993; Chibnik 2003b). Purchases by North American folk art retailers/wholesalers and tourists far outweighed local sales of these crafts and continue to be the driving force for their continued production.

Art historians credit the commercial interests of international art collectors and Western museums in reviving the production of rural crafts that were no longer made after the Mexican Revolution. Mexican art scholar Carlos Espejel notes that in the 1930s, the Austrian art collector René d' Harnoncourt "was instrumental in the revival of certain dying folks arts," as he sought out pieces for tourists, private art collectors, and museums (1986, 2). Another major influence on the popularity of Mexican crafts was the multimillionaire and former U.S. assistant secretary of state Nelson A. Rockefeller who, between 1933 and 1978, developed one of the largest single collections of Mexican folk art in the world. Books written about his collection suggest that Rockefeller's goal in collecting and exhibiting these crafts in U.S. museums was to educate the public to prevent traditional Mexican crafts from disappearing (Delpar 1992; Espejel 1986, 2; C. Fox 1969). According to Espejel, Rockefeller helped open the North American market for Mexican folk art, which at the time was not widely esteemed (1986, 9). The millionaire's patronage of this art, including Day of the Dead crafts, had a far-reaching impact on the popularity of Mexican crafts among international collectors, stimulating future demand and production.[23] This helped increase the esteem that Mexicans themselves had for their country's rural crafts and traditions.

Certain crafts considered to represent the very heart and soul of Mexico would not exist today were it not for market forces. From 1919 onward, U.S.

and other foreign art buyers, as well as Mexican art collectors, approached Mexican artisans asking them to resume the production of defunct folk crafts and create new forms of artistry (Masuoka 1994, 125–126; Delpar 1992, 134–138). Susan Masuoka notes that the Linares family of Mexico, internationally renowned today for their three-dimensional papier-mâché embodiments of nineteenth-century engraver José Guadalupe Posada's calavera drawings, began the large-scale production of these figures only after gaining steady financial patronage from museums and art collectors (from 1968 to the present). Although the Linares family reintroduced and repopularized Posada's calaveras to a world stage decades after the engraver's death, they had not known of Posada's work until 1968, when Diego Rivera's friend (and caretaker of his art collection) Dolores Olmedo asked them to create 3-D renditions of Posada's sketches (1994, 86). Before 1968, the family specialized in making piñatas, masks, and other cardboard crafts for local rather than international buyers.[24] Yet, after the successful public reception of their first group of three-dimensional calaveras, the Linareses received numerous orders from businesses, museums, and private collectors around the world, including a request from Disney World's EPCOT Center. Today, Posada's images have become internationally recognized emblems of Day of the Dead, but the artist's work was not part of the cultural memory of most modern Mexicans before commercial collectors showed an interest and provided a viable market for their production.

In their 1975 documentary film on the Linares family, Bronowski and Grant note that the dying art of papier-mâché was "only being carried out by a few folk artists" in Mexico at the time. In the same film, the patriarch of the Linares family, Pedro Linares, lamented the growing loss of Mexico's traditions. However, with the economic income the Linares family received from national and international commercial art patronage, their collective creativity reached new heights, during which time Pedro Linares invented his famous whimsical *alebrije* figures, and his son, Felipe, created the three-dimensional papier-mâché skull overlaid with bright floral and vine designs that has since become one of the most recognized contemporary symbols of Day of the Dead (Masuoka 1994).[25] A subsequent renaissance of papier-mâché art occurred in Mexico, again the result of the commercialization of this cultural craft. Like José Guadalupe Posada himself, the Linareses are commercial artists, responding to consumer demands for their products. Their Day of the Dead calaveras are embedded in market realities that have generated a national and international renaissance in the popularity of both Posada's work and Day of the Dead.

In addition to the commercialization of Mexican crafts associated with Day of the Dead is the commoditization of the celebration itself. The contemporary prominence of Day of the Dead in Mexico as a *national*, rather than a regional tradition (as it was considered up until the early and mid twentieth century), is due to the heavy promotion of the holiday by the Mexican government and tourism businesses since the 1970s. Prior to this time, Day of the Dead in Mexico was a waning subcultural practice, observed by a dwindling number of rural communities in the south. People who made ofrendas in their homes were not generally respected or admired by the rest of Mexico. This reality began to change when tourism became a booming industry and the Mexican Ministry of Tourism realized that Day of the Dead was a cultural resource that could attract visitors and economic development to the country's impoverished rural regions. Soon, "authentic" cemetery processions were choreographed in picturesque Indigenous towns to please tourist sensibilities. Folk dance shows and the urban play *Don Juan Tenorio*, previously unknown in rural areas, were introduced to Indigenous villages as state strategies to attract Day of the Dead tourists. On seeing the financial success of these events, other towns where the holiday was all but forgotten emulated the model (Brandes 1988, 98–100).

State and commercial promotion of Day of the Dead in national public school curricula, public events, retail sites, literary essay contests, televised programming, newspapers, and other mass media encouraged the mainstream Mexican population to see the custom as something valuable and reflective of the country's national character.[26] Today, Indigenous-style Day of the Dead celebrations occur throughout Mexico, including in areas of the country where the rituals were little known prior to the 1980s and 1990s, such as Tijuana and other northern border regions.[27] (There are now organized tours to Tijuana on November 1 and 2, such as one advertised in the *San Diego Union Tribune* that charges fifty-nine U.S. dollars per person "to preview Tijuana's preparations for Day of the Dead.")[28] During Day of the Dead season, sugar skulls, skeleton figurines, and pan de muerto do a brisk business in Mexico's small shops, while the nationwide department store Sanborn's and transnational chains Wal-Mart and The Price Club display chocolate calaveras and pan de muerto among their gourmet confections. Realizing the holiday's potential to attract customers, restaurants, hotels, and other businesses throughout the country now erect ofrendas and advertise Day of the Dead merchandise and events.[29]

An example of this is Tijuana's Bread for the Dead Festival. Since 1997, Tijuana's Cámara de Industria Panificadora (Industrial Baker's Association) has sponsored an annual "Pan de Muerto Festival," where bread for the dead and other baked goods are promoted.[30] When I attended the event on October 28, 2001, over thirty local bakeries participated, setting up tables in Morelos Park, Tijuana, and distributing free bread samples to several hundred festival attendees against a backdrop of altar exhibits, music, and dance performances. A representative of the Cámara de Industria Panificadora told me that the event was started to familiarize people in Tijuana with Day of the Dead and, specifically, with pan de muerto: "Day of the Dead is not native to this area of Mexico, so a lot of people here do not know about it. They are not familiar with pan de muerto, so we would like to show them."[31]

Two of the most commercialized Day of the Dead sites in Mexico are the now famous towns of Mixquic, a suburb of Mexico City, and Janitzio, in Michoacán—both relentlessly highlighted in glossy photo books and travel articles. Referred to by Mexicans and foreigners alike as *the* places to be to experience an authentic Day of the Dead, these communities have become veritable pilgrimage destinations for tourists in search of "tradition." By the late 1980s, more than a million foreign and Mexican tourists were visiting Mixquic on November 2, and the numbers are even higher today.[32] The island of Janitzio, with a population of about 1,500 inhabitants, receives 100,000 Day of the Dead tourists yearly, making the holiday the biggest annual source of income for the town's poor families (who convert their homes into restaurants and craft booths for the occasion).

Tourists have transformed Day of the Dead in these areas into an unrestrained party that one journalist described as a "chaos of drunken groups of city dwellers and hawkers of such trinkets as small wooden boats and mixed tequila drinks."[33] On a visit to Janitzio in 2005, California resident Maribel Simán DeLucca was deeply disturbed by the disheveled condition in which she found the town's cemetery: "It was filled with broken bottles and beer cans. It made me so upset that I went to the town hall to complain."[34]

In addition to the commercialization of Day of the Dead in many communities throughout Mexico, the country now has a Day of the Dead theme park, located in the Xcaret Amusement Complex, about a forty-minute drive from the tourist haven of Cancún.[35] In the winter of 2005, Xcaret inaugurated its newest attraction, a fabricated cemetery called "El Puente al Paraíso" (The Bridge to Paradise) that allows tourists to experience Day of the Dead year-round. In a prepackaged fusion of ancient and New Age elements, the cemetery was built in the shape of a *caracol* (spiraling conch shell used by the Aztecs and Maya as a form of audio communication) and has an entrance designed with symbols of the four elements of life—according to ancient Mayan cosmology—water, air, earth, and fire. It has seven levels "representing the seven days of the week," 52 stairs "symbolizing the 52 weeks of the year," and 365 tombs, "one for every day of the year," that reflect various tomb styles, decorative practices, legends, humorous epitaphs, and Day of the Dead customs from regions throughout Mexico. There is also "a series of crypts ready to house the incinerated remains of those who visited, enjoyed and loved the park and decided to choose Xcaret as their final resting place."[36]

Thus, we need to be careful about assumptions we make concerning the "noncommercial" nature of the holiday in Mexico, or the "corrupting" influence of all commoditization. Through a variety of commodifying endeavors in the twentieth century, a ritual that was practiced by Mexico's economically and socially marginalized Indigenous peoples has come to be considered the national heritage of all Mexicans. With assorted results, commercial forces have helped bring Day of the Dead to the world stage, through tourist excursions, museum exhibits, or merchandise sales. Even the work of artists and writers associated with Day of the Dead—José Guadalupe Posada, Diego Rivera, Octavio Paz, the Linares family, and others—would not be as widely known today without having been reproduced in commercial products such as books, calendars, T-shirts, posters, souvenirs, newspapers, and magazines.

The commodification of Day of the Dead products and rituals not only revived the celebration in Mexico, but also helped inspire the Chicano artists who initiated Day of the Dead events in the United States. Looking back on the early days of the Chicano Movement, Romo observes that it was the material culture or "visuals" of Day of the Dead that grabbed Chicano artists and inspired them to learn more about the metaphysical aspects of the ritual: "Day of the Dead affected Chicano artists because it gave them a whole bunch of new iconography, new images of death and life, and the whole idea of duality and the life cycle."[37] As Day of the Dead grew more popular in the United States, commodities such as sugar skulls, pan de muerto, marigolds, and papel picado caught the public's attention, spurring some individuals to learn about the tradition and get involved, and others to purchase Day of the Dead objects as mere curiosities.

As mentioned earlier, there are non-Latino companies that hawk Day of the Dead–themed merchandise simply because the "kitsch" value livens up otherwise mundane product lines and increases sales. In such cases, businesses capitalize on Latino culture, with little or no financial benefit going to Latinos themselves (although nonfinancial promotional and educational benefits may accrue simply by having Day of the Dead items more visible in the mainstream). Companies that sell Day of the Dead guitar straps, shot glasses, or cuff links made in China are examples of this. However, most Day of the Dead products in the United States are sold at small folk art stores owned by Latinos or others with a genuine interest in Latin American culture. Along with nonprofit arts organizations, these commercial shops play an important role in educating the public about the holiday, often hiring Latino artisans to teach craft workshops marketed to the public. The sale of sugar skulls, pan de muerto, candles, marigolds and other items at these stores benefits small and informal Latino entrepreneurs (bakers, florists, craftspeople, and artists) working on both sides of the U.S.-Mexican border. Thus, the commercialization of Day of the Dead products is not necessarily exploitative or detrimental to the Latino community.

Despite the fact that Day of the Dead is a lucrative season for these vendors, operating a small, independent shop and staying economically viable is always a struggle. Folk art stores do not receive public or private arts funding and must charge prices that cover the cost of workshop materials and instructors, while still earning a profit. Their prices are higher than those at nonprofit arts organizations, but their for-profit mission does not prevent them from being focal points in their communities. The owners of the shops I visited saw their role as educating the public and building community, as well as selling merchandise. In addition to paid workshops, all of these stores offered free community events such as Day of the Dead altar exhibits, public receptions, lectures, or film screenings. They provided handouts on the meaning of the celebration, and sometimes gave educational talks to local schools and organizations. Because of the visibility of their Day of the Dead products, prominently displayed in store windows, such shops were often the first place approached by students and journalists seeking information about the holiday.

The commoditization of Day of the Dead in fee-based museum exhibits is also not a simple case of cultural exploitation. Although museums benefit economically from the crowds attracted to Day of the Dead exhibits, they also perform key educational and legitimizing functions. As discussed earlier, the presence of Day of the Dead exhibits in museums has been important in popularizing the celebration to wide U.S. audiences, and in providing greater visibility for Latino artists. Moreover, nearly all museums that hold Day of the Dead exhibits offer free tours to school and community groups, and many offer free general admission one day per week and/or free Day of the Dead community events, such as performances, lectures, or workshops. Barbara Henry, educational curator for the Oakland Museum of California, observes that of the twenty thousand visitors the museum receives during its annual six-week Day of the Dead exhibit, "we have about seven thousand school kids come through here each season. Last year we had about ten groups on the waiting list. There's a tremendous response from schools . . . from all different grade levels. . . . We get about three thousand to four thousand people at the free community celebration, just on that one *day*."[38]

Having Day of the Dead represented in museums is beneficial to the Latino community because it provides opportunities for Latinos, especially youth, to see Latin culture esteemed by the larger society. It also creates connections between Latinos and museums. A Guatemalan American in her midtwenties explains, "I live two blocks away from here [the Oakland Museum], but I never stepped foot in this institution until I came to the Day of the Dead celebration they have here. . . . If you come from somewhere where they don't take you to museums, you don't always think of going to museums. . . . So I went, and I was amazed. . . . What was amazing to me was how a public institution took something that was so personal and practiced in the home and turned it into a public interpretation. . . . So I started to be a volunteer here. Then a job opened up and I got a job here."[39] Henry notes, "We know that the Day of the Dead event brings in Latinos, and then once they know about the museum, they come back for other exhibits. We have done surveys that ask if people have come to any previous museum events and, most of the time, they check off Day of the Dead. Four of our staff members have started as volunteer guides at our Day of the Dead exhibit."[40] The exhibit designer at the Peabody Museum of Archeology and Ethnology at Harvard University shared a similar story. When he recruited local Latino youth to help create an altar exhibit, an ongoing relationship began between museum staff and the teens, launching the art career of one young man who did not previously consider himself an artist.[41] As these examples illustrate, institutional sponsorship of ethnic celebrations (whether by museums, municipal governments, or businesses) is a form of validation that can help ethnic minorities resist the social pressure they face to devalue and abandon ethnic traditions.

Although workshops offered by for-profit entities are often too costly for low-income people, these venues are in the minority. In most U.S. cities, especially in California, free Day of the Dead exhibits, performances, poetry events, and craft workshops offered by nonprofit organizations far outnumber the fee-based activities at for-profit stores and museums. As for companies that utilize Day of the Dead to sell products with little or no connection to the holiday, Amalia Mesa Bains, a Chicana artist and visual arts professor at the California State University at Monterey Bay, explains, "We can't prevent corporations and businesses from making money off of the Days of the Dead. We Chicanos don't have control over that. . . . But we *do* have control in making sure that we continue to educate people about the tradition, so that they understand its true meaning. We *do* have control about correcting misinformation. That's *our* responsibility and that's something we need to be vigilant about."[42]

COMMERCIALIZATION VERSUS AUTHENTICITY

During my research in California and elsewhere, I wanted to learn whether commercially sponsored Day of the Dead events organized by chambers of commerce, stores, and tourist bureaus were void of the spirituality and social critique prominent in Chicano altar installations. What I found was that the actual location of an exhibit (whether in a commercial or noncommercial venue, or a Latino or non-Latino space) was less a determining factor than the orientation of the person(s) creating the installations. One of the first commercially sponsored events I observed was the annual Day of the Dead celebration at El Pueblo de Los Angeles Historic Monument, also known as Olvera Street (a re-creation of a Mexican marketplace of stores, vendor carts, and restaurants, located in Los Angeles, California). Organized since the late

1970s by the Olvera Street Merchants Association, the free celebration spans several days and includes a Day of the Dead procession, altar exhibits, craft workshops, movies about Day of the Dead, live music, Aztec danza performances, and *lots* of Day of the Dead merchandise for sale. Despite the celebration's business funding and its location in a tourist area, the ofrenda exhibits I viewed in October of 2003, 2004, and 2005 included politically themed altars. There was one dedicated to labor organizer César Chávez, several altars dedicated to U.S. military servicemembers killed in Afghanistan and Iraq, an altar in memory of the genocide of Native Americans, and one dedicated to the memory of people killed in gay-bashing incidents. The last altar displayed photos of recent gay-bashing victims along with photos of famous gays and lesbians, including Lawrence of Arabia, Oscar Wilde, Andy Warhol, Gertrude Stein, Michelangelo, James Baldwin, Allen Ginsberg, Gianni Versace, and Rock Hudson. The artist's caption stated, "I celebrate their lives and thank them for their example. . . . Far too many gay teens are still contemplating suicide. Too many gay people are still being bashed on the street. It is my hope that this altar will give strength and courage to all people who have been marginalized by society."[43]

At another chamber of commerce–sponsored Day of the Dead celebration in Mesilla, New Mexico, altars honored a spectrum of deceased family, friends, and local political leaders, as well as more general groups, such as victims of domestic violence, homelessness, child abuse, and the Iraq war.[44] An especially large altar was created by the local high school chapter of Amnesty International, in memory of torture victims. It included pamphlets and other written information about human rights abuses worldwide, as well as information about Amnesty International. The weekend-long festival certainly attracted tourist dollars to this historic Spanish colonial town, but it also strengthened community bonds and raised public consciousness about political issues.

Similarly, the Day of the Dead festivals in the cities of Fruitvale and Oceanside, California, both funded through the Mainstreets economic development initiative (discussed in chapter 6), included a mixture of commercial and political aspects. Organized by each city's respective business community with the assistance of local residents, artists, and scholars, both festivals received sizeable monetary and in-kind donations from multinational corporations such as media outlets, soft drink manufacturers, credit card companies, airlines, and grocery stores. For example, the 2004 Fruitvale Day of the Dead festival, widely advertised in commercial media, looked in many ways like any other street festival. Four stages transmitted continuous mariachi, Andean, salsa, reggae, jazz, and rock music throughout the weekend, while social service providers staffed tables offering information on health insurance, immigration services, domestic violence shelters, drug rehabilitation centers, organ donor programs, Latino civic organizations, environmental groups, Catholic Charities' Prison Ministry, the California Highway Patrol, the Girl Scouts, and solidarity groups working on behalf of Chiapas, Guatemala, and Nicaragua. More than 120 vendor booths, selling everything from private mortgage insurance to chiropractic services to cell phones, lined the main street, where walking was laborious because of the enormous crowds.[45] Election volunteers registered people to vote and distributed pamphlets about candidates. The Oakland Raiders' Cheerleaders had a booth selling Raiders' merchandise. Bilingual Citibank employees recruited people for credit card accounts, and the Safeway supermarket chain created a replica "supermercado," where Goya and other Latin American food products were on sale. Hundreds of plastic skeletons and Guatemalan Day of the Dead kites adorned the festival area, frolicking in the wind as people danced, ate at the food pavilions, participated in craft activities, and visited vendor booths.

This was the largest street fair I had ever seen and, given the commercial orientation of the event, I wasn't sure what to expect. What distinguished this festival from others, however, was the fact that in the middle of the main thoroughfare, on both sides of the street, was an exhibit of twenty altar installations created by local artists and community residents. A number of Day of the Dead aficionados in the Bay Area had rolled their eyes when I mentioned the Fruitvale festival, dismissing it as inauthentic. For them, the Mission District procession was the only genuine Day of the Dead event. Nonetheless, the Fruitvale ofrendas reflected an impressive level of artistic creativity, ethnic diversity, and political expression, involving the collaboration of many people over several months. Like similar community rituals in Latin America, it mixed the secular and the sacred. For example, while constructing their street altars the night before the festival, local artists and residents held a communal ceremony and vigil in honor of the dead, with music, prayer, and dance that lasted until dawn. This was an unadvertised, informal, and deeply meaningful ritual held by the altar makers on the eve of the festival—not exactly what one would expect amid the Citibank and Raiders' banners, Kettle Korn booths, and giant stage lights being set up nearby. For the altar makers, the venue was irrelevant to the serious work of commemorating the deceased.

In addition to festival altars that honored family members and friends; an altar created by local schoolchildren for their departed relatives; and altars honoring pop culture stars such as salsa singer Celia Cruz, African musician Malonga Casquelourd, and Chinese artist Mon Gway Wong were various altars commemorating victims of politically related deaths. One installation was created in memory of those who die annually from hunger, emphasizing that hunger is a worldwide and preventable problem. The ofrenda was decorated with flags from many countries, including the United States, listing each country's annual death toll from malnutrition (an eye-opener for passersby who expressed surprise on learning that hunger is a cause of death in the United States). With stand-up panels of text explaining that hunger is a political rather than natural phenomenon, the installation included informational flyers about a nonprofit organization called The Hunger Project.

Another altar was dedicated to more than four hundred murdered female factory workers in Ciudad Juarez, Mexico. Known as "The Women of Juarez," these employees of U.S. and other foreign-owned factories operating just across the border from El Paso, Texas, were raped, mutilated, and murdered on their commute to or from work. Neither the Mexican or U.S. governments nor the multinational corporations on the border have made serious attempts to solve the crimes or increase safety conditions for female workers, who continue to be raped and murdered as they travel to and from work. The installation included poster boards with statistics on the abductions, and provided handouts listing the addresses and Web sites of Sony, Zenith, and Lear—multinational corporations that operate factories in Juarez—urging the public to contact these corporations to demand the implementation of worker safety precautions and an end to corporate union-busting activities.

There was also an altar honoring Rosie Jimenez, a low-income mother and college student who died on October 3, 1977, from a back alley abortion. Believed to be the first woman to die from an illegal abortion after the 1977 Doyle-Hyde Amendment banned the use of Medicaid funds for abortions (disproportionately affecting low-income and minority women's access to the procedure), Jimenez is a symbol, for pro-choice activists, of today's ongoing legal threats to women's reproductive rights.

Perhaps most striking of all the altars was a large installation done by Grupo Maya, a support group of Guatemalan refugees living in the Bay Area. Replicating the feel of a rural Guatemalan cemetery, the exhibit consisted of life-sized mounds of earth formed in the shape of humble rural graves. Decorated with marigolds and wooden crosses, the graves had plates of tamales, corn, fruits, and breads placed on them as typical offerings to the dead. The realism of the scene was heightened by the penetrating smells of melting candle wax, copal incense, and flowers—virtually transporting onlookers from downtown Fruitvale to the Guatemalan mountains. On the graves lay large photos of the real-life skeletal remains of several of the estimated hundred thousand Mayas murdered by the U.S.-supported Guatemalan military during the 1980s. One photo depicted a skull with a pole lodged through the cranium and emerging from one of the eye sockets, where the victim had been stabbed to death. Other photos showed skeletons still wearing decomposing shreds of woven Maya clothing. The photos were taken by forensic experts during recent exhumations of mass graves in Guatemala, conducted by the Guatemalan Foundation for Forensic Anthropology, with support from the United Nations and Amnesty International, attempting to document the extent of the government-sponsored massacres. Next to the installation was information on the Guatemalan military's "scorched earth" campaign that eradicated 440 Mayan villages in the 1980s, as well as recent news clips about ongoing death threats and attacks targeted at Guatemalan forensic investigators conducting these exhumations. Members of Grupo Maya were present to discuss the exhibit and answer questions, as were the creators of all the other altars, converting the festival into a learning experience for attendees.

Because of the beautiful yet gruesome nature of this particular exhibit, it attracted large crowds of spectators, who quietly stared at the photos and read the text. When I asked one of the installation's creators, a native of the Maya Mam Indigenous village of Todos Santos, what he thought of locating such a serious political statement in a carnivalesque setting (with salsa music pulsating in the background and smells of popcorn and fried dough in the air), he responded, "*¡Es lo máximo!*" (It's the best!) He said that he "loved" this venue because "thousands of people from all over pass by the altar and learn something of the traditions and history of Guatemala. Many Guatemalans come and stare, and some start to cry and look away. Others, when they see me dressed in my Mam clothing, start to speak to me in Mam. Others who aren't from Guatemala say that they didn't know Guatemala had Day of the Dead too."[46]

For this Maya immigrant, the commercial, the spiritual, and the political were not mutually exclusive, just as traditional religious fiestas in Latin America are accompanied by *tianguis*—temporary markets that sell holiday and everyday items. The previous examples demonstrate that Day of the Dead activities in commercial venues, like celebrations in nonprofit spaces, exert a Latino presence in the public sphere. Because of the extensive advertising they receive, commercialized events reach larger audiences than are typically drawn to nonprofit gallery exhibits (including people who may never visit museums or galleries), complementing, rather than replacing, oppositional forms of political expression found in more radical art spaces.

An ongoing fear regarding the commoditization of cultural practices is that it destroys the soul of traditions and narrows the range of creative expression. Sometimes, however, the parallel and distinct intentions of commercial forces and cultural practices can be mutually beneficial. In the case of Day of the Dead, a variety of commercial interests from art retailers, book publishers, museums, tourism, and urban renewal organizations have helped popularize the tradition, both in Mexico and the United States, without negating the spiritual, social, and political meanings the celebration holds for individuals and communities. Even the proliferation of Day of the Dead graphics used to sell unrelated commercial products does not nullify the communicative power of the celebration, and familiarizes the public with symbols that may potentially make the audience interested in learning about the actual celebration.

AVANT-GARDE ART, SPIRITUALLY MEANINGFUL RITUALS, and oppositional political work are generally considered to exist outside of dominant institutions and commercial spaces. This can be a deceptive assumption. Art produced in nonprofit spaces is not necessarily exempt from corporate pressures, and does not always represent the interests of disenfranchised populations (Kester 1998), and art produced in commercial spaces is not necessarily inauthentic or apolitical. Holidays or "holy days" in both Western and non-Western societies have been connected to commerce for centuries (Mauss 1967; Waits 1993; Schmidt 1995), with spiritual, social, and commercial phenomena operating simultaneously as individuals choose the level at which they wish to participate. We can distinguish authentic from inauthentic Day of the Dead activities, not by whether or not they occur in commercial venues, but by whether or not they bring individuals into meaningful contact with each other. Despite commercialized aspects of the celebration, people who are serious about the ideas of ceremony, even while adapting them to their own circumstances, cultures, neighborhoods, or political concerns, are engaged in ritual communication, or involvement in "the serious life" (Rothenbuhler 1998). That a Latin American family ritual has become a commoditized spectator event in the United States, attracting large crowds at both nonprofit and commercial venues, does not preclude this meaningful involvement.

Conclusion

What We Can Learn from U.S. Day of the Dead Celebrations

Examining Day of the Dead as a way to critically analyze issues of power, this book has related a complex story about the communicative capacity of cultural ritual in identity construction, education, and political protest. It is a story about the agency of a historically stereotyped and subordinated population with relatively little economic capital and abundant cultural capital to challenge racist, mass-produced discourses of themselves—narratives that have historically reinforced and attempted to legitimize the economic, social, and political subordination of Latinos. The phenomenon of Day of the Dead in the United States encourages a rethinking of what is typically considered "media," to include public ritual celebrations as important forms of grassroots communication, particularly for populations with limited input and access to mainstream media production. It is an example of "politics by other means," in which longstanding norms of cultural devaluation and exclusion are challenged by utilizing traditional forms of social solidarity to create alternative public spheres. Without disregarding the ways that conventional configurations of power create inequitable social conditions, this study shows that political agendas and cultural production are not exclusively determined by dominant stakeholders.

The relatively recent U.S. tradition of Day of the Dead illustrates the power of ritual to expand people's opportunities to exchange ideas and learn from each other. Whether educating the public about aspects of Latino culture, history, and identity, or humanizing abstract political concepts related to contemporary social issues, the creators of Day of the Dead altars, processions, poetry, and art impart a sense of human interconnectedness on a local, regional, national, and even international level. This in turn generates a sense of belonging to and responsibility toward the larger community.

One of the most important implications of this book is that meaningful political communication can happen during activities and in places that are not usually recognized as political. The examples here demonstrate how cultural rituals can inform the public and inspire people to become involved in their communities. Although Day of the Dead celebrations may appear at first glance to be just another form of colorful multicultural entertainment, they do not automatically reinforce the assumptions of equality and peaceful coexistence inherent in many multicultural projects. Messages conveyed at the exhibits, processions, and related rituals frequently elucidate the severe realities of U.S. populations for whom the American Dream did not come true. Information such as this helps cultivate greater understanding and solidarity between diverse populations, creating the groundwork necessary for civic engagement, whether in the form of volunteering at a local community center or getting involved in specific political work.

While this study does not seek to provide quantitative data on the relationship between people's participation in Day of the Dead and subsequent forms of community activism, anecdotal evidence from conversations with participants suggests that, after being profoundly moved by politicized Day of the Dead exhibits or events, some were inspired to become involved in their local community centers, art councils, museums, or chambers of commerce. Others were unexpectedly awakened to disturbing sociopolitical issues while attending these events. For example, a middle-aged Anglo technical writer told me that he had never heard of the Women of Juarez before attending the Day of the Dead exhibit at Cal State San Marcos in the fall of 2004. Three elderly Mexican American women, unable to hold back tears as they helped decorate the unmarked graves of dead migrants at the Holtville cemetery ritual of October 2003, told me that the event made them want to get more active in immigrant rights and social pastoral work along the border. A Guatemalan American told me that he had never considered the connections between race, class, and military recruitment in U.S. high schools before seeing an antiwar altar at the 2004 Oceanside Day of the Dead festival. These people were initially drawn to Day of the Dead activities because of the cultural aspects of the celebration, but left with increased knowledge and political commitment.

Given the pessimism regarding national decreases in traditional forms of civic engagement in the United States, and an increasingly consolidated and monopolistic mass media landscape, more research is needed on unconventional forms of civic participation that occur under the radar of most social science observers. Civic engagement in concrete actions, such as voter turn-out, volunteerism, or political activism, must be preceded by consciousness-raising processes that create a foundation for more elaborate and institutionalized political action. As political scientist James C. Scott notes, "material and symbolic resistance are part of the same set of mutually sustaining practices," with the latter not only supporting practical resistance, but serving as a condition for it (1990, 184–191).

Another important lesson conveyed in the examples of *Day of the Dead in the USA* is that ethnicity is a flexible and changing construct, based on social practices rather than biological characteristics. Mexican Americans and other U.S. Latinos engage with the celebration for a variety of distinct reasons, including spiritual needs, artistic expression, political protest, community development, and commerce. Depending on who is organizing and participating in them, Day of the Dead celebrations can represent "Chicano," "Mexican American," "Latino," or a more general community (neighborhood, town, city) identity, as new relationships develop between ethnically diverse Latino groups and between Latinos and non-Latinos. Thus, ethnic cultures and identities are made and remade in reaction to changing demographic, social, and political circumstances. As in Mexico, the public promotion of Day of the Dead in the United States was a conscious choice on the part of participants who, for the most part, did not grow up in families that practiced the Indigenous rituals of southern Mexico. For these people, the holiday has assumed an ideological symbolism and political value that go far beyond its original religious meaning.

Contrary to romanticized portrayals of Day of the Dead as a relatively uninterrupted continuation of pre-Columbian Indigenous rituals, the historical and ethnographic evidence presented in these pages reveals the decisive roles played by progressive political activists (Chicanos and Mexican nationalists); arts, cultural, and educational institutions; government agency funding; business interests; and the mass media in making the celebration a regular feature of autumn for U.S. Americans of diverse backgrounds. While increasingly popular in Latino communities, Day of the Dead is not universally embraced by all Mexican Americans, or any other group of Latinos. There are differing levels of knowledge about and acceptance/rejection of the celebration within different communities, and even among members of the same family. Meanwhile, many non-Latinos, particularly in California and the Southwest, are as knowledgeable and enthusiastic about the tradition as are many Latinos. All of these developments illustrate how expressions of Latinidad affect not only the Latino community, but the larger U.S. society as well.

Despite fears of the homogenizing influence of U.S. mainstream culture on the rest of the world, the growth of Day of the Dead in the United States makes clear that U.S. culture is not monolithic or homogenous. It is, instead, an evolving hybrid composite of the traditions of the country's diverse inhabitants. In their interactions for more than thirty-five years with mainstream educational, cultural, and media organizations, the Chicano creators of Day of the Dead celebrations have illustrated that when mainstream audiences are exposed to alternative cultural aesthetics and mores, the result can be a subversion of dominant Anglo practices and values. Day of the Dead has helped change mainstream U.S. culture by increasing interest in and tolerance for alternative cultural practices and spiritual beliefs, and by broadening the spectrum of available metaphysical reflections and public rituals related to remembering the dead.

In an increasingly interconnected world, unprecedented levels of transnational exchange over the past three decades have transmitted Day of the Dead to wide publics in both Mexico and the United States, defying previous dichotomies of local versus global, authentic versus commercial, or traditional versus modern. Countering nostalgic portrayals of ethnic communities as insular entities that until recently were untouched by nonlocal influences, these celebrations demonstrate the historical and ongoing influence of nonlocal forces on the formation of local cultural identities and practices. Day of the Dead rituals have flourished in both countries from the 1970s onward in ways that would not have been possible if ethnic groups and their practices existed in "pure" or isolated cultural spaces, untouched by consumerism or the mass media. We can learn much more about the workings of culture by focusing our energy on the political, economic, and social circumstances that produce migrations and transformations of customs than by asking whether or not traditions are "authentic" or "commercial."

Day of the Dead's modern trajectory exemplifies the consequences of accelerated communication processes that used to take place at much slower rates. Rituals practiced in Indigenous communities of Mexico circulated (through improved and more affordable transportation, tourism, commerce, and the mass media) to the United States, where they underwent a cultural and political metamorphosis within the Chicano Movement. Chicano celebrations were later influenced by the Day of the Dead traditions of new waves of Mexican and other Latin American immigrants coming to live and work in the United States. These traditions were widely represented in the U.S. mass media, attracting larger Latino and non-Latino audiences and participants. Through the same communication processes (tourism, commerce, migration, and media flows), Chicano Day of the Dead expressions recirculated to Mexico, influencing artistic and political expressions of the holiday there, and elsewhere. Today, Chicano-style Day of the Dead festivities occur, albeit on a much smaller scale, in places as diverse as Canada, Europe, Australia, New Zealand, and Japan, where they may transform and be transformed by those cultural landscapes.[1] U.S. Day of the Dead celebrations transmit messages about identity, struggle, and universal human experience, making a tangible impact on the lives of participants. As a form of vernacular media, these rituals simultaneously challenge and revitalize mainstream U.S. society.

Methodological Appendix

The methodology for this project entailed (a) library research, (b) textual analysis of Day of the Dead events and media coverage of them, and (c) multi-site ethnographic fieldwork (observation and formal and informal interviews) over a period of eight years. During the autumn of the years 2000 to 2005, I attended Day of the Dead processions, vigils, exhibits, lectures, workshops, film screenings, altar-making ceremonies, poetry readings, and other related activities in California (in the San Diego, Los Angeles, and San Francisco Bay areas), as well as events in New Mexico, Arizona, Texas, and Tijuana, Mexico. Because Day of the Dead exhibits, workshops, vigils, processions, lectures, and other events are now common in California and the Southwest, I was able to attend about twenty different activities each fall, traveling by car and plane. In 2006 and 2007, having moved from California to New Jersey, I attended Day of the Dead celebrations in New York City, New Brunswick, NJ, and Boston, MA. Over eight years, I shot more than sixty rolls of film and hundreds of digital photos.

Having traveled widely throughout Latin America since 1990, I have also observed and discussed Day of the Dead traditions and other death-related rituals (wakes, funerals, and remembrance days) with friends in Mexico, Guatemala, El Salvador, Panama, and Ecuador, providing me with additional insights and background information for this study.

LIBRARY RESEARCH

My library research included readings from a wide variety of sources, starting with a review of literature on pre-Columbian, colonial, and contemporary Latin American rituals for remembering the dead, (most published work concerned Mesoamerican and Andean regions). These ranged from historical accounts of sixteenth-century Indigenous rituals to ethnographic observations of nineteenth- and twentieth-century anthropologists, folklorists, and travelers. To gain additional information on Day of the Dead customs in various areas of Latin America, I searched newspaper coverage (articles and editorials) published from 1998 to 2005 in major Latin American newspapers during the dates of October 30 to November 3, finding relevant articles and commentary in Mexican, Guatemalan,

Nicaraguan, Honduran, Salvadoran, Ecuadorian, Bolivian, Panamanian, and Argentine newspapers.

My investigation of U.S. celebrations began with a review of the relatively few scholarly articles written about U.S. Day of the Dead events. I also collected and analyzed museum exhibition catalogs, promotional posters, post-cards, flyers, newspaper advertisements, newspaper and magazine articles, Day of the Dead Web sites, radio recordings from National Public Radio, footage of TV news coverage of festivities, documentary videos, and elementary school educational curriculum guides.

Scholarly writings from the fields of communication, sociology, anthro-pology, cultural studies, and Chicano/Latino studies enhanced my theoretical understanding of the social and political importance of cultural practices for ethnic minorities in the United States. Readings from the fields of religion and theology provided me with theoretical and historical data on Indige-nous and Mestizo Latin American spirituality and popular religiosity. Literature on the subject of death and dying in the United States, mainly from the fields of sociology and anthropology, gave me an understanding of changing U.S. attitudes, beliefs, and customs around death, from the seven-teenth century until the present. Writings on consumerism and the commercialization of culture, from fields such as sociology, anthropology, history, and cultural studies, informed my reflections on the commoditiza-tion of Day of the Dead.

TEXTUAL ANALYSIS AND MEDIA COVERAGE

I conducted an analysis of altar exhibits and media coverage of Day of the Dead events (in magazine articles, Web sites, and newspaper articles published in the United States over nearly three decades), with a strong emphasis on California events. My research involved photographing altar exhibits, Day of the Dead artwork, processions, and ceremonies; taking notes on the placement of objects and words spoken at performances, lectures, or poetry events; and documenting the visual, olfactory, and auditory details of ceremonies (for example, the types of musical instruments played, songs and dances performed, flowers used, apparel worn, or incense burned). At exhibits, I kept a record of the names of the artists or community groups making the altars and copied (by hand or with a digital camera) the written text that accompanied altar installations. When handouts were available at altar instal-lations (as they frequently were), I gathered copies. These usually consisted of detailed descriptions of an altar's significance, information about the artist(s), and/or information about the person or political cause being honored. When the artists or performers were present at exhibits or events (which is common during exhibit openings and one-day special events), I spoke with them about the meanings of and responses to their work.

To analyze news coverage, I acquired newspaper articles and radio and TV transcripts about Day of the Dead events, predominantly through the Lexis-Nexis and *Los Angeles Times* online archives. U.S. popular magazine articles were acquired from Lexis-Nexis and by purchasing the fall issues of supermarket standards such as *Better Homes and Gardens, Family Circle, Essence, Latina,* and *Parent.*

ETHNOGRAPHIC FIELDWORK

Ethnography made up the bulk of my research. Although I officially initiated my scholarly interest in Day of the Dead in the fall of 2000, I had attended Day of the Dead exhibits in San Diego and Tijuana in the fall of 1999. My ethnographic work entailed attending events (exhibits, festivals, etc.), where I spent several hours (or days) per event observing the environment and participant interactions. When possible, I attended the same event (e.g., a multiday festival or long-running exhibit) on more than one day to observe and take notes. For those events within easy geographic distance, I attended the same events each year, noting changes and continuities over time. My other major ethnographic activity was the conducting of in-depth, recorded interviews with event participants, which I later explain in more detail.

My fieldwork expanded geographically through the years. In the fall of 2000, I attended events in the towns of San Ysidro, Chula Vista, Escondido, Solana Beach, and Oceanside, California, as well as in the cities of San Diego and Tijuana. In the fall of 2001, along with attending the annual events in the previously named communities, I attended several Day of the Dead exhibits, workshops, and altar-making ceremonies in Los Angeles. In the fall of both 2002 and 2003, after attending exhibits and events in San Diego and Los Angeles, I flew to San Francisco to attend the annual Day of the Dead procession on November 2 in the Mission District, spending two weeks visiting and photographing numerous Day of the Dead exhibits in Bay Area community centers, schools, universities, galleries, restaurants, and stores, as well as interviewing artists, curators, staff, students, retailers, and teachers involved in these exhibits/activities.

In the fall of 2003, I participated (from October 26 to November 1) in the weeklong, binational Day of the Dead Border Pilgrimage, spanning the border regions of California, Arizona, New Mexico, and Texas. Participation in this event allowed me to augment my previous research in California with Day of the Dead events and exhibits from southern Arizona, New Mexico, and Texas. It also gave me an opportunity to informally interview participants from the caravan contingency and the hosting churches, universities, social service agencies, community centers, and arts organizations along the way.

In the fall of 2004 and 2005, I attended numerous Day of the Dead exhibits, processions, vigils and other activities in San Diego County (including in downtown San Diego and the cities of Oceanside, Vista, Solana Beach, Escondido, La Jolla, and Chula Vista), as well as several areas of Los Angeles. From 1999 to 2007, I attended a variety of workshops on making sugar skulls, altars, paper flowers, skeleton arts and crafts, masks, and "dead bread." In most cases, I was a participant observer, enjoying the activities while taking notes on the subjects being taught and on the reactions of other participants, their gender, age, race, ethnicity, and other observations. In addition, I took photos at workshops, asking individuals for permission at smaller events or simply taking panoramic shots at larger events.

Because Day of the Dead activities in the United States take place over an extended season of four to eight weeks, it was possible to attend numerous events in different cities each year. Many community centers and museums hold their major Day of the Dead celebrations on the official dates of November 1 or 2, but many others hold their celebrations the week before (or less commonly the week after) because of scheduling difficulties or attempts not to conflict with other well-known Day of the Dead events. (When November 1 and 2 fall on weekdays, most organizations hold their main celebrations on either the preceding or following weekend, to attract larger crowds than would attend on a weekday.) This also made it logistically easier for me to attend multiple events, because not all occurred on the same dates. With assistance from Google.com and Mapquest, I plotted a monthly "schedule" of events to attend each year, organized by dates and geographical distances, and tried to group events in the same cities whenever possible. Each Saturday and Sunday during Muertos season (weekends are especially popular times for workshops and festivals), I attended multiple events, participating in additional exhibits, film screenings, poetry nights, or public lectures during the weekdays. Each year, my friends and family came to expect that I would be unavailable for socializing during the fall weekends due to my Day of the Dead research activities. In the end, I attended more than 150 exhibits and events over eight years (not counting San Diego events I attended casually in 1999, when I had not officially begun my research).

Because I was a transplant from Boston, I was initially unfamiliar with the arts and social service organizations of southern California. (However, I was familiar with community centers and organizations in the Bay Area from having lived there in the 1980s.) During my first year of research, I learned about Day of the Dead events by reading the calendar sections of local newspapers. After meeting more people and becoming familiar with the area, I learned of additional events through word of mouth and from Web sites and from getting the mailing lists of local community centers, galleries, museums, immigrant rights groups, tourist bureaus, and folk art stores. At each event I attended, I took photographs and field notes that were elaborated upon and typed when I returned to my office.

I began my informant interviews by contacting past and present staff at the pioneering Latino art galleries: the Mission Cultural Center for Latino Arts and La Galería de la Raza in San Francisco and Self Help Graphics in Los Angeles. After contacting key personnel affiliated with each site by a letter written on official university stationery, I scheduled dates for face-to-face, tape-recorded interviews via follow-up phone calls and e-mails. All of the organization directors and exhibit curators I contacted for my first round of formal interviews had been involved in their respective organization's earliest Day of the Dead celebrations, and each possessed an average of thirty years of experience working in the Latino arts community. They were able to provide detailed oral histories about Day of the Dead at their institutions and offer views on the ritual's social and political significance. All identified themselves as being long-term activists in the Chicano Movement.[1] After initial interviews with these Day of the Dead "founders," I began interviewing staff from other organizations that had more recently begun to celebrate Day of the Dead. At the end of every interview with staff from these sites, I asked for suggestions of others who might be willing to be interviewed in the future. This yielded recommendations of artists, board members, and program constituents whom I later contacted, allowing me to use "snowball" or network sampling to acquire the bulk of my interview subjects. With the exception of one agency that never responded to my letters and phone calls, nearly everyone I contacted was willing to be interviewed. A few individuals who were unable to meet with me because of time constraints e-mailed their comments or gave me names of other people I could contact in their place.

In total, I conducted seventy-eight interviews (averaging an hour and a half each) with Day of the Dead participants in San Diego County, Los Angeles, and the San Francisco Bay Area. Interviewees included neighborhood residents active in their local community centers or churches, high school and college students, public school teachers and university professors, artists, political activists, librarians, clergy, community development specialists, and vendors of Day of the Dead products. I also held many informal conversations with Day of the Dead celebrants whom I met at altar exhibits, processions, and workshops (some of whom I later interviewed formally).

Because Day of the Dead is one of the busiest periods of the year for those who organize these celebrations and exhibits, I avoided scheduling interviews during this time. Most of my interviews were conducted in the period from January to September, after the rush of the winter holiday season and before the major Day of the Dead activities began.[2] Interviews were conducted in English or Spanish, according to a subject's preference. I met people in their location of choice, which was often a local café, but was sometimes their home or office. In three cases, I conducted formal interviews over the phone because of geographic distances. Interviewees were Mexican Americans and other U.S.-born Latinos; Mexican immigrants (both Mestizos and Indigenous Mixtecs who hailed from urban and rural areas of Mexico); Central Americans from El Salvador, Nicaragua, and Guatemala (including Indigenous Maya: K'iché, Kaqchikel, and Mam); several immigrants from South America (Ecuador, Colombia, Argentina, Bolivia, Brazil); and non-Latino Day of the Dead afficionados. In contrast to most of the immigrants interviewed, the majority of U.S. Latinos were college educated.

The non-Latinos I interviewed were predominantly middle-class, college-educated individuals such as teachers, professors, artists, political activists, or small-scale entrepreneurs. Some described themselves as living alternative lifestyles (e.g., gays and lesbians, neo-pagans, or goths), actively exploring and adopting alternative worldviews. Others were people not affiliated with academia, politics, or the art world, including elderly retirees, military families, and middle-and working-class people generally classified as "Middle America." Many from the latter group learned about Day of the Dead through local newspapers, television, and especially their children's involvement with the celebration at school. Another group of non-Latinos celebrating Day of the Dead were those whose religious congregations held Day of the Dead services, processions, or altar-making events.

To contact non-Latino Day of the Dead participants, I began by interviewing people I knew personally who celebrated Day of the Dead, and asked them to recommend others whom I might contact. Another way I acquired interviewees was by striking up conversations with people at Day of the Dead events that had a noticeably high proportion of non-Latinos in attendance, including the Campo Santo cemetery event in San Diego's Old Town State Park, the Mission District's Day of the Dead Procession in San Francisco, the Participatory Offering at the California Center for the Arts in Escondido, and the Universalist Unitarian Day of the Dead Celebration in Solana Beach, California. Although the majority of non-Latino participants were White, this group also included people of Asian, African American, Native American, Middle Eastern and East Indian descent. Subjects ranged in age from the early twenties to the midseventies, with the majority falling between twenty-four and sixty years old. Everyone quoted by name in this book gave me written permission to do so. The quotes of individuals who did not want their names revealed, or who could not be reached in time for publication, are listed with simply the interview date and location.

Throughout my research, I was deeply impressed by the enthusiasm and candor with which subjects were willing to talk with me, and touched by how many people went out of their way to be helpful, despite the fact that many were extremely busy. Interviews scheduled to be sixty minutes long often lasted much longer. Repeatedly, I received e-mails, postcards, or phone calls from people I interviewed, inviting me to attend upcoming Day of the Dead (and other cultural) events in subsequent months or years. The owner of a San Diego store specializing in Day of the Dead crafts invited me to sit in on the sugar-skull workshops she held during the 2003 season so that I could observe, photograph, and casually talk with participants about their perspectives on Day of the Dead. More than once I was invited to attend planning meetings of community organizations as they prepared for their upcoming Day of the Dead celebrations. Twice, at the end of interviews, the person being interviewed literally walked me to a neighbor's home to introduce me so that I could interview the neighbor as well.

Most sponsoring organizations generously offered to share with me their Day of the Dead press kits, archival photos, flyers, educational curricula, guest book comments, and other information. Three organizations gave me computer discs of photos, sponsorship information, and promotional materials from their celebrations. Some artists and curators spent additional hours, aside from the formal interview, showing me photos of previous years' events. In one case, a curator spent nearly three hours showing me slides of Day of the Dead exhibits he had organized over thirty years, then drove me to my next appointment so I wouldn't be late! Without my asking, two agency directors offered me office space to use as a base for interviewing artists and community people. Other interviewees gave me photocopies of articles they thought would be useful for my project, recommended books for me to read, or offered to make their personal photos available for my research. An artist I had never met before concluded our interview by giving me a small Day of the Dead clay sculpture she made, and the owner of a folk art store made a gift to me of a book on Mexican altars, hoping it would be useful to my work. Decorating my home and office today are Day of the Dead T-shirts, posters, and other souvenirs given to me by artists and staff at nonprofit organizations after I had interviewed them for this book.

It was important for me to treat my research subjects as fellow humans. Because of the common connotation of the term "informant," with "traitor" or "spy," I deviated from standard social science terminology and instead referred to the people I interviewed as "interviewees." And, although it is not standard protocol, I followed up on every formal interview by sending a handwritten thank you card. As an additional way of expressing my gratitude, I offered to let interviewees know about my future publications on the topic, and responded promptly to any requests made of me during the interviews. (In some cases, individuals requested that I send them citations of certain books or Web sites, and two people requested that I send them a typed copy of our interview transcript.) I have maintained e-mail contact with interviewees who expressed interest in staying in touch, and have sent drafts of relevant chapters to certain Chicano/a artists and academics I interviewed, who kindly offered to (and did) provide feedback on my work. Throughout this research, I could not have asked for more generous interviewees, both in terms of their time and spirit of collaboration. I am far more grateful to all of them than words can convey.

Notes

PREFACE

1. Chachayotl is the Nahuatl (Aztec) name for the pod seeds of the giant thevetia tree, which grows throughout central Mexico, Central America, and South America. The seeds have been used as musical instruments since precolonial times. Personal communication with Mario E. Aguilar, founder of the San Diego–based Danza Azteca troupe, Mexi'cayotl, November 26, 2007.
2. Because Day of the Dead extends over a period of several weeks (as opposed to just one day, as in the case of Cinco de Mayo) and is increasingly celebrated by diverse Latino populations in addition to Mexican Americans, it is the largest Latino festivity in the United States.

INTRODUCTION

1. The term "Chicano/a" began to be widely used in the 1970s to describe Mexican Americans who were engaged in struggles to confront the widespread racism and exploitation facing the U.S. Mexican community. Along with political advocacy work, Chicano activists, many of whom were artists, engaged in cultural work such as *teatro popular*, performance art, mural painting, poetry, and ritual celebrations intended to honor Mexican culture.
2. This information is based on personal conversations with dozens of Mexican Americans, including college professors, librarians, and directors of social service agencies. Morrison (1992) also notes this lack of awareness in her research.
3. In *The Enormous Vogue of Things Mexican* (1992), Helen Delpar provides detailed descriptions of early cultural exchanges between U.S. and Mexican artists, writers, and social scientists from 1920 to 1935, noting that in these early years, more Guggenheim fellows and other U.S. researchers went to Mexico than to any other Latin American country.
4. Personal discussion with Professor Celso Lara, director of the Center for Folkloric Studies, University of San Carlos, Guatemala City, July 19, 2001; and also in Lara (2002).
5. See Tagg (1990), Garnham (1992), Negus (1996), Mattern (1998, 1999), and Mattern et al. (2002) for detailed discussions on the role of cultural practices in creating alternative public spheres for political communication.
6. A Google search done on August 10, 2008, using the term "The Days of the Dead," produced some 28.6 million entries.

CHAPTER 1   AN ANCIENT AND MODERN FESTIVAL

1. Although they share certain beliefs, rituals, and the same name, these celebrations are distinct from Mexico's. The literal expression "Day of the Dead" is used in Italy

(il Giorno dei Morti), France and Haiti (Jour des Morts), Portugal and Brazil (Día dos Mortos), and the Philippines (Araw ng mga Patay).

2. Throughout Latin America, including in Mexico, the holiday is described by a variety of names, including Todos Santos or La Fiesta de Todos los Santos (Feast of All Saints' Day), El Día de los Difuntos (Day of the Deceased); El Día de los Fieles Difuntos (Day of the Faithful Departed), La Fiesta de los Finados (Feast of the Deceased), and El Día de las Ánimas Benditas (Day of the Blessed Souls). In Mexico, the expression El Día de los Muertos is common in urban areas, while Todos Santos or El Día de los Difuntos are common in rural areas. In Central and South America, where the expression El Día de los Muertos is considered brusque and rather disrespectful, Todos Santos and El Día de los Difuntos are most often used.

3. Susan Ruiz Patton, Day of the Dead comes to life, *The Plain Dealer*, November 6, 2000, 1B; Maria Elena Baca, Days of the Dead, *Star Tribune*, November 4, 2000, 5B; Karen Pierce Gonzalez, Días de Muertos ceremony keeps Latinos linked to past, *San Francisco Chronicle*, October 27, 2000, 6.

4. According to news articles I collected, Day of the Dead is now celebrated in Omaha, Kansas City, Seattle, Cincinnati, Anchorage, Milwaukee, New Orleans, Atlanta, and elsewhere.

5. Robert Lopez, Family reunions mark Day of the Dead ritual, *Houston Chronicle*, November 2, 2003, A35; Mr. and Mrs. Bones request the pleasure of your company, *L.A. Weekly*, October 24, 2003, calendar, 61; Javier Erik Olvera, A celebration of life on Day of the Dead, *Rocky Mountain News*, November 3, 2003, 5A.

6. In the Catholic Church, novenas are devotions usually consisting of group prayer for nine consecutive days, carried out particularly during times of mourning or when special heavenly assistance is sought. Prayer beads, known as rosary beads, may be used during novenas.

7. Around the world, folk Catholicism entails practices that are commonly carried out but are not officially required or condoned by the Catholic Church.

8. Placing special foods (particularly sweets and breads) on tombs and erecting ancestor altars have been practiced for centuries in places as disparate as Spain (Carmichael and Sayer 1991), Japan (Ivy 1995), Russia (Propp 1987, 236), Ireland (Santino 1994, 1998), Egypt (Richards 2005), and North America (Brandes 1997, 285–286). Altars seen today at Asian restaurants, African American Kwanzaa celebrations, Japanese Obone, Jewish Succoth, and Catholic churches still include flowers, incense, bread, beverages, fruits, or other symbols of life and regeneration.

9. Mole is any of a variety of sauces made of a combination of ground chile peppers, nuts, spices, chocolate, and other ingredients, commonly served over cooked poultry and meats. Although the name "mole" is most commonly used in Mexico, variations of these types of sauces are prepared throughout Mesoamerica; *Pulque* is a Mesoamerican alcoholic drink made of the fermented agave plant, *maguey*; Quinoa is a grain commonly eaten in the Andean countries of South America.

10. Known in Mexico by the Nahuatl name *cempasúchil*, and in Central America as *flor de muerto* or *flor de sempa*, marigolds have been used in Mesoamerica since pre-Columbian times to honor the dead. The same flower is used to honor the dead and decorate graves in India, Russia, and Haiti.

11. Certain beliefs and customs associated with Samhain continued long after Ireland was converted to Christianity. As recently as the mid-twentieth century, for example, arrangements of bread and produce were prepared in rural Irish homes on November 1, "a bowl of water placed on the table," and the doors left unlatched "to let in the souls" (Santino 1998, 90).

12. For young women in traditional Maya villages, this occasion is one of the few times of the year when they can walk unaccompanied at night while parents are busy

talking with neighbors and tending graves. There are jokes, based on reality, about young people losing their virginity in the cemeteries during the Days of the Dead. Similar courtship behaviors occurred during U.S. Memorial Day/Decoration Day celebrations in the mid-twentieth century (Santino 1994, 120).

13. For detailed discussions of the ritual renewal of family and community ties during Day of the Dead in South America, Mexico, and Mixtec communities in the United States, see Buechler (1980), Nutini (1988), and Bade (1997), respectively.

14. Celebrants requesting help from the dead is depicted in the 1990 documentary film, *La Ofrenda: The Days of the Dead*, directed by Lourdes Portillo and Susana Muñoz.

15. The precise dates vary from place to place, but the belief that the souls of children and adults arrive on separate dates exists throughout Mexico, Central America, and the Andes region.

16. Personal discussion with resident of Morales, Izabál, Guatemala, November 5, 1999. The family reunion aspect of Day of the Dead has also been noted by Carmichael and Sayer (1991), Garciagodoy (1998), Greenleigh and Beimler (1991), Bade (1997), and Rogers (2002).

17. In Italy, sugar treats known as *ossi di morti* (bones of the dead) and cookies called *fava dei morti* (beans for the dead) are still made in Trieste, Naples, Palermo, and Sicily during November 1 and 2. In November 2002, friends from Trieste sent me bags of them in the mail.

18. The horse races are not held to honor the dead, but rather to commemorate the feast day for which the town is named. Rituals for honoring the dead (described earlier) occur simultaneously.

19. Personal observation, Guatemala, November 1991–1994.

20. Ritual begging on this day also occurs in Mexico and South America and is reminiscent of the All Souls' Day "souling" practices of England and Ireland that later migrated to the United States to become "trick or treating." The custom of donating to the poor and children on All Souls' Day was originally seen as an indirect way of providing sustenance to the souls in purgatory.

21. Personal interviews with lifelong residents of Huehuetenango, April 7, 2001. This custom also occurs in El Salvador and Mexico.

22. Personal observation, Guatemala, November 1991–1994. According to Guatemalan anthropologist, Celso Lara, the reason the dish is pickled and served cold is so it does not spoil when taken to the cemetery (2002).

23. According to a Garifuna informant from Belize (formerly a territory of Guatemala), many Belizean Garifunas prepare a special family meal on November 1 and create ancestral altars composed of foods, liquor, and clothing of the deceased (personal communication, October 30, 2007).

24. Personal interviews with Salvadoran immigrants residing in San Francisco, CA, May 2001 and October 2003. Articles and photos of the practice were also retrieved from www.ElSalvador.com on November 2, 2004.

25. Personal interview with two natives of Chinandega, Nicaragua, now residing in San Diego, CA, June 1, 2001.

26. A gambling game called "taba" was also played in Mexico in the eighteenth century (Lomnitz 2005, 297).

27. Personal interviews with residents of Quito, Ecuador, April 2001.

28. Discussions with Ecuadorians and photos taken in November 2002 documenting these activities in a cemetery in Otavalo, Ecuador.

CHAPTER 2 MEXICO'S SPECIAL RELATIONSHIP WITH DAY OF THE DEAD

1. For a detailed discussion and critique of the Mexican view of death, see Brandes (2003).
2. Known as *bombas* in Guatemala and El Salvador, these anonymous poems, typically written by university students and published in university newspapers, have provided fleeting opportunities to condemn institutionalized violence and extreme economic disparity within contexts of severe political repression. Personal observation and discussions with university students in Guatemala City and San Salvador, 1990–1994.
3. Calaveritas are now commonly sold in U.S. shops specializing in Latin American folk art and have become trendy collectors' items.
4. Today, the original social commentary of La Catrina is largely lost on the general public, and her image, endlessly reproduced on Day of the Dead promotional posters, flyers, and T-shirts in both Mexico and the United States, has acquired new meaning—a personification of Day of the Dead.
5. LaFaye notes that although Goya's characteristic expressions appear in the work of Posada, this does not necessarily imply imitation (1979, 131).
6. Eventually, as women joined their male relatives, and larger migrant communities from Oaxaca began to form in areas such as Tijuana, Indigenous-style home of rendas began to appear. In Colonia Obrera and Colonia Lomas Taurinas, neighborhoods with the largest Mixtec populations in Tijuana, families from Oaxaca have celebrated Day of the Dead in their homes since the 1980s (personal discussions with residents, Colonia Obrera and Colonia Lomas Taurinas, October 31–November 2, 2001). Aside from Mixtec enclaves, however, most residents of Tijuana were unfamiliar with Indigenous Day of the Dead practices prior to the 1990s.
7. Personal interview, Tijuana, Mexico, October 31, 2001.
8. David Gaddis-Smith, Skeletons out of the closet, *San Diego Union-Tribune*, October 31, 1999, H13.
9. Anne-Marie O'Connor, Traditions collide at Halloween, *Los Angeles Times*, October 31, 1997, Metro, A1.

CHAPTER 3 DAY OF THE DEAD IN THE UNITED STATES

1. Although West and Turner and Jasper refer to these as "Day of the Dead" observances, this term, popularized since the 1970s, was not traditionally used by most Mexican Americans, who instead referred to the holiday as All Saints' Day and All Souls Day (or used the Spanish, Todos Santos and El Día de los Difuntos).
2. When large numbers of Indigenous Oaxacans immigrated to California in the 1980s and 1990s, numbering more than sixty thousand today, they began to construct Day of the Dead altars in their homes. This is a relatively recent phenomenon and does not negate the fact that, prior to the 1970s, Indigenous-style Day of the Dead altars were not part of the average Mexican American experience. For more on the construction of Indigenous altars in private family settings among Oaxacan immigrants in California, see Bade (1997).
3. Decorating graves or home shrines with flowers, candles, and mementos on All Souls' Day has been and continues to be done by Catholics in the United States, Italy, Spain, Portugal, Brazil, Poland, France, Haiti, the Philippines, and elsewhere.
4. Before the affordability of cars, it was common for many ethnic Catholics, such as the Italians, Irish, and Polish, to bring picnics to the cemetery on All Souls' Day, Memorial Day, and other cemetery visits.
5. Personal e-mail communication with John Gonzalez, San Antonio Bureau Chief, *Houston Chronicle*, June 13, 2005.

6. Personal interview with Carmen Lomas Garza, San Francisco, California, May 25, 2006.

7. Comprehensive information on the genesis of the celebration in San Francisco, California, can be found in the doctoral dissertation of theologian Suzanne Morrison (1992). Further historical documentation and curatorial perspective on the California tradition is available in *Chicanos en Mictlán: El Día de los Muertos in California*, a museum catalog edited by Tere Romo and published by the Mexican Museum of San Francisco (2000).

8. Personal interview with Yolanda Garfias Woo, San Francisco, California, June 6, 2003.

9. Personal interview with Nancy Chárraga, San Francisco, California, June 5, 2003.

10. An example of this reappropriation is the now iconic Sun Mad poster (1982) by artist Ester Hernández—a critical spoof of the Sun Maid raisin advertisement. In support of a grape boycott organized by the UFW, the poster portrayed a smiling skeletal maid holding a basket of pesticide-laden grapes, underscoring the sickness and death facing predominantly Mexican farm workers as a result of chemical pesticides. To view the image, see Ester Hernández's home page, www.esterhernandez.com (accessed September 15, 2008).

11. Organic materials are usually prohibited in museums and art galleries to avoid bugs, rodents, or mold that could damage other collections.

12. Modeled on European debutante balls, quinceañeras are "Sweet 15" birthday parties celebrated by families in Latin America as well as by Latinos in the United States. Among Catholics, a special Mass at church is arranged for the occasion.

13. For example, each year a Catholic priest blesses the ofrendas and leads the Day of the Dead procession at El Pueblo de Los Angeles Historical Monument. In 2001, the Day of the Dead festival in Oceanside, California, began with a Catholic Mass. Aztec ceremonial dancers have performed at Day of the Dead celebrations and exhibit openings at the Oakland Museum of California, the Sherman Heights Community Center in San Diego, Chicano Park in San Diego, Self-Help Graphics in Los Angeles, and the Mission Cultural Center in San Francisco.

14. Guadalupanas are religious associations organized by Mexican and Mexican American Catholic women to provide leadership in neighborhood issues, perform charity work, and help organize the annual religious celebration of the Virgin of Guadalupe each December 12.

15. Personal interview with Tere Romo, San Francisco, California, June 2, 2003.

16. Personal interview with David Avalos, San Marcos, California, July 29, 2003.

17. Although the first Chicano Day of the Dead celebrations in Sacramento and Los Angeles included Catholic Masses and some secular Day of the Dead celebrations have included the participation of Catholic clergy (such as the annual celebration at Olvera Street in Los Angeles), most do not. The first Day of the Dead festival in Oceanside, California, in 2000, began with a Catholic Mass and the blessing of ofrendas by a priest, but this was stopped the next year due to complaints that because the event received public funding, it should not include religious activities.

18. Most Chicanos I interviewed considered Day of the Dead more Indigenous than Catholic, while Indigenous Mixtecs and Maya I interviewed called the celebration "*muy* Catolica." In Latin America, people who make Day of the Dead ofrendas are Catholic, whereas in the United States, people of any religion and no religion make them.

19. As Day of the Dead has become better understood in the United States over time, some secular celebrations are now held in cemeteries to simulate the environment of Day of the Dead in Latin America. With the exception of the annual Sacramento celebration held since 1975 at St. Mary's Cemetery, this is a relatively new

development. Recent examples include the Hollywood Forever Cemetery Day of the Dead event in Los Angeles, held since 2000; the annual Day of the Dead celebration sponsored since 2005 by Lazos America Unidos, in New Brunswick, NJ; the Day of the Dead celebration sponsored since 2004 by Mano a Mano at St. Mark's cemetery in the Bowery (New York City); the annual celebration at the Forest Hills Cemetery in Boston, sponsored since the late 1990s by La Piñata; and the annual celebration of the San Diego Historical Society, held since the late 1990s at the Campo Santo Cemetery in Old Town, San Diego.

20. The Day of the Dead calavera is now a common year-round symbol for many Chicano organizations. For example, it is the logo of the Chicano-run Calaca Press, as well as the logo for the Chicano newspaper *Voz Fronteriza*. It is found on the official Web site, letterhead, and flyers of Voz Alta, a Chicano/Latino performance space in San Diego. It is the logo on the Web site and promotional materials of the San Diego café Chicano Perk and is displayed on the Web site of the Chicano/Latino art gallery Self-Help Graphics.

21. Personal interview with an employee of a San Diego art gallery, May 29, 2003.

22. Personal communication with San Francisco sales representative, June 13, 2005.

23. In the 1970s, after decades of promoting assimilationist models, U.S. government and private foundations began funding grassroots multicultural arts and educational initiatives. This came in response to civil rights work and the resulting 1974 Ethnic Heritage Act. The new funding made it possible to conduct the kinds of workshops discussed.

24. These processions usually happen on the evening of November 1 or 2 and are often accompanied by music. Participants may wear skeletal costumes and masks or carry props such as banners, signs, cardboard coffins, or giant skeletal puppets.

25. During the years 2002–2005, this event was advertised in San Diego through newspapers, flyers, the Web, and bulletin boards at local community centers, art galleries, and cafés.

26. For examples of Day of the Dead–themed Web art, see *DNN: Dead News Network*, *Deadtime Stories*, *El Muertorider*, and other political video art by artist John Leaños at www.leanos.net (accessed October 24, 2008).

27. Personal phone interview with Macuilxochil Cruz-Chavez, October 18, 2004.

28. Personal phone interview with Mario Aguilar, November 26, 2007. Aguilar adds, "While today danzantes are called up to dance, we [Danza Mexi'cayotl] are probably the only group that doesn't dance on Día, because it isn't done in Mexico."

29. Personal e-mail communication with Tere Romo, August 13, 2007.

30. Personal conversation, San Francisco, California, November 5, 2002.

31. According to Romo and Garza, La Galería's early Day of the Dead exhibits were instrumental in popularizing Frida Kahlo, who was virtually unknown to the U.S. public in the 1970s (Romo 2000, 38; 2001, 101) and personal interview with Carmen Lomas Garza, San Francisco, May 25, 2006.

32. Personal phone interview with Amalia Mesa-Bains, July 24, 2007.

33. Personal interview with Salvador Acevedo, San Francisco, California, June 3, 2003.

34. Personal interview with Yolanda Garfias Woo, San Francisco, California, June 6, 2003.

35. Allen Myerson, Caressing life on the Day of the Dead, *New York Times*, November 4, 1995, sec. 1, 9.

36. Personal interview, Pasadena, California, June 4, 2004.

37. Personal interview, San Diego, California, April 12, 2001.

38. Personal interview, San Diego, California, April 29, 2003.

39. Personal interview with Tomás Benitez, Los Angeles, California, June 5, 2004.

40. See for example, the work of Pollak-Eltz (1989) on elaborate altars and spirit devo-

tion in Venezuela, Tweed (1997) and Brown (2003) on Cuban altars and ancestor honoring rituals, and Lara (2003, 2008) on altars in Guatemala.

41. Personal interview, San Francisco, California, June 6, 2003.

42. Originating in Italy and Spain, the custom of Christmas posadas, or musical reenactments of Mary and Joseph's search for shelter in Bethlehem (usually ending in a big party) is common throughout Central and South America. Similarly, the European customs of collecting milagros (talismans, often in the shape of human body parts, representing a miracle received or desired) and making ex-votos (decorative plaques created to show appreciation to God or a saint for granting miracles) are practiced in many parts of Latin America, but are usually referred to in the United States as Mexican rather than Latin American traditions.

43. For example, when I invited a friend from Ecuador, who was studying in San Diego, to a Chicano Day of the Dead event, she responded in surprise, "I didn't know Mexicans celebrated it too."

44. Cinco de Mayo (5th of May) is a Mexican holiday celebrating the 1862 victory of Mexicans over the French army in the Battle of Puebla. September 16 is Mexican Independence Day. This celebration in California goes back to at least the 1930s, reflecting the large immigration of Mexicans to the United States during and after the Mexican Revolution. Guelaguetzas are performances celebrating the dances of each region of Oaxaca, held every July. These celebrations in Mexico were originally sponsored by the Mexican government to stimulate national appreciation for Indigenous culture, and are now reproduced by Mexican communities in the United States.

45. Latino Studies programs have recently begun to implement Central American tracks due to requests from growing Central American student populations

46. The English translation of the title is Spirit without Boundaries. The quoted text is from Romo's curatorial statement in the *Espíritu sin Fronteras* exhibit guide, published by the Oakland Museum of California and distributed to patrons from October 12 to December 1, 2002.

47. Personal interview, Oakland, California, June 3, 2003.

48. El Día de los Muertos celebrated October 26 at Sheldon Gallery, U.S. Fed News wire service, October 15, 2007; Town president Dominick, Cicero celebrate Día de los Muertos, U.S. States News wire service, November 2, 2007; Learn about, celebrate "Día de los Muertos," U.S. Fed News wire service, October 8, 2007; See Día de los Muertos display at Indiana University, Kokomo, U.S. States News wire service, November 2, 2007; "Days of the Dead" celebration focus of museum family day, exhibit, U.S. Fed News wire service, October 2, 2007.

49. Personal observation, New Brunswick Public Library, New Brunswick, New Jersey, November 2, 2006.

CHAPTER 4 RITUAL COMMUNICATION AND COMMUNITY BUILDING

1. Eventually, so many people in the Sherman Heights community wanted to make ofrendas that the center couldn't house them all. In response, the Sherman Heights Neighborhood Cultural Council, working with the center, invited neighbors to make ofrendas on their front porches and organized ofrenda tours in conjunction with the center's two-day Day of the Dead festival.

2. Personal interview with Estela Rubalcava Klink, San Diego, California, June 12, 2003. At the time of the interview, Klink was the long-time director of the Sherman Heights Community Center, but has since retired.

3. Community centers and civic organizations serving exclusively Mexican populations tend to create specifically Mexican identity spaces during their Day of the

Dead celebrations, while centers, galleries, and organizations serving diverse Latino populations create Mesoamerican or pan-Latino identity spaces. For a discussion of similar dynamics occurring during Cinco de Mayo celebrations, see Sommers (1991).

4. Indicating the shared importance consigned to this ritual throughout the region, Guatemala, El Salvador, Honduras, Nicaragua, Panama, Bolivia, Ecuador, Brazil, Chile, Colombia, and Peru classify Day of the Dead as a national holiday on which banks, government offices, businesses, and schools are closed.

5. Personal interview, San Diego, California, October 17, 2002.

6. Personal interview with Claudio DeLucca, San Diego, California, April 24, 2003.

7. Personal interview, San Diego, California, April 24, 2003.

8. For example, during the United Farm Workers' union work of the 1960s, the shared Catholic background of Chicanos, Mexicans, and Filipinos in California allowed the Virgin of Guadalupe (representing the mother of Jesus) to serve as a unifying symbol for agricultural workers despite their linguistic and cultural differences. The historical pervasiveness of this image, to which laborers, company owners, and the general public could relate, lent moral authority to the farm workers' struggle. Particularly popular in Mexico, where she is said to have first appeared to an Indigenous man, Juan Diego, in 1531, the Virgin of Guadalupe is also the patron saint of the Philippines and all of Latin America (and is therefore widely respected in these regions).

9. Chicana artists have used the symbol of the Virgin of Guadalupe to represent the power of Latina women, privileging the strength, endurance, and authority associated with Mary over a conventional emphasis on self-sacrifice, passivity, and suffering. Examples are the 1975 print *The Virgin of Guadalupe Defending the Rights of the Xicanos* by Ester Hernández and the 1978 oil painting *Portrait of the Artist as the Virgen de Guadalupe* by Yolanda López. Additionally, writer Gloria Anzaldúa has contested Mexican patriarchal attitudes and reclaimed a historical Latina feminist presence by conflating the Virgin of Guadalupe with the powerful Aztec goddess Coatlalopeuh (Anzaldúa 1999).

10. Personal interview with Tere Romo, San Francisco, California, June 2, 2003.

11. Personal interview with Estela Rubalcava Klink, San Diego, California, June 12, 2003.

12. Election exit poll results, *Los Angeles Times*, November 8, 1994.

13. In interviews conducted with Central American immigrants in Boston and Los Angeles, a common theme was the poor treatment newcomers felt they received from "legal" Latinos who allegedly refused to share information about jobs, English classes, social services, or apartments, and in some cases were seen as exploitative employers. Information based on focus group research conducted by the author with twenty-five Central Americans in Boston in 1996 and personal interviews conducted with nine Central Americans in Los Angeles in 2000.

14. Personal observation, Day of the Dead celebration, Sherman Heights Community Center, San Diego, California, 2000–2005.

15. One of the major Indigenous populations of Oaxaca (a region of southern Mexico internationally known for Day of the Dead celebrations), Mixtecs began migrating to California in the 1970s in search of agricultural jobs. Today there are some three hundred thousand Mixtecs living in the state and about twenty-five thousand living in Oceanside, making them one of the city's largest minority populations. On the opposite coast, Mixtec migrants now account for about two-thirds of all Mexicans living in New York (R. C. Smith 2006, 15).

16. Funding came from the Mainstreets Initiative, a national economic development program designed to breathe new cultural and commercial life into economically

distressed downtown districts. Mainstreets and Day of the Dead will be further discussed in chapter 5.

17. By 2004, the number of ofrendas at the annual celebration had grown to twenty.
18. Personal interview, Oceanside, California, August 5, 2003.
19. While this event was Oceanside's first Day of the Dead procession, the All Saints' Day/Day of the Dead Mass was an annual parish event, around which the procession was planned.
20. This description is based on personal observation and conversations with participants during the event, St. Mary's Star of the Sea Church, Oceanside, California, November 1, 2001.
21. Personal interview, Oceanside, California, August 5, 2003.
22. Personal interview, Oceanside, California, August 5, 2003.
23. Mixtec is the first language of most Mixtec immigrants, some of whom do not speak Spanish.
24. Personal interview with Mary Ann Thiem, Oceanside, California, July 8, 2003.

CHAPTER 5   U.S. DAY OF THE DEAD AS POLITICAL COMMUNICATION

1. Begun in 1994, this program has greatly intensified border surveillance along the historically high-traffic urban areas of the California-Mexico border (increasing the number of patrol agents from 4,200 to more than 10,000). This has pushed crossing attempts into the less patrolled but more desolate desert and mountain areas, where more than 3,000 migrants have died to date. Major causes of death are dehydration and hypothermia, as desert temperatures can exceed 120 degrees in the day and fall below freezing at night. Shootings by bandits, human smugglers, vigilante groups, and border agents also cause migrant deaths along the border.
2. Installation entitled *Life and Death on the Line*, MCCLA Day of the Dead exhibit, October–November 2002.
3. A green card is the colloquial name for the official ID card that allows an immigrant to work legally in the United States.
4. Day of the Dead ofrendas for Digna Ochoa appeared throughout California and the Southwest after her murder. The 2002 Day of the Dead procession in San Francisco, attracting some twenty thousand people, was dedicated to her.
5. Both installations were part of the 2002 Day of the Dead exhibit at MCCLA.
6. Since its founding in 1977, MCCLA has become one of the most prominent art galleries in the Bay Area and, in fact, in the United States, attracting large and diverse audiences and regular media.
7. But, even seemingly nonpolitical activities such as creating altars and making sugar skulls in prestigious museums and other mainstream cultural spaces was itself a form of political work, exerting a Latino cultural presence where there had previously been none.
8. The activities discussed here occurred in California and the Southwest, but my review of national news coverage of Day of the Dead (discussed in the next chapter) shows that similar exhibits and events have taken place in cities across the United States.
9. Statistics on migrant deaths along the U.S./Mexican border were retrieved on October 10, 2008, from the Border Network for Human Rights, 2006 report on migrant deaths at the US Mexico border, www.bnhr.org/index.php?option= com_content&view=article&id=4:2006-report-on-migrant-deaths-at-the-us-mexico-border&catid=1:status-of-human-rights&Itemid=7; and the U.S. Government Accountability Office, August 2006 report, Illegal immigration: Border-crossing deaths have doubled since 1995; Border patrol's efforts to prevent

deaths have not been fully evaluated, www.gao.gov/docsearch/locate?searched
=1&o=0&order_by=rel&search_type=publications&keyword=border+deaths&
Submit=Search.

10. Located in Imperial County, California, Holtville is a farming town on the U.S. side of the border. I attended this event as a participant observer. Similar Day of the Dead events at the Holtville cemetery were held on November 1, 2002, and October 27, 2003. I also attended the 2003 event.

11. Expressed in the event's press release and public speeches given in the cemetery.

12. The death toll was 1,700 as of November 2001.

13. Words spoken by Claudia Smith, a Guatemalan American and immigrant rights activist with the California Rural Legal Assistance Foundation. Personal observation, Holtville, California, November 1, 2001.

14. Personal conversation with Edward Dunn, San Diego, California, November 2, 2001.

15. According to news articles and Web sites I reviewed, such activities have occurred in more than forty U.S. cities, including Phoenix, Austin, Chicago, Seattle, New York, Minneapolis, San Francisco, Los Angeles, and Washington, DC.

16. I attended this event as a participant observer from October 26 to November 2, 2003.

17. From promotional flyer, "The Border Pilgrimage," distributed from August to November 2003, www.rtfcam.org/border/pilgrimage.htm (accessed October 9, 2003).

18. Most participants were from southern California, but some traveled from Sacramento, San Francisco, San Jose, and other parts of northern California to join the pilgrimage. The group, which was roughly half Latino and half Anglo, ranged in age from the midtwenties to the midsixties, and was made up of immigrants rights activists, volunteers working with immigrants, antiglobalization activists, artists, journalists, university students, and religious persons. Some participants were members of the Interfaith Coalition for Immigrant and Refugee Rights while others were atheists.

19. Founded in 1999, with offices in Tucson, Arizona, and Nogales, Mexico, the Border Action Network provides education and advocacy regarding environmental and human rights issues affecting people on both sides of the U.S.-Mexican border.

20. Founded in 1997, Alianza Indigena is a Tucson-based advocacy group and binational alliance of O'odham, Yaqui, and Apache Indigenous peoples living on both sides of the U.S.-Mexican border in California, Arizona, New Mexico, and Texas, and in Baja California, Sonora, and Chihuahua. Working to advance Indigenous rights on both sides of the border, Alianza members oppose anti-immigrant legislation and the militarization of the border.

21. Maquiladoras are factories in Mexico built and owned by transnational corporations to take advantage of the cheap labor and lax environmental laws of Mexico.

22. Kiley Russell, Former migrant workers suing U.S., Mexico for back wages, Associated Press, March 5, 2001; Jerry Bier, $505b suit filed for Mexican workers, *Fresno Bee*, February 24, 2001.

23. Personal observation, Mayapán Women's Collective, El Paso, Texas, November 1, 2003.

24. Ofrendas honoring farm workers have been part of U.S. Day of the Dead exhibits since the 1970s and continue to be commonplace.

25. Because many Chicanos have Indigenous ancestry, the Chicano Movement has received inspiration from and felt solidarity with the cultures and struggles of Indigenous Latin American and U.S. Native American peoples.

26. Danny Lopez describes these traditions among the Tohono O'odham people in

their nation's newspaper: Kokoi Tas: All Soul's Day, *The Runner* 11, no. 12 (2004): 2; I have observed November 2 grave decorations in a Pala Indian cemetery in Pala, California, 2004.

27. The Mayas were members of the International Maya League, a nonprofit organization incorporated in 1990 by Guatemalans living in exile in the United States, working to raise awareness of the violent affects of U.S. foreign policy in Guatemala.

28. School of the Americas Watch, Day of the Dead ceremony in honor of all the Indigenous peoples killed since the arrival of Columbus, www.soaw-ne.org/daydead.html (accessed November 15, 2001).

29. Leonard Peltier is an American Indian Movement (AIM) activist allegedly framed by the FBI because of his political work, and imprisoned for more than thirty years on murder charges. Dubbed the "School of Assassins" by international human rights activists, the U.S. Army's School of the Americas trains Latin American military leaders in counterinsurgency tactics. Its graduates have been responsible for some of the worst human rights abuses in Latin America, including assassinations, torture, and massacres of civilian populations.

30. Carlos Miller, Native Americans honor their ancestors, *Arizona Republic*, October 26, 2001.

31. Personal observation, November 2, 2002. I have also seen Day of the Dead ofrendas honoring Indigenous struggles displayed at the Mexican Cultural Institute in Los Angeles (2003); the Fruitvale Day of the Dead Festival in Oakland, California (2003); the Day of the Dead Festival in Mesilla, New Mexico (2003); the Hollywood Forever Cemetery in Los Angeles (2004); the Centro Cultural de la Raza in San Diego (2004); and the Day of the Dead Festival in Oceanside, California (2004).

32. Personal observation, Sylmar, California, October 30, 2004.

33. A classic example of a ritual that was religious in its native context (Italy), but became an expression of ethnic identity in the United States is seen in *The Madonna of 115th Street*, by Robert Orsi (1985). As with Day of the Dead, completely new ethnic populations have participated in this Italian-initiated festival over time, injecting it with new purposes and meanings.

CHAPTER 6 DAY OF THE DEAD IN THE U.S. MEDIA

1. Personal interview, La Jolla, California, April 29, 2003.

2. Some recent front-page coverage includes the *El Paso Times* (November 2, 2003), *Chicago Weekly* (October 26, 2004), the *San Bernardino Sun* (November 2, 2004), the *Daily News of Los Angeles* (November 1, 2004), the Weekend Calendar supplement of the *Los Angeles Times* (October 27, 2005), and the Calendar Magazine supplement of the *Boston Globe* (November 1, 2006).

3. Many Web sites are created by teachers who freely share their Day of the Dead curricula with the public, offering instructions on how to make ofrendas, papel picado, or traditional foods. Other sites are created by artists, galleries, community centers, or university faculty (often from Spanish language or Latino Studies departments) to display photos of their Day of the Dead exhibits. Commercial sites sell Day of the Dead merchandise and tours.

4. Although Latinos are the largest minority group in the United States, representing 13.9 percent of the national population, they receive the least media coverage of any racial group (Alvear 1998, 49; Gerbner 1993; Hoffman and Noriega 2004, 6; Portales 2000, 56). A UCLA study of prime-time news, reality programming, dramas, situation comedies, sports, variety shows, cartoons, and other television genres

concludes that Latinos are "the most dramatically under-represented racial/ethnic group on prime-time." The report notes that 85 percent of all prime-time shows do not include Latinos as regular characters (Hoffman and Noriega 2004). A 1993 study by the Nieman Center for Journalism at Harvard University found that only 1 percent of national TV news focused on Latinos (Alvear 1998, 49), and research done at the Annenberg School of Communication reveals that on network news, "Latinos make up 1.5 percent of all newsmakers, only 0.3 percent of all news deliverers, and were not cited at all as sources, spokespersons or authorities—by far the lowest proportion of any other group" (Gerbner 1993, quoted in C. Rodriguez 1997).

5. The other spooky holiday, *San Francisco Chronicle*, October 26, 2003, Sunday Datebook, 17; Devorah Knaff, A lively attitude on death: Mexican Day of the Dead celebrations go beyond the ghoulish activities of Halloween, *Press-Enterprise*, Riverside, California, October 16, 1994, A16; Rich Barlow, Spiritual life, *Boston Globe*, November 16, 2002, Metro/Region, B2; Dirk Sutro, Music to go with Raza's Day of the Dead, *Los Angeles Times*, November 1, 1991, Calendar, 1; G. Pabst, Accepting death while celebrating life, *Milwaukee Journal Sentinel*, November 4, 2001, News, 2A.

6. People who are not employees, local residents, or constituents of an arts organization or community center are most likely to rely on media coverage to learn about activities.

7. Personal interview with Mary Ann Thiem, Oceanside, California, July 8, 2003.

8. Personal interview with Estela Rubalcava Klink, San Diego, California, June 12, 2003.

9. Personal interview with Rocky Behr, Pasadena, California, June 4, 2004.

10. Personal interview with René Yañez, San Francisco, California, June 3, 2003. A lack of publicity in the early days is corroborated in the research of Suzanne Morrison, who states that while working in the Mission District from 1974 to 1978, she heard nothing about Day of the Dead at La Galería de la Raza (Morrison 1992, 343).

11. Paying particular attention to the Calendar, Art Walk, and Family Guide to the Weekend sections in the *Times*, and the Events, Art, and Datebook sections in the *Chronicle*, I found that none of the autumn cultural happenings announced in any of these sections took place in the Latino neighborhoods of Los Angeles or San Francisco. Associated with crime, poverty, and violence, these neighborhoods were apparently not yet considered (by mainstream media) as suitable locations for family and arts activities.

12. Personal interview with Yolanda Garfias Woo, San Francisco, California, June 6, 2003.

13. Lon Daniels, The Day of the Dead: Mission district celebrates ancient Aztec festival, *San Francisco Examiner*, November 3, 1990, A1.

14. I surveyed nineteen journalists who have reported on Day of the Dead regarding their views on the rise of Day of the Dead in the news. Journalists were located by their bylines in articles retrieved from Lexis-Nexis. An initial sample of fifty-four journalists was contacted by e-mail. More than half of these no longer worked at the paper in question and could not be reached. Responses were received from nineteen reporters (64 percent of whom were Latinos) with journalistic experience ranging from a few years to more than thirty years in the news business.

15. Personal e-mail communication with reporter at the *Los Angeles Times*, June 10, 2005; personal e-mail communication with reporter at the *El Paso Times*, June 8, 2005; personal e-mail communication with reporter at the *Boston Globe*, June 11, 2005.

16. Personal e-mail communication with reporter at the *San Antonio Express-News*,

June 12, 2005; personal e-mail communication with reporter at the *San Diego Union Tribune*, June 22, 2005; personal e-mail communication with reporter at the *Los Angeles Times*, June 10, 2005; personal e-mail communication with reporter at the *El Paso Times,* June 8, 2005.

17. Personal e-mail communication with reporter at the *San Diego Union Tribune*, June 13, 2005.

18. Personal e-mail communication with editor at the *Houston Chronicle*, June 13, 2005.

19. Personal e-mail communication with a reporter at the *San Diego Union Tribune*, June 24, 2005; personal e-mail communication with reporter at the *San Antonio Express-News*, June 12, 2005; personal e-mail communication with reporter at the *Kansas City Star*, June 27, 2005; personal e-mail communication with reporter at the *San Francisco Chronicle*, June 20, 2005.

20. Personal interviews with Tere Romo, San Francisco, California, June 2, 2003; and Carmen Lomas Garza, San Francisco, California, May 25, 2006.

21. Personal interview with René Yañez, San Francisco, California, June 3, 2002.

22. Personal interview with Yolanda Garfias Woo, San Francisco, California, June 6, 2003.

23. Personal interview with Patricia Rodriguez, San Francisco, California, June 2, 2003.

24. Angelica Martinez, Day of the Dead: A happy day, *San Bernardino Sun*, November 2, 2001, Local, 1; Sandra Guerra-Cline, Altared states: Annual festival for the dead is whimsical, bittersweet, *Fort Worth Star Telegram*, October 13, 2001, Home, 1; Rico Mendez, A Grave Celebration, *San Francisco Chronicle*, October 30, 1997, Daily Datebook, E1; Marita Hernandez, Day of the Dead: Time to Celebrate, *Los Angeles Times*, November 3, 1985, Metro, 1.

25. Day of the Dead news coverage has helped educate the general public about Indigenous spiritual practices that assume a more fluid connection between the living and the dead than do traditional Western religions. Considered "sacrilegious" by mainstream society prior to the 1970s, Latin American Indigenous beliefs and practices now enjoy wider circulation among both Latinos and non-Latinos, in part because of media depictions of Day of the Dead as being spiritually profound. The growth of Day of the Dead in the United States also coincided with a rise in New Age spirituality, in which many baby boomers, disenchanted with traditional Western religions, sought alternative spiritual models from other cultures (to be discussed further in chapter 7).

26. Information based on my conversations with René Yañez, Tere Romo, Carmen Lomas Garza, Yolanda Garfias Woo, David Avalos, Amalia Mesa Bains, and other Chicano/a artists.

27. Personal interview with Louise Torio, San Diego, California, November 15, 2003.

28. Mainstreets is an economic development project that provides funding to economically distressed communities throughout the United States to upgrade commercial infrastructure and public image, reduce crime, build community, and improve business.

29. Library of Congress, California Local Legacies, http://lcweb2.10c.gov/diglib/legacies/CA/200002737.html (accessed October 11, 2008).

30. Personal interview with Terry Alderete, Oakland, California, November 4, 2003.

CHAPTER 7 THE EXPANDING HYBRIDITY
OF AN ALREADY HYBRID TRADITION

1. Personal interview with Johanna Hansen, Lakeside, California, July 22, 2003.

2. Personal conversation with eleven senior citizens (ages 75–92) at the DeFronzo

Senior Center, Boston, July 1, 1999. In the Catholic faith, a "happy death" is possible only by leading a morally correct life and being ready, at the moment of death, to meet a merciful judgment and ascend to heaven. Today, students at U.S. Catholic schools are no longer required to pray daily for a happy death—an example of how death no longer holds the everyday prominence it once did.

3. Starting in Oregon in the early 1990s, Death with Dignity has become a national movement that strives to gain legal rights for dying people to control their own end-of-life care.
4. Personal e-mail communication, April 21, 2001.
5. Personal interview, San Francisco, California, June 5, 2003.
6. Personal interview with Tere Romo, San Francisco, California, June 2, 2003.
7. Personal interview, San Francisco, California, June 4, 2003.
8. So enormous was the national outpouring of offerings to this unplanned commemoration at the site of the 1995 Oklahoma City bombing that the Oklahoma City Memorial Museum was opened in April 2000 to house them all.
9. According to curators I have interviewed, altar making first appeared in U.S. art galleries and museums in the context of Day of the Dead exhibits. Today, altars are widely considered an art form worthy of exhibition year-round (not simply for Day of the Dead). Recent examples are the San Diego Public Library's exhibit, "The Altars Project," shown from December 12, 2004, to January 30, 2005; the San Francisco SomArts Cultural Center's "Native Tears" altar exhibit shown from March 4 to March 24, 2004; Santa Clara University's "Images and Histories: Chicana Altar-Inspired Art," which ran from April 25 to August 4, 2000; and the "Sacred Wild" altar exhibit at the Apexart gallery in New York, running from May 25 to June 25, 2005. For more on the influence of Latino altar-making traditions in the United States, see McMann (1998), Grider (2001), and Salvo (1997). There now are also many books that teach beginners how to make altars, such as Streep (1997), Conway (2000), Owen (2006), Romero Cash (1998), Cano-Murillo (2002), and Cerwinske (1998).
10. Personal interview, San Francisco, California, June 5, 2003.
11. Personal e-mail communication with Sacramento resident, April 21, 2001.
12. Personal interview with Maribel Simán DeLucca, San Diego, California, April 24, 2003.
13. Personal interview with Nancy Chárraga, San Francisco, California, June 5, 2003.
14. Personal interview, Solana Beach, California, August 4, 2003.
15. Personal communication, Los Angeles, California, May 2, 2001.
16. Personal communication, Boston, July 12, 2001.
17. Personal e-mail communication, April 21, 2001.
18. Personal e-mail communication, April 19, 2001.
19. Personal interview with Louise Torio, San Diego, California, November 15, 2003.
20. The annual exhibit is so popular that the museum has had to extend its hours of operation to accommodate all the families, school groups, and others who want to attend. (*Corazon de la Muerte* 2005, 14).
21. Personal interview with Barbara Henry, Oakland Museum of California, June 3, 2003.
22. Personal interview with museum employee, Oakland, California, June 3, 2003.
23. I attended the celebrations in 2001, and from 2003 to 2005. Roughly half of the participants appeared to be non-Latino.
24. The Del Mar Fair is a typical all-American county fair held annually in San Diego County.
25. Personal interview with David Avalos, California State University, San Marcos, July 29, 2003.

26. Personal interview with René Yañez, San Francisco, California, June 3, 2002.
27. During her ethnographic fieldwork in San Francisco in the 1980s and 1990s, Suzanne Morrison noted that non-Latinos of various racial backgrounds enthusiastically participated in both creating and viewing altars at the Mission Cultural Center and made up the majority of annual procession participants: "Non-Latinos initially approached the November 2 procession through the barrio as 'semi-tourists' but are now full-fledged and enthusiastic participants. In fact, every year that I have been present [1984–1987; 1990–1991], Anglos have constituted the majority of the processants" (1992, 2). This situation still appeared to be the case when I attended the Mission procession during the years 2001–2004.
28. By the mid-1990s, responsibility for organizing the Mission procession was assumed by Bay Area artist Rosa de Anda and other artists from the Rescate Culture Collective. Since 2002, the collective has organized the event jointly with the Marigold Project, a group of young artists who organize the outdoor altar exhibits in Garfield Park, where the procession ends. Marigold Project members come from a variety of ethnic backgrounds, including Japanese, Lebanese, Anglo, and Mexican. Personal interviews with four members of the Marigold Project, San Francisco, California, June 5, 2003.
29. Personal interview, San Francisco, California, June 2, 2003.
30. Personal interview, San Francisco, California, June 5, 2003.
31. Personal interview, San Francisco, California, June 6, 2003.
32. Personal interview with René Yañez, San Francisco, California, June 3, 2003.
33. In 1990, I observed Halloween motifs on Day of the Dead ofrendas in the homes of Indigenous Mexicans living in villages around San Cristóbal de las Casas, Chiapas, as well as on altars made by schoolchildren in Oaxaca City. The fusion of Halloween symbols with Day of the Dead ofrendas in Mexico is also documented by Carmichael and Sayer (1991). In 2001, I observed and photographed jack-o'-lanterns on Day of the Dead ofrendas constructed in the homes of Mixtec families living in Tijuana, Mexico. In 2005, I observed and photographed Halloween items on ofrendas created at the Sherman Heights Community Center by working-class Mexican immigrants.
34. Personal interview, San Francisco, California, June 2, 2003.
35. Personal e-mail communication, October 14, 2005.
36. Personal conversation, November 5, 2002.
37. Personal interview with David Avalos, San Diego, California, February 11, 2005.
38. Personal interview, San Francisco, California, June 5, 2003.
39. Personal interview with Salvador Acevedo, San Francisco, California, June 3, 2003.
40. Pocho is a sometimes humorous, sometimes derogatory, term used by Mexicans to describe Mexican Americans, referring to their "Americanized" ways.
41. Personal interview with Carlos Von Son, San Marcos, California, July 29, 2003.
42. Personal interview with Tomás Benitez, Los Angeles, California, June 5, 2004.
43. Personal interview with René Yañez, San Francisco, California, June 3, 2003.
44. Personal interview with Carlos Von Son, San Marcos, California, July 29, 2003.

CHAPTER 8 THE COMMODITIZATION OF A DEATH RITUAL

1. Although these products used to be sold mainly in California and the Southwest, they are now available in museum gift shops in northwestern, midwestern, and eastern cities; in ethnic art stores and curio shops in college towns and gentrifying neighborhoods; and shops in New England towns, the Hamptons, and other upper-income vacation areas. According to Rocky Behr, of The Folk Tree Store, Day of the Dead greeting cards are on the rise: "We're seeing more and more cards

published specifically for the holiday. . . . We even had people from Hallmark go on our Day of the Dead tour. I don't know if they're making cards, but Chronicle [a major press] makes cards." Personal interview with Rocky Behr, Pasadena, California, June 4, 2004.

2. Prices based on personal observation and advertisements from newspapers and promotional flyers found throughout California during the years 2000 to 2005.

3. The most expensive museum admission I encountered to attend Day of the Dead activities was twenty dollars per person, charged by the Metropolitan Museum of Art in New York City in November of 2006 and 2007.

4. Sublime Stitching, www.sublimestitching.com (accessed February 14, 2005).

5. Dunlop Musical Instruments, Price grabber.com, http://musical-instruments. pricegrabber.com/guitar-accessories/m/32537425/ (accessed July 25, 2007).

6. Tim Schafer, Lucas Arts, www.lucasarts.com (accessed October 27, 2005).

7. Designer Diaries, *Game Spot*, www.gamespot.com/features/fandango_dd//11–05–97_2.html (accessed October 27, 2005).

8. AOL City Guide to San Diego, www.digitalcity.com/sandiego/bars/venue.adp? sbid=99509 (accessed March 9, 2005); http://cityguide.aol.com/sandiego/enter-tainment/on-broadway-event-ctr/v-99509 (accessed October 15, 2004).

9. Personal observation in several San Diego Starbucks and personal communication (October 14, 2004) with a representative from Starbucks corporate headquarters who told me that the company was starting a national program celebrating Day of the Dead. The San Diego displays I saw were up from late September until mid-December.

10. Personal interview with Maribel Simán DeLucca, San Diego, California, April 24, 2003.

11. Personal observation in the years 1999, 2000, 2002, 2004, and 2005. The event is one of several annual activities organized by volunteers from the San Diego Historical Society and the Save Our Heritage Organization.

12. Established in 1968, the Unity Council is a nonprofit redevelopment organization dedicated to the economic, social, and physical revitalization of Fruitvale. It promotes low-income home-buyer programs, tree plantings, building renovations, facade enhancements, transit improvements, and financial investment.

13. Personal interview with Terry Alderete, Fruitvale, California, November 4, 2003. In 2006, the festival attracted more than a hundred thousand visitors.

14. A partial list of the sponsoring businesses includes Citibank, Southwest Airlines, Albertson's and Safeway supermarkets, AT&T, Clorox, State Farm Insurance, Pacific Gas & Electric Company, MoneyGram, Wells Fargo Bank, Washington Mutual Bank, Union Bank, Starbucks, AAA, the *Oakland Tribune*, NBC, Univision, Telemundo, and numerous radio stations.

15. Artists Raul Aguilar, Olivia Armas, Yesenia Cardona, Robert Garcia, Robert Karimi, John Leaños, Noelia Mendoza, and Seline Szupinski-Quiroga were from the Regeneration Project, an initiative started by La Galería de la Raza to train and mentor young Chicano artists. The exhibit was displayed at the Yerba Buena Center for the Arts (1998), the Oakland Museum (1999), and the Mexican Museum of Art (2000).

16. Calaca is a Mexican term for skeleton.

17. Raul Aguilar, McMuertos Web site, http://home.pacbell.net/raul_art/Mcad.htm (accessed February 26, 2005). For more information on this exhibit, see Romo (2000, 122–123) and John Leaños's McMuertos Web page, www.leanos.net/projects/mcMuertos/ (accessed February 26, 2005).

18. Personal interview with John Leaños, San Francisco, California, May 29, 2006.

19. Both in the United States and in Latin America, many Latinos have Spanish, German, Italian, Jewish, Irish, or other "White" ancestries, as well as Black, Asian,

Middle Eastern, or other "non-White" ancestries, which may or may not be mixed with Indigenous ancestries. This is especially true for U.S.-born Latinos living in racially diverse cities. For a discussion of racial heterogeneity in Mexico, see Aguilar Rivera (2003).

20. For Oaxacan families, the preparation of the home ofrenda can cost more than US$400, for which they must save all year. Personal conversations with Oaxacan families living in Colonia Turcio Limas in Tijuana, Mexico (where thousands of Oaxacans have settled over the past twenty-five years), November 1, 2003. According to 2006 statistics released by the Mexican government's National Institute of Statistics, Geography, and Informatics (INEGI), 76 percent of Oaxacans live in extreme poverty. Oaxaca's average annual per capita income is the lowest in the country at US$3,400, with many families earning less than this. Information found on the INEGI Web site, Regiones socioeconómicas de México, www.inegi. gob.mx/inegi/default.aspx (accessed October 11, 2008).

21. By the early 1970s, Mexico had "fifty governmental agencies that bought, promoted, exhibited, or were otherwise related to folk art" (Espejel 1986, 9–10). These and other folk art retailers stimulated national and international interest in Mexican crafts that kept traditional craftspeople employed.

22. For more on Mexican middle-class attitudes toward rural people and folk customs, see Beezley (1987) and Friedlander (2006).

23. Rockefeller was one of the most prominent U.S. collectors to criticize divisions between "high" and "low" art, and actively advocated placing Mexican folk art in prestigious U.S. museums such as the Metropolitan Museum of Art and the New York Museum of Modern Art (in 1940).

24. For years, the Linares family's economic mainstay was the production of papier-mâché Judas effigies, popularly burned in Mexico City during Holy Week. When the burning of Judases was outlawed by the Mexican government in 1957 after a devastating fire, the family turned more of their attention to fulfilling art collectors' requests for both traditional and original papier-mâché pieces.

25. Alebrijes are fantastical animal-like creatures, first created by Pedro Linares. See Masuoka (1994) for a thorough documentation of the Linares family's papier-mâché work.

26. The process of promoting regional traditions into national ones, through media and business interests, is described in the now classic book *The Invention of Tradition* (Hobsbawm and Ranger 1983).

27. The relatively recent advent of Day of the Dead celebrations in Mexico's northern border region is also discussed by Brandes (1998a, 374) and Childs and Altman (1982, 53–60).

28. Caroline Dipping, Tijuana day trip will preview Day of the Dead holiday, *San Diego Union Tribune*, September 21, 1996, Local, B1.

29. Aspects of Day of the Dead are also commercialized in other Latin American countries. Since at least the 1980s in Guatemala, Coca-Cola, Kodak, and Nescafé have sponsored enormous kites emblazoned with corporate logos for the Day of the Dead kite festivals held in San Lucas Sacatepequez. Guatemalan supermarkets hold promotional sales of flowers, candles, and meats used to prepare the traditional Day of the Dead meal, el fiambre. In Ecuador, guaguas (Day of the Dead bread) and colada morada (a Day of the Dead blackberry drink) are advertised in shops, and the transnational company Nestlé sells instant colada morada powdered drink mix.

30. Both the Bread for the Dead Festival and altar exhibits in Tijuana area hotels, such as the Rosarito Beach Hotel a half hour south of Tijuana, are advertised in San Diego newspapers to attract U.S. tourists. I learned about this event by reading the *San Diego Reader* (a weekly cultural events publication).

31. Personal conversation with a member of the Cámara Industria Panificadora, Tijuana, October, 28, 2001.
32. Day of the Dead expected to draw million visitors, *Los Angeles Times*, October 26, 1987, 20.
33. Masses celebrate: Culture of Mexican holiday drowned out by sea of tourists, *Ventura County Star,* October 31, 2000, Life, E1.
34. Personal phone communication with Maribel Simán DeLucca, San Diego, California, March 8, 2005.
35. A Mexican-style Epcot Center that opened in 1990, Xcaret's attractions include replicas of a Mayan village; a Spanish mission; a traditional Mexican plaza with strolling musicians and craft vendors; a Mayan archeological site (with restored and replica pyramids); a museum; bird aviary; butterfly pavilion; botanical garden; aquarium; charrería (traditional horsemanship show); reenacted village festivals; jungle ecotours; spelunking, snorkeling, scuba, and "swim with the dolphins" tours; folkloric entertainment; five restaurants and "Get married in Xcaret" packages. Admission is US$49 per person. Information retrieved from www.xcaret.com (accessed March 25, 2005).
36. Translation is mine. All quotations are from El puente al paraíso (2005).
37. Personal interview with Tere Romo, San Francisco, California, June 2, 2003.
38. Personal interview with Barbara Henry, Oakland, California, June 3, 2003.
39. Personal interview, Oakland, California, June 3, 2003.
40. Personal interview with Barbara Henry, Oakland, California, June 3, 2003.
41. Personal discussion with Sam Tager, Cambridge, Massachusetts, December 16, 2003.
42. Personal phone interview with Amalia Mesa Bains, July 24, 2007.
43. Altar by Tony de Carlo, El Pueblo Gallery, Olvera Street, October 17–November 30, 2003.
44. I attended the Mesilla event in November 2003.
45. Booths also sold clothing (from India, Africa, Latin America, and the United States), toys, jewelry (including Irish and African jewelry and Italian good luck charms), newspaper subscriptions, phone cards, massages, and more.
46. Personal conversation, Fruitvale, California, November 2, 2003.

Conclusion

1. Besides the United States, Mexico, and other Latin American countries, Day of the Dead is increasingly observed in Canada. The Lexis Nexis database yields various articles in the *Toronto Star*, the *Ottawa Citizen*, and the *Globe and Mail*, about celebrations in Canadian cities. The same database has articles on Day of the Dead exhibits in London, Sydney, and Wellington. According to Tomás Benitez, there have also been Chicano-style Day of the Dead celebrations in Scotland and Japan (personal interview with Benitez, Los Angeles, California, June 5, 2004).

Methodological Appendix

1. Although all interviewees involved in the earliest Day of the Dead exhibits in California identified as Chicano/a, not all event organizers of Mexican heritage whom I later interviewed did. Many instead identified as Mexican American, Mexicano, or Latino.
2. Exceptions were during my trips to San Francisco, where I interviewed some people in November (after November 2, when activities were not as hectic), and the interviews I held with people during the November 2003 Border Pilgrimage car caravan.

Glossary

atole de maíz: A warm, thick, porridge-like corn drink made in Mexico and Central America.

calavera: The Spanish word for "skull" and also "rakish person." In Mexico, the term refers to skull-shaped toys, figurines, art, and sweets; to political and humorous skull and skeleton drawings in the style of José Guadalupe Posada; and to satirical poems created for the Days of the Dead.

calaveritas: Miniature skeleton-shaped figures, usually positioned in humorous, lifelike scenes.

Central America: The isthmus between southern Mexico and northern Colombia, comprising the countries of Guatemala, Belize, El Salvador, Honduras, Nicaragua, Costa Rica, and Panama.

Chicano/a: Also sometimes spelled "Xicano/a." This term is used as a marker of self-determination and ethnic pride by Mexican Americans who identify with the political and cultural goals of the Chicano Movement. Not all Mexican Americans identify as Chicanos. Chicanos are a subset of Mexican Americans dedicated to progressive or radical political organizing work and/or the creation of politically meaningful public art. In California and the Southwest, some non-Mexican Latinos, who identify with the Chicano Movement's history and goals, also identify themselves as Chicanos.

Chicanismo: "Chicano-ness." The term refers to Chicanos or the Chicano Movement.

Chicano Movement: Political and cultural movement that blossomed in the 1970s (with roots going back to the 1930s), celebrating Mexican American histories and cultural traditions, and working on a broad cross section of issues affecting the Mexican American and larger Latino community, including improved educational opportunities, voting and political rights, farm workers' rights, and Native American land rights. The movement seeks to address discrimination and negative stereotypes of Mexicans and other Latinos in the mass media and the general U.S. consciousness by means of political organizing, scholarship, and the creation of literary and visual art that validates

Mexican American and Latino cultures. Political transformation through collective efforts, and spiritually influenced artistic expression (particularly visual art) are major themes of the movement.

chicha: An alcoholic, fermented corn drink made in various countries of Latin America.

guaguas: In Andean countries, refers to breads baked in the shape of babies or animals.

Indigenous: For the purposes of this book, a noun or adjective referring to the autochthonous peoples of the Americas (those whose ancestors had the earliest human presence in the geographical region where they live). This includes people who identify as Indigenous, speak Indigenous languages, and live in relatively isolated Indigenous communities, as well as those who do not identify as Indigenous or live in Indigenous areas, but maintain Indigenous linguistic or cultural practices. "Indian," often used synonymously with "Indigenous," is considered an inaccurate and derogatory term by Latin American Indigenous rights organizations.

Latin America: In most contemporary usage, refers to those territories in the Americas where the Spanish or Portuguese languages are dominant.

Latino/a: A noun or adjective that refers to a person of Latin American ancestry living in the United States. This includes people of Cuban, Dominican, Puerto Rican, Mexican, Central American, or South American heritage, regardless of race. It applies to native-born U.S. citizens and Latin Americans who have immigrated to the United States. Although often used interchangeably with "Hispanic" (a word that comes from the Latin word for Spain), "Latino" is the preferred term by those who resent the historical privileging of Spanish over Latin American cultures.

Latinidad: A noun used primarily by researchers studying ethnic and racial identity, to refer to a collective sense of pan-Latino "Latin-ness."

Mesoamerica: Means "Middle America" in Greek. This term is used by archeologists, anthropologists, and ethnologists to describe a cultural zone comprising southern Mexico, Guatemala, Belize, El Salvador, western Honduras, the Pacific lowlands of Nicaragua, and northwestern Costa Rica, where Indigenous inhabitants share cultural similarities brought about by centuries of intra- and interregional interaction. These include agricultural techniques (particularly a heavy reliance on the cultivation of maize), similar calendar and numerical systems, similar pictographic and hieroglyphic writing systems, shared grammatical traits, and shared ideological and spiritual concepts.

Mestizo: Describes peoples and/or cultures that are the product of racial mixing.

ofrenda: The Spanish word for "offering." In Mexico and elsewhere, the word refers to altars laden with foods, flowers, candles, and other offerings made to deceased relatives during the Days of the Dead.

pan de muerto: Ornately shaped sweet bread baked in Mexico for the Days of the Dead.

papel picado: Intricate, brightly colored tissue-paper cutouts made to adorn homes, churches, schools, and town squares for festive occasions in Mexico and Central America.

pulque: Mesoamerican alcoholic drink made of the fermented agave plant.

References

Aguilar Rivera, J. 2003. Diatriba del mito nacionalista. *Nexos: Sociedad, Ciencia, Literatura* 25:36–40.

Alvear, C. 1998. No Chicanos on TV. *Nieman Reports* 52 (Fall): 49–51.

Anderson, B. 1991. *Imagined communities: Reflections on the origin and spread of nationalism.* New York: Verso.

Andrade, M. 2003. *Day of the Dead in Mexico: Through the eyes of the soul; Yucatán.* San Jose, CA: La Oferta Review.

Anzaldúa, G. 1999. *Borderlands: La frontera, the new mestiza.* San Francisco: Aunt Lute. (Orig. pub. 1987.)

Aparicio, F., and S. Chávez-Silverman. 1997. *Tropicalizations: Transcultural representations of Latinidad.* Hanover, NH: University Press of New England.

Appadurai, A. 1986. *The social life of things: Commodities in social perspective.* New York: Cambridge University Press.

———. 1996. *Modernity at large: Cultural dimensions of globalization.* Minneapolis: University of Minnesota Press.

Ariés, P. 1981. *The hour of our death.* New York: Knopf.

Bade, B. 1997. The dead are coming: Mixtec Day of the Dead and the cultivation of community. In *Proceedings of the 1995 and 1996 Latin American Symposia: Death, burial, and the afterlife; Landscapes and mindscapes of the ancient Maya,* ed. A. Cordy-Collins and G. Johnson, 7–20. San Diego: San Diego Museum of Man.

Bailey, J. 1979. The penny press. In *Posada's Mexico,* ed. R. Tyler, 85–122. Washington, DC: Library of Congress.

Bakhtin, M. 1984. *Rabelais and his world.* Bloomington: Indiana University Press.

Barbash, S., and V. Ragan. 1993. *Oaxacan wood carving: The magic in the trees.* San Francisco: Chronicle Books.

Baron, R., and N. Spitzer. 1992. *Public folklore.* Washington, DC: Smithsonian Institution Press.

Barron, S., S. Bernstein, and I. Fort. 2000. *Made in California: Art, image and identity 1990–2000.* Los Angeles: Los Angeles County Museum of Art; Berkeley: University of California Press.

Baumann, G. 1992. Ritual implicates "Others": Rereading Durkheim in a plural society. In *Understanding rituals,* ed. D. Coppet, 97–116. New York: Routledge.

Beezley, W. 1987. *Judas at the Jockey Club and other episodes of Porfirian Mexico.* Lincoln: University of Nebraska Press.

———. 1994. *Rituals of rule, rituals of resistance.* Wilmington, DE: Scholarly Resources.

Belasco, W. 1987. Ethnic fast foods: The corporate melting pot. *Food and Foodways* 2:1–30.

Bellah, R. 1980. *Varieties of civil religion,* San Francisco: Harper and Row.

Bendix, R. 1997. *In search of authenticity: The formation of folklore studies*. Madison: University of Wisconsin Press.

Berrin, K. 1988. *Feathered serpents and flowering trees: Reconstructing the murals of Teotihuacán*. San Francisco: Fine Arts Museum of San Francisco.

Bird, F. 1995. Ritual as communicative action. In *Ritual and ethnic identity: A comparative study of social meaning of liturgical ritual in synagogues*, ed. J. Lightstone and F. Bird, 23–52. Waterloo, Ontario: Wilfrid Laurier University Press.

Boase, T. 1972. *Death in the Middle Ages: Mortality, judgment and remembrance*. New York: McGraw-Hill.

Bonfil Batalla, G. 1996. *México profundo: Reclaiming a civilization*. Austin: University of Texas Press.

Bourdieu, P. 1984. *Distinction: A social critique of the judgment of taste*. Cambridge, MA: Harvard University Press.

Brandes, S. 1988. *Power and persuasion: Fiestas and social control in rural Mexico*. Philadelphia: University of Pennsylvania Press.

————. 1997. Sugar, colonialism, and death: On the origins of Mexico's Day of the Dead. *Comparative Studies in Society and History* 39:270–297.

————. 1998a. Day of the Dead, Halloween, and the quest for Mexican national identity. *Journal of American Folklore* 111:359–380.

————. 1998b. Iconography in Mexico's Day of the Dead: Origins and meaning. *Ethnohistory* 45:182–218.

————. 2003. Is there a Mexican view of death? *Ethos* 31 (1): 127–144.

————. 2006. *Skulls to the living, bread to the dead: The Day of the Dead in Mexico and beyond*. Malden, MA: Blackwell.

Brody Esser, J. 1988. *Behind the mask in Mexico*. Santa Fe, NM: Museum of International Folk Art.

Bronowski, J., and R. Grant. 1975. *Pedro Linares: Folk artist*. VHS. San Francisco: Works.

Brown, D. 2003. *The light inside: Abakuá society arts and Cuban cultural history*. Washington, DC: Smithsonian Institution Press.

Buechler, H. 1980. *The masked media: Aymara fiestas and social interaction in the Bolivian highlands*. New York: Mouton.

Buechler, H., and J. Buechler. 1971. *The Bolivian Aymara*. New York: Holt, Rinehart, and Winston.

Cadavál, O. 1985. The taking of the Renwick: The celebration of the Day of the Dead and the Latino community in Washington, DC. *Journal of Folklore Research* 22:179–193.

————. 1991. Making a place home: The Latino festival. In *Creative ethnicity: Symbols and Strategies of Contemporary Ethnic Life*, ed. S. Stern and J. Cicala, 204–222. Logan: Utah State University Press.

————. 1998. *Creating a Latino identity in the nation's capital: The Latino festival*. New York: Garland.

Cameron, S. 1999. Todos Santos. In *Mexican and Central American Handbook*, 705. Bath, England: Footprint Handbooks.

Cano-Murillo, K. 2002. *Making shadow boxes and shrines*. Gloucester, MA: Rockport.

Cardona, A. 1950. Muertos y muertitos. *Voz* 1:17–21.

Carey, J. 1989. *Communication as culture: Essays on media and society*. New York: Routledge.

Carmichael, E., and C. Sayer. 1991. *The skeleton at the feast: The Day of the Dead in Mexico*. Austin: University of Texas Press.

Carrasco, D. 1990. *Religions of Mesoamerica: Cosmovision and ceremonial centers*. San Francisco: Harper and Row.

———. 1998. *Daily life of the Aztecs: People of the sun and earth*. Westport, CT: Greenwood.

Carrasco, D., and E. Matos Moctezuma. 2003. *Moctezuma's Mexico: Visions of the Aztec world*. Boulder: University Press of Colorado.

Carveth, R., and D. Alverio. 1997. *Network brownout: The portrayal of Latinos in network television news*. Washington, DC: National Association of Hispanic Journalists; Washington, DC: National Council of La Raza.

Cerwinske, L. 1998. *In a spiritual style*. New York: Thames and Hudson.

Chakravartty, P., and M. Castañeda-Paredes. 2002. Globalization and critical media. *Southern Review: Communication Politics and Culture* 35:63–79.

Chen, K. H. 1998. Introduction: The decolonization question. In *Trajectories: Inter-Asia cultural studies*, ed. K. H. Chen, 1–54. New York: Routledge.

Chibnik, M. 2003a. *Crafting tradition: The making and marketing of Oaxacan wood carvings*. Austin: University of Texas Press.

———. 2003b. Crafts and commodities: Oaxacan wood carvings. In *Encuentros*, 1–13. Washington, DC: Inter-American Development Bank. Published text of lecture given at IDB Cultural Center, May 29, 2003.

Childs, R., and P. Altman. 1982. *Vive tu recuerdo: Living traditions in the Mexican Days of the Dead*. Los Angeles: Museum of Cultural History, UCLA.

Christian, W. 1981. *Local religion in sixteenth-century Spain*. Princeton, NJ: Princeton University Press.

Clark, L. S. 2003. *From angels to aliens: Teenagers, the media, and the supernatural*. New York: Oxford University Press.

Collins, C., and C. Rhine. 2003. Roadside memorials. *Omega* 47:221–244.

Coluccio, F. 1991. *Fiestas y costumbres de Latinoamérica*. Buenos Aires, Argentina: Corregidor.

———. 1995. 2 de noviembre. In *Fiestas y costumbres de la república Argentina*, 141–146. Buenos Aires: Editorial plus Ultra.

Combating the network "Brownout." 1999. *Hispanic Business* 21:46.

Conway, D. J. 2000. *A little book of altar magic*. Freedom, CA: Crossing.

Cook, T., and B. Hartnett. 2001. Splitting images: The nightly news network and the politics of the Lesbian and Gay Movement 1969–1978. In *Sexual identities, queer politics*, 286–317. Princeton, NJ: Princeton University Press.

Cooper Alarcon, D. 1997. *The Aztec palimpsest: Mexico in the modern imagination*. Tucson: University of Arizona Press.

El corazon de la muerte: Altars and offerings for Day of the Dead. 2005. An exhibition catalog. Oakland: Oakland Museum of California; Berkeley, CA: Heyday Books.

Curran, J. 1991. Rethinking the media as a public sphere. In *Communication and citizenship*, ed. P. Dahlgren and C. Sparks, 27–57. New York: Routledge.

Dahlgren, P. 1991. Introduction. In *Communication and citizenship*, ed. P. Dahlgren and C. Sparks, 1–24. New York: Routledge.

Davies, J. 1991. *Sergei Esenin: All Souls' Day*. Liverpool, England: Lincoln Davies.

Dávila, A. 1999. Latinizing culture: Art, museums, and the politics of U.S. multicultural encompassment. *Cultural Anthropology* 14 (2): 180–202.

———. 2001. *Latinos Inc.: The marketing and making of a people*. Berkeley and Los Angeles: University of California Press.

Davis, S. 1986. *Parades and power: Street theater in nineteenth-century Philadelphia*. Philadelphia: Temple University Press.

Dawson, A. 2004. *Indian and nation in revolutionary Mexico*. Tucson: University of Arizona Press.

Dayan, D., and E. Katz. 1992. *Media events: The live broadcasting of history*. Cambridge, MA: Harvard University Press.

de Coppet, D. 1992. *Understanding rituals*. New York: Routledge.

de la Fuente, B. 1974. *Arte prehispánico funerario: El occidente de México*. Mexico City: Universidad Nacional Autónoma de México.

Del Castillo, R., T. McKenna, and Y. Yarbro-Bejarano. 1991. *Chicano art: Resistance and affirmation 1965–1985*. Los Angeles: Wight Art Gallery, UCLA; Los Angeles: CARA National Advisory Committee.

Delpar, H. 1992. *The enormous vogue of things Mexican*. Tuscaloosa: University of Alabama Press.

Dewey, J. 1916. *Democracy and education*. New York: Macmillan.

———. 1927. *The public and its problems*. New York: Henry Holt.

Día de los Muertos (Day of the Dead). 1991. An exhibition catalog. Chicago: Mexican Fine Arts Center Museum.

Durand Ponte, V. 2000. *Etnia y cultura política: Los Mexicanos en Estados Unidos*. Mexico City: Regional Center for Multidisciplinary Research, Universidad Nacional Autónoma de México.

Durkheim, E. 1965. *The elementary forms of religious life*. New York: Macmillan.

Elderhostel. 2004. The world is our classroom. In *United States and international programs 2004–2005* (August). Boston, MA: Elderhostel.

Eliade, M. 1959. *The sacred and the profane*. New York: Harcourt, Brace, Jovanovich.

Errington, S. 1998. *The death of authentic primitive art and other tales of progress*. Berkeley: University of California Press.

Espejel, C. 1986. *The Nelson A. Rockefeller collection of folk art*. San Francisco: Mexican Museum and Chronicle Books.

Ewen, S. 1976. *Captains of consciousness: Advertising and the social roots of the consumer culture*. San Francisco: McGraw-Hill.

Eyerman, R., and A. Jamison. 1998. *Music and social movements: Mobilizing traditions in the twentieth century*. New York: Cambridge University Press.

Falassi, A. 1987. *Time out of time: Essays on the festival*. Albuquerque: University of New Mexico Press.

Feintuch, B. 1988. *The conservation of culture*. Lexington: University Press of Kentucky.

Fine, J. 2004. WSJ allots more space for soft news: Lifestyles sections to expand in Fall. *Advertising Age* 75:4.

Fishman, J., and H. Casiano. 1969. Puerto Ricans in our press. *Modern Language Journal* 53:157–162.

Fiske, J. 1989. *Understanding popular culture*. Boston: Hyman.

Flores, J. 1993. *Divided borders: Essays on Puerto Rican identity*. Houston: University of Texas Press.

———. 2000. The Latino imaginary: Meanings of community and identity. In *From bomba to hip hop: Puerto Rican culture and Latino identity*, 191–203. New York: Columbia University Press.

Flores, W. 1997. Citizens vs. citizenry: Undocumented immigrants and Latino cultural citizenship. In *Latino cultural citizenship: Claiming identity, space, and rights*, ed. W. Flores and R. Benmayor, 255–277. Boston: Beacon.

Flores, W., and R. Benmayor, eds. 1997. *Latino cultural citizenship: Claiming identity, space, and rights.* Boston: Beacon.

Forgacs, D., ed. 1988. *An Antonio Gramsci reader.* New York: Schocken Books.

Fox, C. 1969. Introduction. In *The Nelson A. Rockefeller collection of Mexican folk art.* New York: Museum of Primitive Art.

Fox, G. 1996. *Hispanic nation: Constructing an identity.* Tucson: University of Arizona Press.

Frank, T. 1997. *The conquest of cool: Business, culture and counterculture and the rise of hip consumerism.* Chicago: University of Chicago Press.

Fregoso, R. 1993. *The bronze screen: Chicana and Chicano film culture.* Minneapolis: University of Minnesota Press.

Friedlander, J. 2006. *Being Indian in Hueyapan.* New York: Palgrave Macmillan. (Orig. pub. 1975).

Friedman, L., ed. 1991. *Unspeakable images: Ethnicity and the American cinema.* Chicago: University of Chicago Press.

Fuente, B. 1974. Arte prehispánico funerario: El occidente de México. Mexico City: Universidad Nacional Autónoma de México

Gans, H. 1979. *Deciding what's news.* New York: Pantheon Books.

Garafalo, R. 1992. *Rockin' the boat: Mass music and mass movements.* Boston: South End.

García Canclini, N. 1987. *Políticas culturales en América Latina.* Mexico City: Grijalbo, S.A.

———. 1993. *Transforming modernity: Popular culture in Mexico.* Austin: University of Texas Press.

———. 1995. *Hybrid cultures: Strategies for entering and leaving modernity.* Minneapolis: University of Minnesota Press.

———. 2001. *Consumers and citizens: Globalization and multicultural conflicts.* Minneapolis: University of Minnesota Press.

Garciagodoy, J. 1998. *Digging the Days of the Dead.* Niwot: University Press of Colorado.

Garnham, N. 1990. *Capitalism and communication.* Newbury Park, CA: Sage.

———. 1992. The media and the public sphere. In *Habermas and the public sphere,* ed. C. Calhoun, 359–376. Cambridge, MA: MIT Press.

Gaspar De Alba, A. 1998. *Chicano art: Inside/outside the master's house; Cultural politics and the CARA exhibition.* Austin: University of Texas Press.

Geertz, C. 1973. *The interpretation of cultures.* New York. Basic Books.

Gerbner, G. 1993. *Women and minorities on television: A study in casting and fate.* Philadelphia: Annenberg School of Communication, University of Pennsylvania.

Gilroy, P. 1993. *The black Atlantic: Modernity and double consciousness.* London: Verso.

Gitlin, T. 1980. *The whole world is watching: Mass media in the making and unmaking of the new Left.* Berkeley and Los Angeles: University of California Press.

Gluckman, M. 1962. *Essays on the ritual of social relations.* Manchester, UK: Manchester University Press.

Gómez-Peña, G. 1986. A new artistic continent. In *Made in Aztlán,* ed. P. Brookman and G. Gómez-Peña, 86–97. San Diego: Centro Cultural de la Raza.

———. 1996. *The new world border: Prophecies, poems, and loqueras for the end of the century.* San Francisco: City Lights.

———. 2005. *Ethno-techno: Writings on performance, activism, and pedagogy.* New York: Routledge.

González, R. 1972. El plan espiritual de Aztlán. In *Atzlán: An anthology of Mexican American literature,* ed L. Valdez and S. Steiner, 402–406. New York: Vintage Books.

Gosnell, L., and S. Gott. 1989. San Fernando Cemetery: Decorations of love and loss in a Mexican American community. In *Cemeteries and gravemarkers: Voices of American culture*, ed. R. Meyer, 217–236. Ann Arbor, MI: UMI Research Press.

Graburn, N., ed. 1976. *Ethnic and tourist arts: Cultural expressions from the Fourth World*. Berkeley: University of California Press.

Gray, H. 1995. *Watching race: Television and the struggle for "blackness."* Minneapolis: University of Minnesota Press.

Greenleaf, R. 1971. *The Roman Catholic Church in colonial America*. New York. Knopf.

Greenleigh, J., and R. Beimler. 1991. *The Days of the Dead: Mexico's festival of communion with the departed/Los Días de Muertos: Un festival de comunión con los muertos en México*. San Francisco: Collins.

Grider, S. 2001. Spontaneous shrines: A modern response to tragedy and disaster. *New Directions in Folklore* 5:1–13

Griffith, J. 1995. *A shared space: Folklife in the Arizona-Sonora borderlands*, 13–34. Logan: Utah State University Press.

Grimes, R. 1990. *Ritual criticism: Case studies in its practice, essays on its theory*. Columbia: University of South Carolina Press.

———. 1995. *Beginnings in ritual studies*. Columbia: University of South Carolina Press. (Orig. pub. 1982.)

Gutierrez, D. 1995. *Walls and mirrors: Mexican Americans, Mexican immigrants, and the politics of ethnicity*. Berkeley and Los Angeles: University of California Press.

———. 1997. *Between two worlds: Mexican immigrants in the United States*. Wilmington, DE: Scholarly Resources.

Habermas, J. 1989. *The structural transformation of the public sphere: An inquiry into a category of bourgeois society*. Trans. T. Burger. Cambridge, MA: MIT Press.

———. 1991. The public sphere. In *Rethinking popular culture*, ed. C. Mukerji and M. Schudson, 398–404. Berkeley and Los Angeles: University of California Press.

Hackett, R. 1991. *News and dissent: The press and the politics of peace in Canada*. Norwood, NJ: Ablex.

Hall, S. 1997. *Representation: Cultural representations and signifying practices*. Thousand Oaks, CA: Sage.

———. 1998. A Tokyo dialogue on Marxism, identity formation and cultural studies. In *Trajectories: Inter-Asia cultural studies*, ed. K. H. Huang, 360–378. New York: Routledge.

Hall, S., and T. Jefferson. 1976. *Resistance through rituals: Youth subcultures in post-war Britain*. London: Hutchinson.

Hallin, D. 1994. *We keep America on top of the world: Television journalism and the public sphere*. New York: Routledge.

———. 2000. Commercialization and professionalization in the American news media. In *Mass media and society*, ed. J. Curran and M. Gurevitch, 218–235. New York: Oxford University Press.

Halter, M. 2000. *Shopping for identity: The marketing of identity*. New York: Schocken Books.

Hamill, P. 1999. *Diego Rivera*. New York: Abrams.

Hebdige, D. 1979. *Subculture: The meaning of style*. New York: Methuen.

Hinds, H., and C. Tatum, eds. 1990. *Studies in Latin American popular culture*. Minneapolis: University of Minnesota.

Hoare, Q., and N. Smith, eds. 1999. *Selections from the Prison notebooks*. New York: International.

Hobsbawm, E., and T. Ranger. 1983. *The invention of tradition*. New York: Cambridge University Press.

Hoffman, A., and C. Noriega. 2004. Looking for Latino regulars on prime-time television: The Fall 2003 season. In *Chicano Studies Research Center research report*, 1–24. Los Angeles: Chicano Studies Research Center, UCLA.

Hoover, S., and L. Clark. 2002. *Practicing religion in the age of the media: Explorations in the media, religion, and culture*. New York: Columbia University Press.

Hoover, S., and K. Lundby. 1997. *Rethinking media, religion, and culture*. Thousand Oaks, CA: Sage.

Howley, K. 2005. *Community media: People, places, and communication technologies*. New York: Cambridge University Press.

Ivory, C. 1999. Art, tourism, and cultural revival in the Marquesas Islands. *Unpacking culture: Art and commodity in colonial and postcolonial worlds*, ed. R. Phillips and C. Steiner, 316–334. Berkeley: University of California Press.

Ivy, M. 1995. *Discourses of the vanishing: Modernity, phantasm, Japan*. Chicago: University of Chicago Press.

Jackson, C. 1977. *Passing: The vision of death in America*. Westport, CT: Greenwood.

Jordan, T. 1982. *Texas graveyards*. Austin: University of Texas Press.

Kaniss, P. 1991. *Making local news*. Chicago: University of Chicago Press.

Kastenbaum, R. 1989. Dance of Death (Danse Macabre). In *Encyclopedia of death*, ed. B. Kastenbaum and R. Kastenbaum, 67–70. Phoenix, AZ: Oryx.

Kester, G. 1998. *Art, activism, and oppositionality: Essays from afterimage*. Durham, NC: Duke University Press.

Kirshenblatt-Gimblett, B. 1998. *Destination culture: Tourism, museums, and heritage*. Berkeley: University of California Press.

Klor de Alva, J. 1998. Aztlán, Borinquen, and Hispanic nationalism in the United States. In *The Latino Studies reader: Culture, economy and society*, ed. R. Anaya and F. Lomelí, 135–163. Malden, MA: Blackwell.

Kraeplin, C., and F. Subervi-Velez. 2003. Latinos in the mainstream media: A case study of coverage in a major Southwestern daily. In *Brown and black communication: Latino and African American conflict and convergence in mass media*, ed. D. Rios and A. Mohamed, 105–122. Westport, CT: Praeger.

LaFaye, J. 1979. From daily life to eternity. In *Posada's Mexico*, ed. R. Tyler, 123–140. Washington, DC: Library of Congress.

Lara C. 1996. Tradiciones Guatemaltecas para el Día de Todos los Santos. *Siglo Veintiuno*, November 1. p. 1.

———. 1998a. *Significados del Día de los Santos y de los Difuntos*. Guatemala City: University of San Carlos Press.

———. 1998b. *Tradiciones de Guatemala*. Guatemala City: University of San Carlos Press.

———. 2000. El origen de Todos los Santos y la Fiesta de los Difuntos. *La Hora*, October 30. p. 2.

———. 2002. *Fieles difuntos, santos y ánimas benditas en Guatemala: Una Evocación Ancestral*. Guatemala City: Artemis Edinter.

Lara Figueroa, C. 2003. *Fieles difuntos, santos y ánimas benditas en Guatemala: Una evocación ancestral*. Guatemala City: Artemis Edinter.

———. 2008. Tradiciones de Cuaresma en Guatemala: Huertos y velaciones populares de Cuaresma. *La Hora*, February 22. Nacionales, p. 1.

Leach, W. 1993. *Land of desire: Merchants, power, and the rise of a new American culture*. New York: Vintage.

Lee, R. 1999. *Orientals: Asian Americans in popular culture*. Philadelphia: Temple University Press.

Limón, J. 1983. Western Marxism and folklore: A critical introduction. *Journal of American Folklore* 96:34–52.

———. 1994. *Dancing with the devil*. Madison: University of Wisconsin Press.

Lipsitz, G. 1990. *Time passages: Collective memory and American popular culture*. Minneapolis: University of Minnesota Press.

———. 2001. Not just another social movement: Poster art and the Movimiento Chicano. In *¿Just another poster? Chicano graphic arts in California*, ed. C. Noriega, 71–87. Santa Barbara: University Art Museum, University of California.

Litwicki, E. 2000. *America's public holidays 1865–1920*. Washington, DC: Smithsonian Institution Press.

Llamas, V. 1989. *La muerte viva, the Day of the Dead: A living tradition*. VHS. New York: Gessler.

Lok, R. 1991. *Gifts to the dead and the living, forms of exchange in San Miguel Tzinacapan*. Leiden, Netherlands: Leiden University.

Lombardi-Satriani, L. 1974. Folklore as culture of contestation. *Journal of the Folklore Institute*. Special issue, *Folklore Studies in Italy* 11:99–121.

Lomnitz, C. 2005. *Death and the idea of Mexico*. New York: Zone Books.

Lomnitz-Adler, C. 1992. *Exits from the labyrinth: Culture and ideology in the Mexican national space*. Berkeley and Los Angeles: University of California Press.

Lopez, A. 1991. Are all Latins from Manhattan? Hollywood, ethnography, and cultural colonialism. In *Unspeakable images: Ethnicity and the American cinema*, ed. L. Friedman, 404–424. Chicago: University of Illinois Press.

Lopez, D., and Y. Espiritu. 1990. Pan ethnicity in the United States: A theoretical framework. *Ethnic and Racial Studies* 13:198–224.

Lopez, F. and D. Runsten. 2003. Mixtecs and Zapotecs working in California: Rural and urban experiences. Paper presented at the conference Indigenas Mexicanos Migrantes en Estados Unidos: Construyendo Puentes entre Investigadores y Lideres Comunitarios, UC Santa Cruz, October 11–12, 2002. Los Angeles: North American Integration and Development Center, School of Public Policy and Social Research, UCLA.

Lukes, S. 1977. Political ritual and social integration. In *Essays in social theory*, 52–73. New York: Macmillan.

Lukic, R., and M. Brint. 2001. *Culture, politics and nationalism in the age of globalization*. Quebec City: University of Laval.

MacAloon, J. 1984. Olympic games and the theory of spectacle in modern societies. In *Rite, drama, festival, spectacle: Rehearsals toward a theory of cultural performances*, 241–280. Philadelphia: Philadelphia Institute for the Study of Human Issues.

MacAloon, J., M. de Moragas, and M. Llines. 1996. *Olympic ceremonies: Historical continuity and cultural exchange*. Barcelona, Spain.

Marchi, R. 2006. El Día de los Muertos in the USA: Cultural ritual as political communication. In *Spontaneous shrines and the public commemoration of death*, ed. J. Santino, 261–283. New York: Palgrave.

———. 2007. Day of the Dead as a new U.S. holiday. In *Religion, media, and the marketplace*, ed. L. Clark, 280–307. New Brunswick, NJ: Rutgers University Press.

Marciel, D., and M. Herrera-Sobek. 1998. *Culture across borders: Mexican immigration and popular culture*. Tucson: University of Arizona Press.

Marcuse, H. 1969. *An essay on liberation*. Boston: Beacon.

Martín-Barbero, J. 1993. *Communication, culture and hegemony: From the media to mediations*. Newbury Park, CA: Sage.

Martínez Nova, C. 2003. The "culture" of exclusion: Representations of Indigenous women street vendors in Tijuana, Mexico. *Bulletin of Latin American Research* 22 (3): 249–268.

Masuoka, S. 1990. Calavera miniatures: Political commentary in three dimensions. *Studies in Latin American Popular Culture* 9:263–278.

———. 1994. *En calavera: The papier-mâché art of the Linares family*. Los Angeles: Fowler Museum of Cultural History, UCLA.

Mattelart, A. 1979. *Multinational corporations and the control of culture: The ideological apparatuses of imperialism*. Sussex: Harvester; Atlantic Highlands, NJ: Humanities.

Mattern, M. 1997. Let the good times unroll: Music and race relations in southwest Louisiana. *Black Music Research Journal* 17:159–168.

———. 1998. Cajun music, cultural revival: Theorizing political action in popular music. *Popular Music and Society* 22:31–48.

———. 1999. John Dewey, art and public life. *Journal of Politics* 61:54–75.

Mattern, M., J. Gregory, A. Lewton, S. Schmidt, and D. Smith. 2002. Body politics with feeling: The power of the clothesline project. *New Political Science* 24 (3): 433–448.

Mauss, M. 1967. *The gift: Forms and functions of exchange in archaic societies*. New York: Norton.

McDannell, C. 1995. *Material Christianity: Religion and popular culture in America*. New Haven, CT: Yale University Press.

McIlwain, C. 2005. *When death goes pop: Death, media and the remaking of community*. New York: Lang.

McMann, J. 1998. *Altars and icons: Sacred spaces in everyday life*. San Francisco: Chronicle.

Medina, L. 1994. Días de Muertos da puebla a Los Angeles: Migrazione e rigenerazione identitaria di un complesso rituale. *Religioni e Societa* 18:6–23.

Medina, L., and G. Cadena. 2002. Días de Muertos: Public ritual, community renewal, and popular religion in Los Angeles. In *Horizons of the sacred: Mexican traditions in U.S. Catholicism*, ed. T. Matovina and G. Riebe-Estrella, 69–94. Ithaca, NY: Cornell University Press.

Metcalf, P., and R. Huntington. 1991. *Celebrations of death: The anthropology of mortuary ritual*. New York: Cambridge University Press.

Meyer, R., ed. 1989. *Cemeteries and gravemarkers: Voices of American culture*. Ann Arbor, MI: UMI Research Press.

Mills, K., and W. Taylor. 1998. *Colonial Spanish America: A documentary history*. Wilmington, DE: Scholarly Resources.

Milne, J. 1965. November: All saints and all souls. In *Fiesta time in Latin America*, 162–172. Los Angeles: Ritchie.

Mindich, D. 2005. *Tuned out: Why Americans under 40 don't follow the news*. New York: Oxford University Press.

Molina Guzmán, I. 2006. Mediating Frida: Negotiating discourses of Latina/o authenticity in global media representations of ethnic identity. *Critical Studies in Media Communication* 23 (3) 232–251.

Molina Guzmán, I., and A. Valdivia. 2004. Brain, brow, and booty: Latina iconicity in U.S. popular culture. *Communication Review* 7:205–221.

Monsiváis, C. 1987. Look death, don't be inhuman: Notes on a traditional and industrial myth. In *El Día de los Muertos: The life of the dead in Mexican folk art*, ed. M. Pomar, 9–16. Fort Worth, TX: Fort Worth Art Museum.

Moore, S., and B. Myerhoff. 1977. *Secular ritual*. Assen, Netherlands: Van Gorcum.

Morrison, S. 1992. Mexico's Day of the Dead in San Francisco, California. PhD diss, Theology Department, UC Berkeley.

Mosco,V., and H. Schiller. 2001. Introduction: Integrating a continent for a transnational world order. In *Continental order? Integrating North America for cybercapitalism,* ed. V. Mosco and H. Schiller, 1–34. Lanham, MD: Rowman and Littlefield.

Mosquera, G. 1996. *Beyond the fantastic: Contemporary art criticism from Latin America.* Cambridge, MA: MIT Press.

Navarette, C. 1982. *San Pascualito Rey y el culto a la muerte en Chiapas.* Mexico City: Universidad Nacional Autónoma de México.

Negus, K. 1996. Globalization and the music of the public spheres. In *Globalization, communication, and transnational civil society,* ed. S. Braman and A. Sreberny-Mohammadi, 179–198. Cresskill, NJ: Hampton.

Noriega, C., ed. 2001a. *Chicano Studies reader: An anthology of Aztlán, 1970–2000.* Los Angeles: Chicano Studies Research Center, UCLA.

———, ed. 2001b. *¿Just another poster? Chicano graphic arts in California.* Santa Barbara, CA: University Art Museum, University of California.

Noriega, C., and A. López, eds. 1996. *The ethnic eye: Latino media arts.* Minneapolis: University of Minnesota Press.

Nutini, H. 1988. *Todos santos in rural Tlaxcala: A syncretic, expressive, and symbolic analysis of the cult of the dead.* Princeton, NJ: Princeton University Press.

Oboler, S. 1995. *Ethnic labels: Latino lives.* Minneapolis: University of Minnesota Press.

Omi, M., and H. Winant. 1993. The Los Angeles "race riot" and contemporary U.S. politics. In *Reading Rodney King: Reading urban uprising,* ed. R. Gooding-Williams, 97–114. New York: Routledge.

Orsi, R. 2002. *The Madonna of 115th Street: Faith and community in Italian Harlem 1880–1950.* New Haven, CT: Yale University Press.

Owen, C. 2006. *Crafting personal shrines: Using photos, mementos and treasures to create artful displays.* New York: Sterling.

Padilla, F. 1985. *Latino ethnic consciousness: The case of Mexican Americans and Puerto Ricans in Chicago.* Notre Dame, IN: University of Notre Dame Press.

———. 1990. Latin America: The historical base of Latino unity. *Latino Studies Journal* 1:7–27.

Paredes, A. 1993. *Folklore and culture on the Texas-Mexican border.* Austin: University of Texas Press.

Paz, O. 1981. *The labyrinth of solitude.* New York: Grove.

Pollak-Eltz, A. 1989. *Las ánimas milagrosas en Venezuela.* Caracas, Venezuela: Fundación Bigott.

Pomar, M. 1987. *El Día de los Muertos: The life of the dead in Mexican folk art.* Fort Worth, TX: Fort Worth Art Museum.

Portales, M. 2000. *Crowding out Latinos: Mexican Americans in the public consciousness.* Philadelphia: Temple University Press.

Portes, A., and R. Rumbaut. 2001. *Legacies: The story of the immigrant second generation.* Berkeley: University of California Press.

Portillo, L., and S. Muñoz. 1990. *La ofrenda: The Days of the Dead.* VHS. San Francisco: First Run Features.

Prior, M. 2003. Any good news in soft news? The impact on soft news preference on political knowledge. *Political Communication* 20:149–171.

Propp, V. 1987. The commemoration of the dead. In *Time out of time: Essays on the festival,* ed. A. Falassi, 236–260. Albuquerque: University of New Mexico Press.

El puente al paraíso: Un vistazo al más allá desde Xcaret. 2005. *Paquetes Gran Plan* 10 (Winter): 24–25. The official flight magazine of Aero Mexico.

Quiroga, J. 1997. Hispanic voices: Is the press listening? In *Latin looks: Images of Latinas and Latinos in the US media*, ed. C. E. Rodríguez, 36–55. Boulder, CO: Westview.

Ramírez Berg, C. 2002. Categorizing the other: Stereotypes and stereotyping. In *Latino images in film*, 13–37. Austin: University of Texas Press.

Reuter, J. 1979. The popular traditions. In *Posada's Mexico*, ed. R. Tyler, 59–84. Washington, DC: Library of Congress.

Ricard, R. 1982. *The spiritual conquest of Mexico*. Berkeley: University of California Press.

Richards, J. 2005. *Society and death in ancient Egypt: Mortuary landscapes of the Middle Kingdom*. New York: Cambridge University Press.

Ricourt, M., and R. Danta. 2003. *Hispanas de Queens: Latino panethnicity in a New York neighborhood*. Ithaca, NY: Cornell University Press.

Rochfort, D. 1993. *Mexican muralists: Orozco, Rivera, Siquieros*. San Francisco: Chronicle.

Rodriguez, A. 1999. *Making Latino news: Race, language, class*. Thousand Oaks, CA: Sage.

Rodriguez, C., ed. 1997. *Latin looks: Images of Latinos and Latinas in the U.S. media*. Boulder, CO: Westview.

Rogers, N. 2002. *Halloween: From pagan ritual to party night*. New York: Oxford University Press.

Romero Cash, M. 1998. *Living shrines: Home altars of New Mexico*. Santa Fe: Museum of New Mexico Press.

Romo, T., ed. 2000. *Chicanos en Mictlán: El Día de los Muertos in California*. San Francisco: Mexican Museum of San Francisco.

———. 2001. Points of convergence: The iconography of the Chicano poster. In *¿Just another poster? Chicano graphic arts in California*, ed. C. Noriega, 91–115. Santa Barbara: University Art Museum, University of California.

———. 2002. *Espíritu sin fronteras*. Exhibit guide. Oakland: Oakland Museum of California.

Rosaldo, R. 1994a. Cultural citizenship and educational democracy. *Cultural Anthropology* 9 (3): 402–411.

———. 1994b. Cultural citizenship in San Jose, California. *Polar* 17 (2): 57–63.

———. 1994c. Social justice and the crisis of national communities. *Colonial discourse/postcolonial theory*, ed. F. Barker, P. Hulme, and M. Iversen, 239–252. Manchester, UK: Manchester University Press.

Rosaldo, R., and W. Flores. 1997. Identity, conflict, and evolving Latino communities: Cultural citizenship in San Jose, California. In *Latino cultural citizenship: Claiming identity, space, and rights*, ed. W. Flores and R. Benmayor, 57–96. Boston: Beacon.

Rose, T. 1994. *Black noise: Rap music and black culture in contemporary America*. Middletown, CT: Wesleyan University Press.

Rothenbuhler, E. 1998. *Ritual communication: From everyday conversation to mediated ceremony*. Thousand Oaks, CA: Sage.

Ryan, C. 1991. *Prime time activism: Media strategies for grassroots organizing*. Boston: South End.

Salvo, D. 1997. *Home altars of Mexico*. Santa Fe: University of New Mexico Press.

Sanchez, G. 1993. *Becoming Mexican American: Ethnicity, culture, and identity in Chicano Los Angeles, 1900–1945*. New York: Oxford University Press.

Santa Ana, O. 2002. *Brown tide rising: Metaphors of Latinos in contemporary American public discourse*. Austin: University of Texas Press.

Santino, J. 1988. The tendency to ritualize: The living celebrations series as a model for cultural presentation and validation. In *The conservation of culture: Folklorists and the public sector*, ed. B. Feintuch, 118–131. Lexington: University Press of Kentucky.

———. 1994. *Halloween and other festivals of death and life*. Knoxville: University of Tennessee Press.

———. 1998. *The hallowed eve: Dimensions of culture in a calendar festival in northern Ireland*. Lexington: University Press of Kentucky.

———. 2004. Performative commemoratives, the personal and the public: Spontaneous shrines, emergent ritual, and the field of folklore. *Journal of American Folklore* 117 (466): 363–372.

Sassen, S. 1997. U.S. immigration policy towards Mexico in a global economy. In *Between two worlds: Mexican immigrants in the United States*, 213–227. Wilmington, DE: Scholarly Resources.

Schiller, H. 1969. *Mass communication and American empire*. Boston: Beacon.

———. 1976. *Communication and cultural domination*. White Plains, NY: International Arts and Sciences.

———. 1989. *Culture Inc.: The corporate takeover of public expression*. New York: Oxford University Press.

Schmidt, E. 1995. *Consumer rites: The buying and selling of American holidays*. Princeton, NJ: Princeton University Press.

Schudson, M. 2003. *The sociology of news*. New York: Norton.

Scott, J. 1990. *Domination and the arts of resistance: Hidden transcripts*. New Haven, CT: Yale University Press.

Simpson, D. 1992. Raymond Williams: Feeling for structures, voicing "history." *Social Text* 30:9–25.

Smith, R. C. 2006. *Mexican New York: Transnational lives of new immigrants*. Berkeley: University of California Press.

Smith, W. 1977. *The fiesta system and economic exchange*. New York: Columbia University Press.

Sommers, L. 1991. Inventing Latinismo: The creation of "Hispanic" panethnicity in the United States. *Journal of American Folklore* 104:32–51.

———. 1995. Día de los Muertos en Detroit. In *Fiesta, fe y cultura: Celebrations of faith and culture in Detroit's colonia mexicana*, 35–63. Detroit, MI: Casa de Unidad Cultural Arts and Media Center.

Sreberny-Mohammadi, A. 1996. Globalization, communication and transnational civil society. In *Globalization, communication, and transnational civil society*, ed. S. Braman and A. Sreberny Mohammadi, 1–20. Cresskill, NJ: Hampton.

Stannard, D. 1975. *Death in America*. Philadelphia: University of Pennsylvania Press.

Stern, S. 1987. *Resistance, rebellion and consciousness in the Andean peasant world, 18th to 20th centuries*. Madison: University of Wisconsin Press.

———. 1993. *Peru's Indian peoples and the challenge of Spanish conquest*. Madison: University of Wisconsin Press.

Stern, S., and J. Cicala. 1991. *Creative ethnicity: Symbols and Strategies of Contemporary Ethnic Life*. Logan: Utah State University Press.

Stoeltje, B. 1983. Festival in America. In *Handbook of American folklore*, ed. R. Dorson, I. Carpenter, E. Peterson, and A. Maniak, 239–246. Bloomington: Indiana University Press.

Storey, J. 1998. *Cultural theory and popular culture*. New York: Prentice Hall.

Streep, P. 1997. *Altars made easy*. San Francisco: Harper.

Suarez-Orozco, M. 2001. Mexican immigration and the Latinization of the United States. *ReVista, Harvard Review of Latin America* (Fall): 40.

Suarez-Orozco, M., and M. Paez. 2002. *Latinos: Remaking America*. Berkeley: University of California Press.

Tagg, P. 1990. Music in mass media studies. In *Popular music research*, ed. K. Roe and U. Carlsson, 103–114. Gothenburg, Sweden: Nordicom.

Taussig, M. 1980. *The devil and commodity fetishism*. Chapel Hill: University of North Carolina Press.

———. 1994. Violence and resistance in the Americas: The legacy of conquest. In *Violence, resistance and survival in the Americas: Native Americans and the legacy of conquest*, ed. W. Taylor and F. Pease, 269–284. Washington, DC: Smithsonian Institution Press.

———. 1997. *The magic of the state*. New York: Routledge.

———. 2004. Dying is an art, like everything else. In *Things*, ed. B. Brown, 381–392. Chicago: University of Chicago Press.

Taylor, C., and H. K. Bang. 1997. Portrayals of Latinos in magazine advertising. *Journalism and Mass Communication Educator* 52:285–304.

Taylor, W. 1979. *Drinking, homicide, and rebellion in colonial Mexican villages*, Palo Alto: Stanford University Press.

Taylor, W., and F. Pease. 1994. *Violence, resistance and survival in the Americas: Native Americans and the legacy of conquest*. Washington, DC: Smithsonian Institution Press.

Thompson, E. P. 1991. *Customs in common*. London: Merlin.

Tinker, E. 1961. *Corridos and calaveras*. Austin: University of Texas Press.

Toelken, B. 1996. *The dynamics of folklore*. Logan: Utah State University Press.

Toor, F. 1947. *A treasury of Mexican folkways*. New York: Crown.

———. 1953. *Festivals and folkways of Italy*. New York: Crown.

Trim, Kathryn. 2002. Día de los Muertos. *Holiday Celebrations* (Fall): 60–67.

Tuchman, G. 1978. *Making news: A study in the construction of reality*. New York: Free Press.

Turk, J., J. Richstad, and R. Bryson. 1989. Hispanic Americans in the news in two Southwestern cities. *Journalism Quarterly* 66:107–115.

Turner, K. 2001. Mexican American home altars: Toward their interpretation. In *The Chicano Studies reader: An anthology of Atzlán*, ed. C. Noriega, E. R. Avila, K. M. Davalos, and C. Sandoval, 327–344. Los Angeles: Chicano Studies Research Center.

Turner, K., and P. Jasper. 1994. Day of the Dead: The Tex-Mex tradition. In *Halloween and other festivals of death and life*, ed. J. Santino, 133–151. Knoxville: University of Tennessee Press.

Turner, V. 1977a. *Ritual process: Structure and anti-structure*. Ithaca, NY: Cornell University Press.

———. 1977b. Variations on a theme of liminality. In *Secular ritual*, ed. S. Moore and B. Myerhoff, 36–52. Assen, Netherlands: Van Gorcum.

———. 1982. *Celebration: Studies in festivity and ritual*. Washington, DC: Smithsonian Institution Press.

Tweed, Thomas. 1997. *Our lady of the exile: Diaspora religion at a Cuban Catholic shrine in Miami*. New York: Oxford University Press.

Tyler, R., ed. 1979. *Posada's Mexico*. Washington, DC: Library of Congress.

Urlin, E. 1990. All Souls Days. In *Festivals, holy days and saints days: A study in origins and survivals in church ceremonies and secular customs*, 200–204. Detroit, MI: Omnigraphics.

Valdivia, A. 2003. Salsa as popular culture: Ethnic audiences constructing an identity. In *A companion to media studies*, ed. A. Valdivia, 399–418. Malden, MA: Blackwell.

Vargas, L. 2000. Genderizing Latino news: An analysis of local newspaper's coverage of Latino current affairs. *Critical Studies in Media Communication* 17 (3): 261–293.

Venegas, S. 2000. The Day of the Dead in Aztlán: Chicano variations on the theme of life, death, and self-preservation. In *Chicanos in Mictlán*, ed. T. Romo, 42–54. San Francisco: Mexican Museum of San Francisco.

Vergara, C. 1997. Tullu Pallay: Ritual de reciprocidad entre la vida y la muerte. In *El cuerpo humano y su tratamiento mortuario*, ed. E. Malvido, G. Pereira, and V. Tiesler, 51–66. Mexico City: Centro de Estudios Mexicanos y Centroamericanos.

Viquiera, J. 1984. Religión popular e identidad. *Cuicuilco: Revista de la Escuela Nacional de Antropología e Historia* 14–15:7–14.

Waits, W. 1993. *Modern Christmas in America: A cultural history of gift giving.* New York: New York University Press.

Warner, L. 1962. *American life, dream and reality.* Chicago: University of Chicago Press.

West, J. 1989. *Mexican-American folklore.* Little Rock, AR: Little Rock.

White, A., ed. 2001. *Frida Kahlo, Diego Rivera, and Mexican modernism.* Canberra, Victoria: National Gallery of Australia.

Wilentz, S. 1985. *Rites of power: Symbolism, ritual, and politics since the Middle Ages.* Philadelphia: University of Pennsylvania Press.

Williams, R. 1961. *The long revolution.* New York: Columbia University Press.

———. 1962. *Communications.* New York: Penguin Books.

———. 1973. Knowable communities. In *The city and the country*, 165–181. New York: Oxford University Press.

———. 1979. *Politics and letters: Interviews with New Left Review.* London: Lowe and Brydone.

———. 1991. Base and superstructure in Marxist cultural theory. In *Rethinking popular culture*, ed. C. Mukerji and M. Schudson, 407–423. Berkeley: University of California Press.

Willis, T. 1978. *Profane culture.* New York: Routledge.

———. 1990. *Common cultures: Symbolic work at play and the everyday cultures of the young.* Milton Keynes, UK: Open University Press.

Wilson, C., and F. Gutierrez. 1985. *Minorities and media.* Beverly Hills, CA: Sage.

Wilson, C., F. Gutierrez, and L. Chao. 2003. *Racism, sexism and the media: The rise of class communication in multicultural America.* 4th ed. Thousand Oaks, CA: Sage.

Winning, H. 1987. El simbolismo del arte funerario de Teotihuacán. In *Arte funerario*, ed. L. Noelle, 55–63. Mexico City: Universidad Nacional Autónoma de México.

Wollen, P. 1989. Introduction. In *Posada: Messenger of mortality*, ed. J. Rothenstein, 14–23. Boston: Redstone.

Ybarra-Frausto, T. 1996. The Chicano Movement/The movement of Chicano art. In *Beyond the fantastic: Contemporary art criticism from Latin America*, ed. G. Mosquera, 165–182. Cambridge, MA: MIT Press.

Yudice, G. 1996. The transnational culture brokering of art. In *Beyond the fantastic: Contemporary art criticism from Latin America*, ed. G. Mosquera. Cambridge, MA: MIT Press. 196–216.

Index

aboriginal peoples. *See* Indigenous peoples
advertising, 85–86
aesthetic distancing, 117
affirmative action, 91
Afghanistan war protests, 80
African Americans, 82
Aguera, Francisco, 26
Aguilar, Mario E., 46
AIDS victims, 81
Alderete, Terry, 96
Alianza Indigena, 76, 158n20
All Saints' Day, 10–11
All Souls' Day, 10–11, 13–14, 152nn3–4
altar installations: Guatemalan and Salvadoran, 54, 134; honoring Latino cultural icons, 6; Indigenous peoples, 152n2; international, 150n8; McMuertos, 120–121; and Mexico's Day of the Dead customs, 23, 40; political, 132–135, 138; public shrine making as, 102; in San Diego Day of the Dead celebrations, 56–58; traditional, 12–13, 17; year-round installations, 162n9. *See also* ofrendas
Altman, P., 27
American Indian Movement, 38
ancestor altars, 12–13, 150n8
anticolonial liberation movements, 38
Anzaldúa, Gloria, 82
Appadurai, Arjun, 117
Argentina, 19
Arroyo, Antonio Vanegas, 27–28, 43
Arroyo, Arsacio Vanegas, 43

art as means of communication, 57–58, 71, 79, 137
artists: increasing recognition of, 64, 95–96; inspired by Day of the Dead, 129; reclamation of cultural history and identity, 29, 38–39, 86
atole de maiz (corn-based drink), 16, 48, 167
authenticity, 7, 112–113, 121, 131–136
Avalos, David, 43, 106, 110
Aymara. *See* Indigenous peoples
Aztecs, 21, 24–25, 46. *See also* Indigenous peoples

Barraza, Jesus, 71
Benitez, Tomás, 52, 111
Bilingual Education Act (Title VII), 90
Binational Oaxacan Indigenous Front, 65
Black Power Movement, 38
Boccalero, Sr. Karen, 47
Bolaños, Fray Joaquín, 26
Bolivia, 3, 10, 13, 17–18
books about the Day of the Dead, 45
Border Action Network, 76, 158n19
Border Pilgrimage, 75–77, 158n18
Bourdieu, Pierre, 117
los braceros, 78–79
Brandes, Stanley, 2, 25–26, 30–31
Brazil, 59
Bread for the Dead Festival (Tijuana), 126–127, 165n30
Bronowski, J., 126
Buddhism, 101

Buechler, Hans, 17–18
Bueno, Carlos, 47

Cadavál, Olivia, 62, 64
El Calavera (literary magazine), 27
calavera (skull) imagery, 23–27, 40, 44, 154n20, 167
calaveritas (miniature skeleton figures), 24, 167
California Arts Council, 93
California Rural Legal Assistance Foundation, 74
Canclini, Néstor García, 22
car caravan processions, 45, 75–77, 158n18
Carey, James, 57–58
Carmichael, E., 30
Carrasco, Davíd, 60
Caso, Alfonso, 124
Catholicism: All Saints' Day, 10–11; All Souls' Day, 10–11, 13–14, 152nn3–4; happy death, 100, 161–162n2; iconography, 60, 117, 156nn8–9; Roman Catholic rituals, 10–11
La Catrina, 27–28, 152n4
Celts, 13, 150n11
cemetery rituals, 16–20, 153–154n59. *See also* graves, cleaning and decorating of
Central America, 16–17. *See also specific countries*
Chárraga, Nancy, 38
Chávez, César, 78
Chicanismo, 167
Chicanos: artists, increasing recognition of, 64, 95–96; artists inspired by Day of the Dead, 129; Chicano Movement, 167–168; cultural pride and celebration of identity, 29, 38–40, 86; *danza* performances, 46, 56; and Day of the Dead iconography, 39–47; definition of, 149n1, 167; and ethnicity as a flexible construct, 4, 139; and Neo-Indigenism, 39; and solidarity with oppressed peoples, 80; and spiritual

nationalism, 41; and spread of Day of the Dead celebrations, 3, 5–6, 37–47, 50, 140; women, 156n9. *See also* Latinos
chicha (fermented corn drink), 168
Childs, R., 27
Cinco de Mayo, 155n44
citizenship, cultural, 59
"City of Miracles" (Yañez), 108
civic engagement, 138
civil rights movement, 37–38, 82
Cleveland, OH, 10
colonialism, 43
Coluccio, Felix, 18
Columbus Day, 82
commercialization of Day of the Dead, 115–122, 131–136, 165n20, 165n29
commoditization of Day of the Dead, 7, 115–122, 131–136
communal healing process, 102–103
communication: art as means of, 57–58, 71, 79, 137; political, 1, 5–6, 70–73, 138; public rituals as means of, 57–58, 137. *See also* ritual communication
communitas and leveling of social hierarchies, 61–64
community, imagined, 58–60, 84, 86, 96
community building, 6, 121, 137
copal incense, 12
Covarrubias, Miguel and Rosa, 124
Cruz, Celia, 57
Cruz-Chavez, Macuilxochitl, 46
Cuba, 48
cultural capital, 117–118, 137
cultural citizenship, 59, 122
cultural hybridity, 1
cultural nationalism in Mexico, 28, 30–31
cultural pride, 29, 38–40, 84, 86, 121, 130–131
cultural purity and globalization, 112–113
cultural ritual and political communication, 1

cultural solidarity, 73
culture and commerce, 122–131

Dance of Death motifs, 26
Danza Mexi'cayotl, 46
danza (prayer dancing), 46, 56
Day of the Dead Border Pilgrimage, 75–77
Day of the Dead murals (Rivera), 29
Day of the Dead theme park, Mexico, 128
dead, commemorating of, 13, 46, 74–77, 80–81, 102–103
de Anda, Rosa, 163n28
death: attitudes toward in U.S., 7, 98–101; conceptualization of, 15; and Day of the Dead iconography, 44; happy death, 100, 161–162n2; Indigenous peoples' representations of, 25; as part of cycle of life, 95, 101; relationship of Mexicans with, 21; sociopolitical causes of, 47
Death with Dignity, 100, 162n3
DeLucca, Maribel Simán, 118, 128
Dewey, John, 57
d'Harnocourt, René, 125
Diaz, Porfirio, 27–28
Diego, Juan, 156nn8–9
Doyle-Hyde Amendment, 134
Dunn, Edward, 75

Ecuador, 19
education: about Day of the Dead celebrations, 6–7, 45, 48; role of media, 7, 85, 93–95. *See also* museums
El Salvador, 17, 54
Espejel, Carlos, 125
ethnicity as a flexible construct, 4, 139
Eurocentric racism, 37–38, 72
Europe and Day of the Dead celebrations, 5, 14–15, 26, 37–38
Eyerman, Ron, 113

farm workers, 78–79
feminist reappropriations of the Virgin of Guadalupe, 156n9

fertility dances, 13
Fiske, John, 40
Flores, Juan, 60
folk art, 117, 124–125, 165n21, 165n23
folk Catholicism, 11, 150n7
Forest Hills Cemetery, Boston (MA), 102–103
Fruitvale Day of the Dead festival, Oakland, CA, 96, 119–120, 132–133
funding for Day of the Dead events, 93
funeral industry, 99
fusion of Indigenous, Catholic, and folk practices, 11–12

La Galería de la Raza, 48–49
Garciagodoy, Juanita, 22–23, 26, 123
Garza, Carmen Lomas, 36, 48
Gaspar de Alba, Alicia, 43
globalization, 5, 112–113, 140
Gonzalez, John, 35–36
Gosnell, L., 35
Gott, S., 35
Goya, Francisco de, 27
Gramsci, Antonio, 41
Grant, R., 126
grant funding, 93
graves, cleaning and decorating of: Mexican American customs, 34–36; and Mexico's Day of the Dead cus-toms, 22–23, 123; traditional practices, 11–12, 16–20; unidentified migrant gravesites in Holtville, CA, 74–75
Grim Fandango (computer game), 117
Grupo Maya, 134
Guadalupanas, 42, 153n14
guaguas (baby- or animal-shaped breads), 168
Guatemala and Guatemalans: altar installations, 54, 134; commercialization of Day of the Dead, 165n29; courtship rituals, 13–14; Day of the Dead celebrations, 10, 16–17, 79–80; Guatemala City, 17

Guelaguetza, 155n44
Guevara, Che, 57

Halloween: celebrated in Mexico, 31–33, 49; Day of the Dead celebration as alternative ritual, 86–87; devoid of connection with death, 100; iconography used in ofrendas, 109, 163n33
harvests, 13
heaven, 14
Hebdige, Dick, 44
Henry, Barbara, 105, 130
Hernández, Ester, 153n10
historical background of Day of the Dead celebrations, 11–12
Hobsbawm, Eric, 43
Holtville, CA, unidentified migrant gravesites, 74–75, 138
Honduras, 10
hospice care programs, 100
Huehuetenango (Guatemala), 17
Hunger Project, 134
Huntington, Richard, 98

Ibañez, Antonio, 47
iconography, Catholic, 60, 117, 156nn8–9
iconography of Day of the Dead, 39–47, 60, 116–117. *See also calavera* (skull) imagery
imagined community, 58–60, 84, 86, 96
immigrants vs. U.S.-born, 63, 156n13
Indigena, Alianza, 76, 158n20
Indigenous peoples: Day of the Dead as family reunion, 15; definition, 168; folk art, 117, 124–125; harmony with world of the dead, 11–12; and Mexican popular arts, 28–29; and Mexico's Day of the Dead customs, 23; and racism, 30; and representations of death, 25; rights of, 79–80; spiritual beliefs, 161n25; spread of Day of the Dead customs to the U.S., 37–47; and traditional ofrendas, 123–124, 152n2

Interfaith Coalition for Immigrant and Refugee Rights (ICIR), 74
invented tradition, 43
Iraq war protests, 80
Irish Americans, 81–82
Italian Americans, 82
Italy, 13, 15, 151n17

Jamaica, 48
Jamison, Andrew, 113
Janitzio, Mexico, 127
Jasper, Pat, 24, 31
Jimenez, Rosie, 134
Junior Reserve Officers Training Corps, 80

Kahlo, Frida, 57, 124, 154n31
kite flying, 10, 16, 79, 165n29
kitsch, 116–117, 129
Klink, Estela Rubalcava, 57, 62, 89, 155n2

La Faye, Jacques, 27–28
Lara, Celso, 3, 17, 151n22
Latin America: Day of the Dead celebrations, 5, 10–11, 14–20; immigration to the U.S., 53, 63; protests of U.S. military interventions, 81
Latinos: ancestry of, 164–165n19; artists, increasing recognition of, 64, 95–96; conflicts between recent immigrants and U.S.-born, 63; cultural pride, 86; definition of, 168; and ethnicity as a flexible construct, 4, 139; farm workers, 78–79; honored in altar installations, 6; and imagined community, 58–60, 84; movies and TV shows about, 63; population growth, 92; portrayed in advertising, 85–86; reporters, 91; resentment toward non-Latino participants, 106–107; underrepresented by media, 7, 159–160n4. *See also* Chicanos
Leaños, John, 121

legitimization through media coverage, 84
leisure rituals, 60–61
Linares, Pedro, 126
Linares family, 43, 126, 165nn24–25
living wills, 100
Lomnitz, Claudio, 25, 123
Lomnitz-Adler, Claudio, 42
Los Angeles, CA, 47–48, 119, 131–132

MacAloon, John, 68
magazine coverage, 85, 89
maguey (agave plant), 150n9
Mainstreets Initiative, 96, 119–120, 132–133, 156–157n16, 161n28
Manilla, Manuel, 27
maquiladoras, 77, 158n21
Maradiaga, Ralph, 48
marginalized populations, 58, 64, 71
Marigold Project, 163n28
marigolds, 12, 150n10
Martín-Barbero, Jesús, 71
Martineau, Harriet, 99
Martin Luther King Jr. Day, 82
Masuoka, Susan, 126
Mayans, 79–80, 134. *See also* Guatemala and Guatemalans; Indigenous peoples
Mayapán Women's Collective, El Paso, TX, 78
McMuertos (altar installations), 120–121
media coverage, 5–7, 83–96
Medina, Lara, 62
Memorial Day, 100
merchandising of Day of the Dead products, 89, 103, 116–132. *See also* commercialization of Day of the Dead
Mesa-Bains, Amalia, 48, 49, 131
Mesilla, NM, 119, 132
Mesoamericans, 13–14, 17, 25, 39, 54–55, 168. *See also* Indigenous peoples
Mestizos, 19–20, 28, 38, 41, 169
Metcalf, Peter, 98

methodology, 4, 141–148
Metropolitan Museum of Art, NYC, 102, 164n3
Mexican Americans: and cleaning of graves, 34–36; conflicts between recent immigrants and U.S.-born, 63; and Day of the Dead celebrations, 2–3; ethnicity as a flexible construct, 139; learning about Day of the Dead celebrations, 37–47, 50–52; and ownership of Day of the Dead celebrations, 52–53
Mexican Independence Day, 155n44
Mexican Renaissance, 28–29
Mexican Revolution, 22
Mexican-U.S. border region, 31–32, 34–36, 74–77, 157n1
Mexico and Mexicans: commercialization of Day of the Dead celebrations, 123–129, 165n20; cultural nationalism, 28, 30–31; Day of the Dead customs, 15, 22–26, 40; and Day of the Dead tourism, 2–3, 124–129; ethnicity as a flexible construct, 139; fatalism, 22; folk art, 124–125; and Halloween, 31–33; influenced by Chicano Day of the Dead celebrations, 49–50; national pride and Day of the Dead, 126; ownership of Day of the Dead celebrations, 52–53; pre-Columbian iconography, 29; relationship with death, 21; and tourism, 2–3, 29–33, 124–129
migrant deaths, 74–77, 157n1
Milne, Jean, 18
Minneapolis, MN, 10
Mission Cultural Center for Latino Arts (MCCLA), 70–71, 107–108, 157n6
Mixquic (Mexico), 127
Mixtecs, 64–68, 156n15. *See also* Indigenous peoples
mole (type of sauce), 23, 65, 150n9
Monsiviaís, Carlos, 22
Moore, S., 62
Morrison, Suzanne, 47, 63

movies: about Day of the Dead, 45–46; about Latinos, 63; with Day of the Dead imagery, 84

Mujeres against Militarism, 80

multiculturalism, rising interest in, 90

murals, 29

El Museo del Barrio, NYC, 102

museums: and altar installations, 9, 105, 162n9; Day of the Dead exhibits, 54, 72, 130–131; and education about Day of the Dead, 2, 4, 89–90; fees charged, 116, 130; and recognition of Latino artists, 64, 95–96. *See also specific museums*

Myerhoff, B., 62

National Foundation for the Arts, 93

nationalism, 32–33

National Museum of the American Indian, NYC, 102

National Public Radio, 85

Native Americans, 79–80, 82

Neo-Indigenism, 39

New Age spirituality, 161n25

New Brunswick, NJ, 46

news organizations, 85, 88–89

newspaper coverage, 83–84, 88–90, 92

Nicaragua, 17

Nogales, AZ, 36

Nogales (Mexico), 36

non-Latinos and Day of the Dead celebrations, 4–5, 97, 101–114, 118

nontraditional religions, 100–102

nontraditional vs. traditional interpretations, 108–113

Nutini, Hugo, 25

Oakland, CA, 96, 119–120, 132–133

Oakland Museum, CA, 105

Oceanside, CA, 46, 64–68, 106, 120, 132–133, 138, 156n15

Ochoa, Digna, 71, 157n4

ofrendas: definition of, 169; Guatemalan and Salvadoran, 54; honoring farm workers, 78–79, 81; honoring victims of society, 81; Indigenous traditions, 12–13; Latin American traditions, 16–20; Mexican American traditions, 40; at Mission Cultural Center for Latino Art, 70–71, 107–108; Mixtec, 65–68; in San Diego, 56–58; in Sherman Heights, 155n1; traditional Mexican, 23, 123–124; in U.S., 45; use of Halloween iconography, 109, 163n33. *See also* altar installations

Oklahoma City bombing site, 102, 162n8

Old Town State Park, San Diego, CA, 119

Olmedo, Delores, 126

Olvera Street, Los Angeles, CA, 119, 131–132

Operation Gatekeeper, 70–71, 74–77, 157n1

Operation Hold the Line, 75

oppressed peoples, solidarity with, 80

ownership of Day of the Dead celebrations, 52–53

pan de muerto (sweet bread), 17–18, 36, 127–128, 169

pan-Latino, 4, 10, 53, 155–156n3

papel picado, 22–23, 56, 169

Papel Picado para Digna Ochoa (Vargas), 71

papier-mâché crafts, 43, 126, 165n24

pasquines (Spanish lampoons), 24

Paz, Octavio, 21, 52

Peabody Museum, Boston, 102, 131

Peltier, Leonard, 79, 159n29

Peru, 13, 18

Pinochet, Augusto, 10

El plan espirituál de Aztlán (The spiritual plan of Aztlán), 41

political communication, 1, 5–6, 70–73, 138

popular culture vs. folk culture, 40

population growth, Latino, 92

Posada, José Guadalupe, 27–28, 40, 43, 126

prayer dancing (*danza*), 46, 56
public rituals, power of, 5, 68, 81–82, 137
public shrine making, 102
public space, access to, 7, 53, 64
El Pueblo de Los Angeles Historic Monument (CA), 119, 131–132
Puerto Rico, 59
Pulido, Guillermo, 49–50
pulque (alcoholic drink from the agave plant), 12, 150n9, 169
purgatory, 14–15

Quechua. *See* Indigenous peoples
quinceañeras, 153n12
quinoa, 150n9
Quito (Ecuador), 19

racism, 30, 38, 60
radio coverage, 89
Ranger, Terrance, 43
Raza Unida Coalition, 80
Regeneration Project, 164n15
religious imagination, 60
reporters, Latino, 91
Rescate Culture Collective, 163n28
Reuda de la Muerte (Barraza), 71
Reuter, Jas, 26
ritual begging, 18, 79, 151n20
ritual communication: art as means of, 57–58, 71, 79, 137; and commoditization, 121; and community building, 6; as political commentary, 81–82; and positive representation in the media, 96; reinforcing social identity, 57–58
Rivera, Diego, 28–29, 52, 124
roadside shrines, 102
Rockefeller, Nelson A., 125
Rodriguez, Patricia, 71, 94
Roman Catholic rituals, 10–11
Romero, Oscar, 57
Romo, Tere, 37–39, 41–42, 47, 49, 54, 62, 101
"Rooms for the Dead" (Yañez), 108
Rosaldo, Renato, 59

Sacatepequez (Guatemala), 16
Sacramento State University, 102
Salcajá (Guatemala), 16
Samhain, 13, 150n11
San Antonio, TX, 35, 115, 119
San Diego, CA, 45, 50–51, 56–58, 119
San Francisco, CA, Mission District, 48–49, 106–107, 163n28
San Rafael, CA, 10
Santa Fe, NM, 119
Santería, 48
Santiago (Guatemala), 16
Santino, J., 68
satirical art, 27–28
Sayer, S., 30
Schafer, Tim, 117
Scott, James C., 138
secularization of Catholic iconography, 117
secular vs. spiritual significance of Day of the Dead, 40, 42–43, 94, 132–135
Self-Help Graphics, 47–48, 52, 62
September 11, World Trade Center site, 102
Sherman Heights, San Diego, CA, 120, 155n1
Sherman Heights Community Center (San Diego), 51, 56–58
shrines, 11–12
skull imagery. *See calavera* (skull) imagery
Smithsonian Institution's museums, 9, 64, 68, 72
social hierarchies, leveling of, 61–64
social identity, reinforced by rituals, 58
social space, access to. *See* public space, access to
SomArts Cultural Center, 108
South America, Day of the Dead customs, 17–20
Southwestern style, 117
spirituality, growing interest in, 100–102, 140, 161n25
spiritual nationalism, 41
spiritual vs. secular significance of Day of the Dead, 40, 94, 132–135

St. Mary's Star of the Sea Church
(Oceanside, CA), 65–68
St. Patrick's Day Parade, 81–82
steel-drum bands, 48
stereotypes, 29, 85–86
street processions, 11–12, 23, 45, 48,
66–67. *See also specific cities*
sugar skulls, 15, 23–25, 103
Sumpango (Guatemala), 16
Sun Mad Poster, 153n10
syncretism and Day of the Dead celebrations, 11–12, 46

El Teatro Campesino, 48
television coverage, 89–90
television shows: about Day of the
Dead, 84; about Latinos, 63
Terrance Park Cemetery, CA, 74–75
Thiem, Mary Ann, 68, 88–89
Thompson, E. P., 73
Tijuana (Mexico), 32–33, 126, 152n6,
165n30
Title VII (Bilingual Education Act), 90
Todos Santos (Guatemala), 16
Torio, Louise, 96
tourism: and Day of the Dead, 118–120;
and Day of the Dead in Mexico, 2–3,
29–33, 124–129
traditional vs. nontraditional interpreta-
tions, 108–113, 120–121
Turner, Kay, 24, 31
Turner, Victor, 60–62
Tzintzuntzan (Mexico), 30–31
tzompantli (skull racks), 25

Unitarian Universalist Fellowship, Solana
Beach, CA, 104
United Farm Workers (UFW), 78,
153n10
Unity Council, 164n12

urban redevelopment strategy. *See* Fruit-
vale Day of the Dead festival,
Oakland, CA
U.S. Army's School of the Americas,
79–80, 159n29
U.S.-born vs. immigrants, 156n13
U.S.-Mexican border region, 31–32,
34–36, 74–77, 157n1

Vargas, Eva, 71
Vasconcellos, José, 28–29
Venegas, Sybil, 37, 47
Vergara, César Abilio, 18
Vietnam War Memorial (Washington,
D.C.), 102
Vigil against Militarism, Los Angeles,
CA, 80
Virgin of Guadalupe, 117, 155n44,
156nn8–9
volunteerism, 57, 131, 138
Von Son, Carlos, 111
Voyage pour l' éternité (literary magazine),
27

Washington, DC, 64
Williams, Raymond, 57–58
witchcraft, 94
Wollen, Peter, 28
Women of Juarez, 134, 138
Woo, Yolanda Garfias, 38, 48, 50, 89, 94
workshops teaching Day of the Dead
crafts, 42–50, 72, 116, 119–120, 129
World Trade Center site, 102

Xcaret Amusement Complex (Mexico),
128, 166n35

Yañez, René, 48–49, 93, 106, 108–109,
112
Yerba Buena Cultural Center, CA, 108

About the Author

REGINA M. MARCHI is an assistant professor in the Department of Journalism and Media Studies at Rutgers University. She holds a PhD in communication from the Department of Communication at the University of California, San Diego, and an MA in English literature from San Francisco State University. Dr. Marchi's teaching and research focus on the intersections of culture, politics, and media.